HANDS-ON INCIDEN
RESPONSE AND DIG
FORENSICS

BCS THE CHARTERED INSTITUTE FOR IT

BCS, The Chartered Institute for IT, champions the global IT profession and the interests of individuals engaged in that profession for the benefit of all. We promote wider social and economic progress through the advancement of information technology science and practice. We bring together industry, academics, practitioners and government to share knowledge, promote new thinking, inform the design of new curricula, shape public policy and inform the public.

Our vision is to be a world-class organisation for IT. Our 70,000-strong membership includes practitioners, businesses, academics and students in the UK and internationally. We deliver a range of professional development tools for practitioners and employees. A leading IT qualification body, we offer a range of widely recognised qualifications.

Further Information
BCS, The Chartered Institute for IT,
First Floor, Block D,
North Star House, North Star Avenue,
Swindon, SN2 1FA, United Kingdom.
T +44 (0) 1793 417 424
F +44 (0) 1793 417 444
www.bcs.org/contact

http://shop.bcs.org/

HANDS-ON INCIDENT RESPONSE AND DIGITAL FORENSICS

Mike Sheward

bcs
The
Chartered
Institute
for IT

Published by BCS Learning & Development Ltd, a wholly owned subsidiary of BCS, The Chartered Institute for IT, First Floor, Block D, North Star House, North Star Avenue, Swindon, SN2 1FA, UK.
www.bcs.org

PDF ISBN: 978-1-78017-4211
ePUB ISBN: 978-1-78017-4228
Kindle ISBN: 978-1-78017-4235
Paperback ISBN: 978-1-78017-4204

Ebook available

British Cataloguing in Publication Data.
A CIP catalogue record for this book is available at the British Library.

Disclaimer:
The views expressed in this book are of the author(s) and do not necessarily reflect the views of the Institute or BCS Learning & Development Ltd except where explicitly stated as such. Although every care has been taken by the authors and BCS Learning & Development Ltd in the preparation of the publication, no warranty is given by the authors or BCS Learning & Development Ltd as publisher as to the accuracy or completeness of the information contained within it and neither the authors nor BCS Learning & Development Ltd shall be responsible or liable for any loss or damage whatsoever arising by virtue of such information or any instructions or advice contained within this publication or by any of the aforementioned.

Publisher's acknowledgements
Reviewers: Martin Heyde and Dale McGleenon
Publisher: Ian Borthwick
Commissioning Editor: Rebecca Youé
Production Manager: Florence Leroy
Project Manager: Sunrise Setting Ltd
Cover work: Alexander Wright
Picture credits: ArtOlympic

Typeset by Lapiz Digital Services, Chennai, India.

CONTENTS

LIST OF FIGURES

AUTHOR

Mike Sheward CISSP, CISM, CCFP-US, CISA, HCISPP, CEH, OSCP, CHFI is Director of Information Security at Seattle-based Accolade Inc., and runs a digital investigation consultancy, Secure Being LLC.

Mike has worked in information security, primarily in incident response and digital forensics roles, in both the UK and USA, and in both the public and private sectors.

FOREWORD

Industry definitions have been in place for as long as there have been industries: auto, travel, finance, fashion or technology. But when the chief executive officer (CEO) of General Motors (GM) announces that they are hiring 12,000 IT engineers, the world has clearly changed. GM is no longer just a car company – it is a technology company. And the same could be written about companies in every industry. With technology comes opportunity, innovation and efficiency. And risk. Today, information security issues are more complex than most executives have the knowledge and experience to comprehend, in just about every industry.

The reality of today's business climate is that information security needs to be a core focus of every business, in every industry. When every company in the world is a technology company, every company requires the culture of awareness created by a strong information security focus.

As a co-founder of Concur and the current CEO of healthcare tech company Accolade, I've had the pleasure of working with Mike Sheward for nearly 10 years, and in that time we've watched the haphazard scramble of companies working to leverage the power of the internet, followed almost immediately by massive information security incidents that put their customers and employees at risk. Throughout it all, Mike has been an excellent advocate and practitioner of information security while at the same time acknowledging the needs of a business to continue to innovate and move with pace. Information security in today's age requires that balance. And it also requires the ability to partner with executive management as well as with every employee in the business to create a culture of awareness and vigilance. In my experience, there is no better practitioner of those skills than Mike Sheward. The lessons outlined in this book express those skills with Mike's trademark dry English wit and I am confident you will find them valuable.

Rajeev Singh
CEO, Accolade

ACKNOWLEDGEMENTS

A lot of people are responsible for supporting, encouraging and allowing me to work in this field that I love so dearly.

First and foremost, my family, Jessica and Oliver, thank you for giving me the time to write and run off and respond to things.

My parents Geoff and Angela, thank you for providing everything I needed to tinker, explore and break from a young age.

Rajeev Singh and Mike Hilton have provided me with two great companies at which to ply my trade.

I'd also like to thank Mike McGee, Chris Jennings, Darcey Axon, Tony McDowell and Campbell Murray for being my work families at various points in my career.

Finally, I'd like to thank BCS and Rebecca Youé for turning this career goal into a reality.

GLOSSARY

Application security (AppSec) A subdiscipline of information security focused on developing security into an application, or testing the security of an application.

Artefact A data item, such as a file or log entry, that may be relevant to an investigation or incident.

Attack vector A means leveraged by an attacker, such as a malicious hacker, to compromise a target. For example, this could include a flaw in a web application, or delivering malware via email.

Baseline A measurement of a typical behaviour which can be used to make comparisons, and therefore detect abnormal behaviour.

Bourne-again shell (Bash shell) A commonly used Unix shell, the Bourne-again shell is the default shell on many modern Unix-like operating systems. The shell allows a user to type commands into a terminal window.

Chief information security officer (CISO) A position within an organisation that typically bears overall responsibility for an organisation's information security programme.

Confidentiality The state of secrecy or privacy of a given piece of information.

Debugger A software tool used to deconstruct running applications for the purposes of detecting, understanding and fixing errors.

Decryption The process of taking encrypted information and converting it back to a format that is human readable, or otherwise usable by a computer, such as to a given file format.

Defacement A type of attack in which the attacker alters the appearance of a website.

Denial of service A condition caused when a system is unable to service legitimate requests because it is overwhelmed by malicious traffic, or otherwise taken offline.

Due diligence The steps taken by a person, or business, to ensure that they are acting in a safe and legal manner.

Encryption The process of taking a piece of information and encoding it in such a way that only authorised parties are allowed to view it.

Ephemeral Something that lasts for a very short time. Commonly used when describing container images.

Exfiltration The act of surreptitiously removing data from a computer or network.

Exploit A piece of software written to take advantage of a vulnerability in a computer system.

False positive An incorrect indication that a condition is occurring. Commonly associated with intrusion detection systems or vulnerability scanners.

Grep A Unix command used to search for a string of characters in a file. An abbreviation of the term 'globally search for a regular expression and print'.

Hardware security module (HSM) A physical device that stores, protects and manages the use of encryption keys.

Hashing A mathematical process performed on data of any size, which results in the generation of data that is a fixed size, otherwise known as a hash digest. Frequently used to ensure data integrity.

HTTP HyperText Transfer Protocol, the primary protocol used by web browsers and servers to communicate. A set of standards for transferring text and other media across the internet.

Hypervisor Computer software that is responsible for running and managing virtual machines.

Initial public offering (IPO) A period in which shares in a private company are offered for sale to the general public for the first time.

Internet service provider (ISP) A company that provides customers with access to the internet.

IT asset Any hardware, software or data owned by an organisation that is used to conduct business.

Jailbreaking The process of bypassing restrictions imposed by the manufacturer of an electronic device (such as a smartphone), usually for the purposes of installing software outside that approved by the manufacturer.

Kernel The core component of an operating system, responsible for managing hardware resources such as CPU and RAM.

Micro-services An application architecture model that leverages multiple small components, or services, to implement a function, as opposed to building a single large application.

Network-attached storage A hardware device that provides file storage services to one or more clients across a network.

Open Systems Interconnection (OSI) model   A conceptual model that describes seven layers of communication functions to be implemented by an operating system or a telecommunications system for the purposes of inter-system communication. The OSI model covers everything from data input at the application level to physical transmission of data as an electrical signal.

Packet   A formatted unit of data carried across a packet-switched network. A packet includes addressing information, to help it get to where it needs to go, as well as the data it is transmitting.

Penetration test   An authorised test that is designed to simulate actions taken by a malicious attacker attempting to gain access to an organisation, application or network.

Phishing   An attack that involves sending phony emails purporting to be from a legitimate source, such as a financial institution. The intent of the attack is for the victim to respond with sensitive information, such as a set of credentials. A spear-phishing attack is a phishing attack that is targeted at a specific victim.

Post-traumatic stress disorder (PTSD)   A mental illness that occurs as the result of an injury or other severe psychological shock; it can result in frequent recall of the event that caused the condition.

Process   In a computing context, used to describe an instance of a running program.

Radio frequency (RF)   An electromagnetic wave with a frequency of 20 kHz to 300 GHz, used in wireless communication. An RF-shielded bag is designed to block waves at these frequencies.

Security operations   A subdiscipline of information security focused on the day-to-day management and monitoring of an organisation's security controls and procedures. A security operations centre (SOC) may be responsible for triggering an incident response upon the discovery of a specific condition.

Storage area network (SAN)   A specialised network used to connect storage devices, such as disk arrays and tape libraries. This network of connected storage devices can then appear to multiple clients as if it were a locally attached storage device. The benefits of such a setup include improved performance and redundancy.

Structured Query Language (SQL)   A programming language used to manage relational database platforms, it can be used to create databases or alter the structure of an existing database, as well as perform operations on the stored data itself. A SQL injection attack occurs when an attacker finds a vector in which to insert their own SQL commands for interpretation by a database server.

Subpoena   A legal document that requires a witness to attend court or produce other evidence for court. Failure to comply with the requirements of a subpoena can result in a legal penalty.

Systems administrator   A position within an organisation that is generally responsible for the day-to-day management and maintenance of computer systems.

The Onion Router (TOR)   A free piece of software that allows a user the ability to redirect traffic through a wide array of geographically disparate, volunteer-run nodes, known as relays. This helps the user maintain anonymity online, and is frequently used to avoid network-based surveillance.

Tradecraft   In computer security, a term used to describe the tools, techniques and processes used by an attacker.

Usability   Refers to the ease of use of a given product, typically a piece of software or a device.

Volatile data   Information stored in memory, or in transit, that will be lost when a computer is powered off. For example, the contents of random access memory (RAM).

Vulnerability   A weakness, typically within a piece of software, that can be exploited by an attacker to create an unwanted condition. For instance, a vulnerability in a web application could allow an attacker the ability to bypass authentication and access sensitive information.

USEFUL WEBSITES

Brett Shavers' Blog (http://brettshavers.cc/index.php/brettsblog)
A blog maintained by the highly engaging digital forensics professional Brett Shavers.

Cyber Forensicator (http://cyberforensicator.com/)
A site run by Mikhaylov and Oleg Skulkin that aggregates a wide range of digital forensics and incident response content.

Digital Forensic Diaries (www.digitalforensicdiaries.com)
Homepage of this author's other work, a series of short stories based on real-life forensic investigations.

Forensic Focus (www.forensicfocus.com/)
A great news resource and online community for digital forensics professionals.

Forensics Wiki (www.forensicswiki.org/)
A Creative-Commons-licensed site that tracks various tools, techniques and papers on digital forensics.

Lesley Carhart (https://tisiphone.net/)
The homepage/blog of Lesley Carhart, a highly respected and articulate digital forensics and incident response professional. Leslie is also on Twitter: @hacks4pancakes.

mac4n6 (https://www.mac4n6.com/)
A blog devoted to macOS and iOS forensic research, written and maintained by Sarah Edwards.

SANS Digital Forensics (https://digital-forensics.sans.org/)
A collection of digital forensics resources provided by the SANS organisation.

Shodan (https://www.shodan.io/)
An extremely valuable search engine for internet-connected devices that can provide insight during an incident response.

This week in 4n6 (https://thisweekin4n6.com/)
A weekly roundup of relevant digital forensics and incident response news.

ThreatMiner (https://www.threatminer.org/)
A free (donation suggested) resource for searching across an aggregated collection of threat intelligence data.

Windows Incident Response Blog (http://windowsir.blogspot.com/)
A blog devoted to Microsoft Windows incident response techniques, written by acclaimed forensics author Harlan Carvey.

PREFACE

It is often said there are two types of organisation: those who have experienced an information security incident, and those who don't know they've experienced a security incident. From this, and the constant barrage of information-security-related news stories that fill our timelines, news feeds and television screens, it should be very clear to everyone that we live in a time when the information security incident is extremely relevant. This is not going to change any time soon. Incidents will continue to occur, and organisations will be judged on how they react to a given incident. Throughout this book, we're going to be deconstructing security incidents – how they're discovered, what to do and what not to do when they strike and, perhaps most importantly, how to learn from them.

There are countless books on information security theory, and many of them are dedicated to incident response (IR). So, what makes this one any different? The aim of this book is to take the theory and show how it applies to various real-life incidents and investigations, in a hands-on fashion. Throughout my career I've been faced with a number of security incidents and investigations, and have served as both an outside consultant and an internal incident lead at various organisations. These experiences have taught me a lot about the way different businesses react, especially when faced with the prospect of having to explain to customers, regulators or employees that something undesirable has happened to their data.

In all of the cases that I can recall, there is a sort of tipping point: a moment when the realisation occurs that what was just considered 'data' prior to the incident actually represents human lives and livelihoods, and will have a material impact on a real person. It is unfortunate that for most organisations it takes an incident to get to this point. My hope is that by telling the stories of those events, and showing how the theory of incident response applies to them, all in a single publication, we can go some way to demonstrating how this all plays out in reality. Hopefully eyes will be opened to the fact that with some smart design, and planning, we can actually prepare for and face down incidents head-on, all the while capturing evidence that can assist us in preventing a recurrence of the incident.

No matter the scenario, one thing I've learned is that the only way to resolve an incident is through well-executed teamwork – no individual can stand between chaos and normality for an organisation. The team of people charged with responding to a security incident will include professionals who encompass varying functions within the organisation; to be a team player as a security professional means learning to work with all of these people. If you can make them successful, they'll make you successful. The foundations of this teamwork start a long time before an incident strikes. Exposing the traditionally technically minded security professional to the wider scope of pressures that shape how an organisation chooses to act is another aim of this book.

Another key theme, as you can probably guess from the title, is exploring the relationship and transition between incident response and digital forensics. These two disciplines actually have very similar goals but require different approaches – it is this difference that can lead to the friction between them. Incident response involves eradicating the evidence that digital forensics relies on, but both strive for resolution.

As we move into the second half of the book, focused on digital forensics, you'll notice a shift in style. Whereas organisations have the freedom to completely develop their own incident response processes, digital forensics is a branch of forensic science and therefore the steps taken become more prescriptive.

Digital forensics is another area I've been fortunate to work in during my career. It is an addictive, rewarding, but time-consuming and anxiety-ridden occupation. I absolutely love it, but there are plenty of things I wish I had known at the start of my career. Perhaps the most prominent example of this is just how personal an investigation can become. Digital forensics pertains to crimes committed in digital realms, but those crimes are committed by real people. Sometimes it is easy to forget that, until you see that person sat opposite you as you collect evidence that could ultimately cost them financially, or in some other way.

Throughout the digital forensics section of this book I've included various case studies and personal anecdotes that demonstrate how real people, both victims and perpetrators, are affected by digital forensics investigations. The final chapter is dedicated to this topic.

WHO SHOULD READ THIS BOOK?

I've written this book to appeal to a number of different audiences. If you're new to the industry, it will serve as a realistic introduction to the various technologies and skills you will need to understand and ultimately master. If you're someone who works in an IT role, perhaps not dedicated to security or forensics, it will help you to confidently leverage those technical skills for security or forensics purposes. After all, everyone is on the security team, whether or not it is in their job title. Finally, if you've worked in IR or forensics for a while, my hope is that the case studies and war stories in this book will be relatable and help you to explore new ways to use the tools and technologies that you're already familiar with.

It is an honour and a privilege to work in this industry. It was a dream I pursued for a long time. It is even more of an honour to be able to write this book and share with you my experiences and advice. I really hope you enjoy what you're about to read and learn a great deal from it.

INTRODUCTION

This book covers two closely intertwined, yet regularly competing, disciplines: incident response and digital forensics. One often leads to, or from, the other, and to say that their relationship is complex would be an understatement.

On paper these two topics would seem go together, in perfect harmony, rather than up against each other as combatants. The truth is, however, that in the midst of a security incident, in a time of always-on services and applications, most organisations will take the path of least resistance to getting back to an operational state, and frequently this means not properly conserving potential evidence that is vital for a successful forensics investigation. After all, most organisations aren't in business to respond to security incidents or run forensics investigations.

In one corner, we have incident response. Those who engage in security incident response are charged with detecting that something is wrong, containing the issue and steering an organisation back to business as usual, with minimal impact to daily operations.

In the opposing corner, we have digital forensics, the part artistic, part scientific process that seeks to conclusively and meticulously prove why a security incident occurred in the first place. Commonly, the ultimate aim is to find the specific party responsible for an incident, for the purposes of disciplinary or criminal action.

Imagine, if you will, a scene in your favourite television crime drama in which the crime scene technician is meticulously dusting for fingerprints, while bullets from an ongoing shootout with the police continue to fly around them. The primary objective would be to bring the situation to a safe conclusion, not spend time collecting evidence. That would come later in a criminal investigation. Of course, organisations don't have to hold themselves to such stringent investigative standards, and therefore might not investigate at all, even when it could be the right thing to do.

That said, I do have better news. It is entirely possible to strike the perfect balance between incident response and digital forensics needs at your organisation. It just takes planning, business savviness, trust, appropriately deployed technologies and human practitioners who understand how all these pieces fit together.

The aim of this book is to arm you with the knowledge you need to become one of those practitioners, because the world needs you now more than ever.

INCIDENT RESPONSE

Anyone who has ever dealt with an information security incident would likely agree on one thing – they are incredibly stressful for everyone involved. They typically involve long conference calls on the 'P1', 'Sev1', 'Code Red' or 'whatever else your organisation chooses to call it' phone bridge. Occasionally an executive will speak up, asking for an update or suggesting a course of action with varying degrees of helpfulness, all adding to the pressure on those actively fighting the fire.

Preparation is key

This pressure intensifies if the organisation hasn't adequately prepared for an incident. Preparation can be as simple as ensuring someone documented how a given business process works, and stored that documentation in an accessible location. It sounds like common sense, but all too often we find incident response planning to be lacking.

I once handled an incident in which a financial business process was suspected of being compromised, resulting in the potential theft of many millions of dollars. The first thing I asked for on the incident bridge was a description of the process, and any documentation that would help me, as an outsider to this particular organisation, understand the potential attack vectors that I needed to investigate. Aside from one person who understood the mechanics of the process at a very high level and was able to give a description, there was no documentation, no written procedures and no plan in place to respond to an issue with this key financial process. Therefore, before we could officially start the incident response process, we had to sit down and figure a few fundamental things out, wasting valuable time.

Time is precious

Time is not on your side during an information security incident. The longer you leave things uncontained, the worse they will become. The ticking clock provides an additional layer of pressure on those who are charged with incident handling, as if they needed another.

The definition of what constitutes a security incident can be so varied that a lot of time can be wasted deciding if a security incident really is a security incident at all.

Another complicating factor is that information security incidents frequently manifest in other, 'non-security', ways, such as servers crashing or strange behaviour attributed to software bugs. This can lead to more confusion, panic, and to incidents breeding other incidents as teams struggle to understand what exactly is going on.

Incredibly, despite a marked increase in negative and embarrassing headlines related to security incidents in the last five years, some organisations still delay in bringing incident handlers with a security specialism into incidents that cannot be easily attributed to a known cause. This is something we, as security incident handlers, must overcome. After all, a security incident should have to be 'ruled out', rather than 'ruled in'.

So, why don't more organisations approach incident response with security in mind from the beginning?

Perception is a factor

The root cause of this reluctance is, more often than not, directly related to the perception of the security team within the organisation. Quite frankly, security teams are often seen as a roadblock, an afterthought, nosey and determined to catch people out.

Many security teams started life with a compliance-driven mindset. A series of checkboxes to be checked and audits to be passed, with very little desire to think past the initial work and build a lasting technical security infrastructure that can grow with the organisation. Compliance-driven security teams are great at dishing out requirements to other teams, but rarely deliver anything themselves. Who'd want to hang out with those types of people? Who'd want to invite them to scrutinise an incident in progress? No one.

On a more positive note, I can report with high levels of confidence that the times are a-changing. More and more organisations have realised the value of security above and beyond a compliance-driven function. In doing so, they've made investments in security that have allowed talented security professionals to break through and have more seats at more tables.

Having a seat at the table is huge, but doesn't always guarantee that the security professional will be the first one to be notified when a potential security incident occurs. That trust must be earned, and value must be demonstrated early.

There is no better way to earn trust than to be a competent security incident handler. If you can keep cool under pressure, find the problem, help contain it, and remediate the root cause, all while fielding questions from executives and customers, you'll be the most popular person in the room, trust me. This feeling is also highly addictive, and one of the reasons why incident response is one of the most exciting and rewarding aspects of information security.

Become a brilliant incident responder and you'll also elevate the perception of the security team within the organisation, which leads to better integration between security and other teams. This results in an organisation becoming more proactive in addressing security concerns, which in turn leads to fewer incidents.

A lot of people would have you believe that if a company is responding to a security incident then there are a lot of things wrong in its security programme. Don't listen to those people. Every company has to deal with security incidents; if they aren't, they probably aren't doing a good enough job of detecting them. Given this, you should treat the incident response phase as the first opportunity to get things right. Bear this in mind as we work through the incident response portion of this book (Part 1).

DIGITAL FORENSICS

Generally speaking, there are two categories of people who get involved in digital forensics. There are those who seek it out as a career, working in either the private sector at specialist consultancies or in the public sector for government departments such as the police or the security and intelligence agencies, and then there are those who become involved almost accidentally, or happen to be in a non-dedicated forensics role but find themselves having to collect and preserve evidence in the face of some unexpected shenanigans.

Personally, I first became involved in digital forensics accidentally. A few months into a network engineering job, I unknowingly caught someone doing something they really shouldn't have been doing on a public-sector network. I didn't think much of it until an HR representative came down for a chat about the event a few months later.

When I found out that the behaviour I'd initially believed to have been attributable to a piece of malware was actually caused by a human being violating a pretty significant policy, not to mention a criminal law, I was blown away. In fact, that was the exact moment I knew that I wanted to move from the occasional category to the full-time category of digital forensics practitioner!

This is forensic science

Whereas the standards for incident response can vary between organisations, when it comes to digital forensics we're dealing with a legitimate branch of forensic science. Just as a murder suspect can be nailed by DNA found at a crime scene, a cybercriminal can be traced by their digital fingerprints.

Accusing someone of a murder based on your science is a pretty big deal – you'll want to make sure that you've handled the evidence properly and run your tests on it in a defined, repeatable and proven fashion. The same standards apply to computer crimes and digital forensics, and this is why it is such an interesting and rewarding field to engage in.

Running a digital forensics investigation can be a time-consuming and costly undertaking, which is why it's not always the first priority for an organisation. That said, it has been proven time and time again that cybercrimes committed by supposedly anonymous actors can be accurately attributed to a specific person. After all, people are people, and people make mistakes.

Cybercrimes can be committed either directly against a computer system (such as hacking into a website) or by leveraging a computer system as an accessory in a different type of crime (such as distributing child pornography). As a forensic investigator, either full-time or occasional, this is an important distinction to remember. You usually don't have the choice of which type of crime you investigate. This has led to many in the profession who are specialists in crimes against computers, technologists by nature, being slightly caught out when crimes that use computers as an accessory have fallen into their laps for investigation. An example of this is when you are suddenly asked to investigate a fellow employee for suspected wrongdoing.

The insider threat

Organisations are realising, thanks to famous cases such as the tale of Edward Snowden, the now infamous National Security Agency (NSA) secrets leaker, that insiders can pose the most serious threat. Those who have been trusted with the access required to do their jobs can, if driven by nefarious motivations, become the most damaging presence on a network.

In June 2013, Edward Snowden was a systems administrator for a subcontractor providing services to the NSA, the United States' equivalent of the Government Communications Headquarters (GCHQ) in the UK. Motivated by his belief that the NSA was violating the rights of ordinary American citizens, he leveraged his privileged access to obtain and leak a number of highly classified documents.

Ask anyone who has worked as an IT administrator at an organisation without a dedicated security team, and they'll probably have plenty of stories of the times they were asked to collect evidence to help support disciplinary or even legal proceedings against someone within the organisation. This is a common scenario and, depending on the experience, one that can shape that person's perception of digital forensics. It can become a messy business that people want no part of, but, with a bit of insight and preparation, you can spare yourself some of the less desirable aspects and make your role in the forensics process very clear.

Often people approach the investigator with a non-specific ask, something like, 'Hey, we know this guy is doing something dodgy at work, can you tell us what it is?' This isn't the way things should work, at all. Instead, the first thing you should demand as an investigator is a very specific allegation. Something like, 'On Wednesday we believe X did Y, can you find evidence of that?' If this can't be provided, it is best to step back from the investigation and not become involved. This simple rule will help to ensure your digital forensics experience remains a positive one.

Digital forensics has evolved

Just as technologies evolve, so do the challenges faced by digital forensic investigators. These days, the answers can be found in many places, not just on the hard disks of computers. Cloud storage and services, while highly convenient and cost-effective from a business perspective, are a game changer from an evidence preservation perspective. Similarly, smartphones and tablets, now in widespread use, provide yet another in-scope source of potential evidence that require a whole new set of tools.

As we work through the digital forensics section of this book (Part 2), we're going to look at the various tools and techniques, along with the scientific and legal aspects to the process. The aim is to equip you with the knowledge you'll need to make your case and not leave you open to questioning. You should always, always, conduct your actions as if you'll have to defend them in a legal setting. If you do this, you'll be set up for success.

WHY BOTH?

Now that we've talked about the two fundamental topics we're going to cover in this book, let's revisit why we're packaging them together, especially given my earlier statement that they can sometimes be at odds with one another.

Let's be clear. There is a definite overlap between the incident response and digital forensics realms. Knowing how to recognise this overlap and understand when an incident response is turning into a digital forensics investigation, or, conversely, when an investigation requires that an incident response is triggered, will unquestionably help you to deliver value to your organisation.

Business pressures and workloads might try to steer you in one direction or another, but if you have a good understanding of both incident response and digital forensics, you'll be able to make the right choices for your given scenario.

Every organisation is different. The information security needs for a healthcare company are very different from the information security needs at a cloud services provider. Some companies have significant security resources, whereas others scrape by with the bare minimum. Just as you must balance risk in other aspects of information security, you must also balance the risk of not completing a digital forensics investigation as a follow-up to an incident.

HANDS-ON

The fact that this book has 'hands-on' in the title is very deliberate. There are plenty of textbooks that cover incident response and digital forensic theory. In this book, we're going to go a step further. We will take the theory and, using case studies and examples, apply it to real-life scenarios.

When I started in this field I'd studied a great deal of theory, but absolutely none of the books I read could prepare me for some of the real-life, human pressures I'd face in the field. Sure, knowing how to properly prepare a forensic image of a suspect's laptop is a core skill for any forensic investigator, but no one mentioned that at times I'd be doing so in front of a suspect with their legal representation, and even with a young child present. This actually happened, and on more than one occasion. I wish I'd had a heads-up that this might be the case before I'd got started!

That said, despite the awkward and sometimes uncomfortable situations that can be associated with an investigation, nothing comes close to the satisfaction you experience when your work helps bring a wrongdoer to justice.

Incident response and digital forensics are, in my opinion, the most interesting aspects of information security. Even when things start to get close to mundane, they won't stay that way for long. If you like to be challenged, think fast, and be on the cutting edge of technology, I can assure you that you're in the right place.

HOW THIS BOOK FITS IN

There is a significant amount of material pertaining to these two topics that we will cover over the next 16 chapters. There are two parts to the book, as already mentioned: the first focuses on incident response and the second on digital forensics. Although the parts are distinct and clearly have a primary focus, you will see multiple instances of overlap throughout. This is by design, and illustrates how you can make the jump from one discipline to the other.

In both parts, the chapters are laid out to mirror the typical chronologies of both incident response and digital forensics processes. Given this, it is highly recommended that the book is read in sequence, as the chapters build on material covered previously.

Intertwined with the theory, I've included a number of my own first-hand experiences in both incident response and digital forensics. There are also a number of relevant case studies from incidents and investigations that I've researched as part of the writing process for this book. These anecdotes and case studies are presented in boxes, associated with a relevant section of text.

PART 1
INCIDENT RESPONSE

1 UNDERSTANDING INFORMATION SECURITY INCIDENTS

Information security is a broad topic, with many subdisciplines. You could work in application security, network security, compliance, forensics or a security operations role, or be a lawyer specialising in information security and data privacy. All of these information security roles appeal to people with different skill sets, experience levels and interests.

An organisation can have one person spending some time on security where possible, or a dedicated security team (this could be as large as several thousand full-time employees), with budgets that vary just as broadly. Despite all the differences between these roles, and the resources available to a given security team, one event that binds us all together is the security incident. We're all working to reduce the likelihood of them occurring in the first place, and to minimise the impact they cause when they do happen. In this chapter, we're going to be looking at what exactly makes a security incident a security incident, common methods of detection, and why they will continue to occur.

WHAT IS AN INFORMATION SECURITY INCIDENT?

Before we can respond to, or even attempt to plan for, an information security incident, we must first define what exactly an information security incident is. Various standards and publications have their own definition, but many of these definitions are variants of the definition afforded by NIST (National Institute of Standards and Technology) Special Publication (SP) 800-61, *Computer Security Incident Handling Guide*:

A security incident is the act of violating an explicit or implied security policy.

In this book we'll be using this NIST definition of an information security incident.

The beauty of this definition is that it can be applied globally to any organisation, but by referencing a security policy it accommodates the significant differences between individual organisations and their risk profiles. For example, at most Silicon Valley start-up offices you'll see people using their smartphones freely in their work areas without issue. Doing so at the office of a defence contractor handling classified information would very likely be considered a serious security incident. The same activity, in two different environments: one is acceptable, the other is a security incident. Policy is the differentiator.

This should serve to reinforce the importance of security policies for all organisations, no matter the size or industry. After all, you can't take action against someone for violating a policy if there aren't any policies for them to violate. The first step in creating an incident response plan should be revisiting other information security policies, first to make sure that they are in place, and secondly to ensure that they are up to date.

TYPES OF INCIDENT

Although the detail of what makes a security incident a security incident may vary from organisation to organisation, we can still classify several types of security incident that are universally considered as such.

At the highest level security incidents fall into two categories. The first of these categories is incidents with internal origins, meaning an incident caused by an insider to an organisation. An example of this would be an employee mishandling data, either deliberately or accidentally. The second category is incidents with external origins, meaning, as you can probably guess, an incident caused by an outsider to an organisation. An example of this type of incident would be if a user is phished by a malicious attacker who goes on to use stolen credentials to obtain unauthorised access to data.

All security incidents are sensitive matters, but some are more sensitive than others. The external versus internal classification scheme also serves as a guide to the level of confidentiality that should be applied to an incident. As a security incident handler, you will likely have access to a great deal of sensitive information. This is often a necessary side effect of being effective in detecting security incidents. Given that internal security incidents often involve the actions of a single employee, they are typically much more sensitive and are treated on a 'need to know' basis. Simply put, this means that only the people who 'need to know' the details of the incident will be informed. Conversely, if an external attacker defaces a web page, the chances are that more people will be involved in the clean-up operation, from both technical and public relations perspectives, and therefore more people will 'need to know'.

Let's run through some examples of incidents that fall into these two categories.

Internal incident types

In information security it is often said that your people are your greatest asset, as well as your greatest risk. The types of security incident caused by insiders to an organisation can range from innocent mistakes made while trying to do the right thing to purposefully malicious actions designed to cause harm.

Inappropriate data handling

Data is the lifeblood of most organisations: payment card data, healthcare data, customer data, analytical data and financial data, to name but a few types of the stuff. With data come various rules and requirements for how it is handled. For example, in the case of payment card data the Payment Card Industry Data Security Standard (PCI DSS) rules supreme; this contains a number of requirements an organisation must meet if they wish to handle credit card numbers and process payments.

General legal requirements for the handling of data about individuals, such as the Data Protection Act (1998) in the UK and its Europe-wide replacement that took effect in 2018, the General Data Protection Regulation (GDPR), contain provisions and penalties for non-compliance and must be adhered to.

An organisation may also have certain contractual requirements it must meet when handling customer data, for example a requirement not to share customer data with a third party for analytical purposes.

If any of these industry, legal or contractual requirements are violated by an insider at an organisation, either intentionally or accidentally, this could constitute a security incident. Mistakes such as storing sensitive data on removable storage media without proper encryption are more common than people would like to admit, and could be highly damaging to a business.

In recent times, the rapid growth of cloud services has led to some significant data handling mistakes as operators get to grips with doing things in new ways. There have been many reported cases of massive data files being made accessible to the entire internet because an incorrect permission setting was being used on the cloud storage service they were being stored in.

'Shadow IT' is another trend that can lead to this type of security incident. People get used to using a service personally, for example using Google Drive to store files, and want to use it for work too. Rather than getting approval from an IT authority within the company, they take the path of least resistance and just use the service anyway. Without the appropriate security, compliance and legal review and oversight, this can lead to significant problems for an organisation.

Mishandling security credentials

Credentials, such as user account names and passwords, uniquely identify a user within an organisation, and are all that stand between the user and the data they are allowed to access to be able to do their job. Despite this, people commonly mishandle their credentials. Remember, people are people, and people make mistakes (this is going to be a common theme in this book!).

The improper storage, transmission and disclosure of passwords are significant challenges for any organisation. As an example, many have dealt with employees sharing passwords with fellow employees while on holiday to facilitate some type of access to cover a given task.

Service accounts are user accounts that are used by computers to log in to other computers to perform a function. An example of this would be a service account used to deploy a piece of software across every machine on a network. Service accounts frequently have elevated permissions when compared to the accounts used by their human counterparts, so are a particularly enticing target for an attacker. It is for this reason that service account passwords should be securely shared between the systems administrator and the team requesting the account. All too often, these passwords are shared via instant message or email rather than a secure password vault tool.

A lost, stolen or otherwise mishandled set of credentials should always be treated as a security incident.

Acceptable use policy violations

Organisations leverage acceptable use policies to govern what employees can and cannot do when using their computer equipment. This can be highly important in creating a safe work environment for everyone. Common examples of things that are prohibited by acceptable use policies include:

- accessing pornography using work computers;
- illegally downloading copyrighted materials;
- sending abusive emails to others using work email systems;
- installing hacking tools or malicious software on the computer;
- disabling security features on the computer such as antivirus protection or encryption.

A violation of an acceptable use policy can be considered a security incident.

Unauthorised access

Sometimes, an insider can leverage their access, or the access afforded to a fellow employee, to obtain data they are not normally authorised to obtain. For example, why would someone in the sales department need access to another employee's payroll information? There are various malicious motivations that may lead to someone obtaining unauthorised access to data, and there are many different ways that it can happen. Sometimes it can even happen accidentally.

If unauthorised access to data is detected then that is a security incident, and it must be treated as such to ensure that any follow-up actions needed to prevent a repeat incident are conducted.

It is also worth noting that unauthorised access incidents can also exist in the physical realm. Unauthorised access to a data centre could lead to unwanted physical access. If a malicious attacker has physical access to a server, the chances of being able to successfully protect it are greatly reduced.

External incident types

Every single business, across every type of industry, should consider themselves a target for malicious external actors leveraging technology to cause harm. When discussing what motivates those outside a business to break in, common themes include financial motivators, intellectual property theft, data exfiltration and compromise of IT assets for reuse in other cybercrimes. In other words, there is no shortage of reasons why, and given the amount of interconnectivity in the modern world, there is no shortage of potential attack vectors for them to exploit.

A hacking attack against a web application or network

This is the 'classic' incident. A malicious actor finds a vulnerability in a web application, then exploits the vulnerability to compromise the application. From there, depending on the motivation of the attacker, the outcome could be something as simple as website defacement, perhaps in an act of hacktivism,[1] or something as complex as establishing a persistent presence to be able to steal credit card information.

There are various types of vulnerability that could be present in a web application, and we'll look at these in more detail in the incident response process and network forensics section of Chapter 11.

Phishing or spear-phishing attack

This is the most common method for an attacker to gain access to an organisation. Phishing attacks are dirt cheap, require minimal technical skill and rely on the omnipresent trusting nature of humans, particularly those who are less technically savvy.

In a phishing attack, the victim is sent a nefarious email that is crafted to look like it is from a trusted source. This could be a bank, a government department or even a social media site. The email will usually indicate that something requires the victim's action to resolve promptly to avoid some sort of disruption to their daily lives, usually involving money – 'Your bank account is about to be frozen' or 'we're issuing you a fine' are common examples. The resolution requires the victim to log in to a fake version of the site that allegedly sent the email, and in doing so they hand over their valuable credentials to the phisher.

Spear phishing is a variant on phishing, and is essentially a more targeted phishing email in which the attacker has done additional research, and may try to exploit a relationship between the victim and a third party. A classic example of this is posing as the chief executive officer of a company and asking an employee to reply with sensitive information. Similarly, chief financial officers are constantly targeted by spear-phishing emails asking them to make payments, because they are known to have the ability to make large cash withdrawals or transfers with minimal oversight.

Malware/ransomware attack

Some of the earliest examples of malware were produced in the late 1980s, and just as computers and the internet have evolved, so too has malware. Malware, or malicious software to use its full moniker, is a computer program built for the sole purpose of damaging or otherwise compromising a computer system. Every day, organisations are bombarded by emails that contain malware-laden attachments. All it takes for disaster to strike is for one of these to slip through the cracks and perhaps land on a machine that hasn't received all the relevant security updates.

Malware is a complex topic, and there are many different variants to get to grips with. Wiper malware is designed to destroy data; remote-access malware can be used by an attacker to remotely control a computer or silently watch as the victim goes about

---

[1] Hacktivism is a portmanteau of 'hacker' and 'activism', and is used to describe hackers working in support of a political cause.

their business, and then there is the latest trend – ransomware. This is a particularly nasty type of malware because it exploits both the actual and sentimental value of data that people generate. Once on a victim machine, ransomware works by encrypting files, usually images, movies, documents and spreadsheets, with a key that is known only to the attacker. The victim is then forced to pay real money to get that key so that they can safely decrypt their files. Of course, there is no guarantee that the victim will receive the key.

In early May 2017 a ransomware strain known as WannaCry began targeting machines running the Microsoft Windows operating system. The ransomware exploited a significant vulnerability in the operating system's implementation of the Server Message Block protocol. WannaCry was a worm, which meant it self-replicated and was able to spread around networks to other vulnerable machines.

The ransomware encrypted files on machines and demanded a ransom, to be paid in Bitcoin, of around £385, increasing to £770 after three days.

WannaCry is estimated to have affected around 400,000 machines in total, and claimed several high-profile victims. The National Health Service (NHS) of the United Kingdom was particularly badly affected, and even had to cancel planned medical operations as staff scrambled to run on backup paper systems.

Denial of service (DoS) attack

If you've ever spent time on the platform of Paddington station during peak commuting hours, you've likely experienced a denial of service as you try to board the train. All those additional people cramming through a small number of doors mean that things move slowly, and you may even have to wait for a train or two to get on.

In the digital realm a denial of service attack follows the same pattern, but with packets, not people. A denial of service occurs when a system is overwhelmed by traffic and is unable to function as it should. If this occurs on an ecommerce site it will result in lost revenue, as shoppers will be unable to shop and will therefore go elsewhere.

Attackers often use malware to 'recruit' victim machines into large networks of compromised computers. These victim machines are known as zombies, and the networks are known as botnets. One of the most common uses for a botnet is to launch a denial of service attack. An attacker may control a botnet of some tens of thousands of machines. If all those machines start sending malicious or malformed traffic to a victim website, it is likely to experience a denial of service. This particular approach, using many machines, is also known as a distributed denial of service (DDoS) attack.

Denial of service attacks can also be used as a diversionary tactic to draw the incident responder's attention away from whatever other activity the attacker is engaged in.

In October 2016, a highly significant denial of service attack caused disruption to various internet services in North America and Europe. The denial of service was sourced from Mirai, a botnet made up of tens of millions of compromised 'internet of things' (IoT) devices. These included printers, security cameras and even baby monitors.

The target of the attack was a company called Dyn, which provides Domain Name System (DNS) services to many major internet sites such as Twitter, Netflix and Airbnb. This is the technology used to translate domain names to Internet Protocol (IP) addresses on the internet through a series of lookup queries.

The infected devices overwhelmed Dyn's DNS infrastructure, causing legitimate DNS queries to time out and making them inaccessible to most users.

Serious vulnerability discovered in externally facing application

Software vulnerabilities are nothing new, and by now most people, whether technical by nature or not, will have experienced having to install an urgent software update to address a security vulnerability. An organisation will typically have programmes in place for handling software vulnerabilities in third-party software they run, such as operating systems or web server software.

If an organisation is in the business of developing their own software, then they should also have hooks into various parts of their software development life cycle (SDLC) to handle security vulnerabilities that may be discovered and reported either during development or after release.

So why would a newly discovered software vulnerability be considered a security incident? To answer this question, I'd like to go back to 7 April 2014. This was the day a highly significant vulnerability, dubbed 'Heartbleed', was disclosed to the world. Heartbleed was a vulnerability in a very popular open-source software library, OpenSSL. The job of OpenSSL is to handle connections to web servers that leverage the Secure Sockets Layer (SSL) protocol for encrypted data transmission. In other words, OpenSSL is responsible for protecting sensitive information sent between a client computer and a web server.

If exploited, the Heartbleed vulnerability could be used to access a chunk of the vulnerable web server's memory, which could include sensitive data such as passwords submitted by users.

Half a million web servers were estimated to be at risk from Heartbleed, and attackers started to exploit the bug within hours of it being disclosed. Given this, organisations were forced to patch fast, and those who couldn't patch quickly enough, or didn't take the vulnerability seriously enough, placed themselves at huge risk. In many organisations the only way to get the expeditious reaction required for Heartbleed was to declare a security incident and get everyone who could help involved in the recovery effort.

A lot of lessons were learned from the Heartbleed vulnerability, perhaps the biggest being the realisation that there is so little time to react when something like it is disclosed. For this reason, incident response plans were updated to include 'Heartbleed-like' issues.

Figure 1.1 shows an application that is vulnerable to a command injection attack. It is highly likely that if this application was in production use, and exposed to the internet, an automated scan would discover the vulnerability and begin exploitation attempts within minutes.

Figure 1.1 A command injection vulnerability is used to expose the Linux /etc/ passwd file via a web application

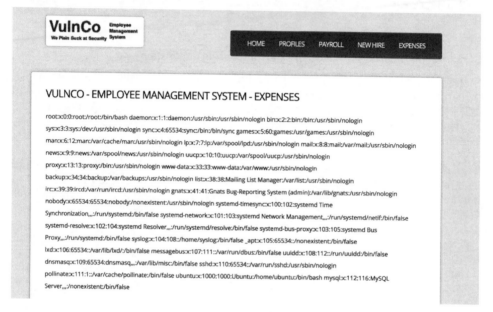

False positives

As a security incident handler, I can assure you that the most common type of security incident you'll work on will not be malware related, or phishing related, or even insider threat related. Instead, it'll be a false positive. A false positive, in this context, is a condition that might suggest an incident is occurring, but can actually be attributed to some legitimate activity or event that poses no risk to the organisation.

False positives are common and are not an indicator of failure on the part of the incident handler or reporter. I'll happily take picking up on 10 false positives in a given day over not having the visibility or insight to notice something that could be an incident. That said, steps should be taken to reduce the number of false positives. This can involve tuning your monitoring equipment, such as intrusion detection systems (IDS), to weed out alarms caused by legitimate traffic (we'll talk more about this later in this chapter).

I was out mowing the lawn one Saturday morning when a call came in on the security on-call number. A relatively new systems administrator was on the other end of the line. He explained to me how he'd just rebooted a VMware ESX hypervisor server for the first time since he started at the company. On boot-up, he'd noticed an ominous message in the server's BIOS messaging. It read 'ALL YOUR SERVERS ARE BELONG TO US', an apparent reference to the famous line from the 1992 video game *Zero Wing*. The original line was 'ALL YOUR BASES ARE BELONG TO US', a phrase in broken English that eventually found a second life as an internet meme.

Believing, quite understandably, that some malicious actor had taken control of the VMware server and was responsible for the taunting BIOS message, he called the security team per our established procedures. A breach of a hypervisor would be a very serious issue, as it could potentially impact all the virtual machines it was responsible for running.

I started to run through our breach checklist, but in the back of my mind I was confident that I could attribute this boot-up message to a former systems administrator who, although not malicious, was, shall we say, a bit of a character. With this in mind, I put in a call to a more senior systems administrator who'd been at the company for a longer period of time. The breach checklist revealed no evidence of compromise, and a few minutes later I received confirmation that our 'zany' former systems administrator used to put this message on all servers as 'standard'.

A classic false positive, that could really have been avoided. Despite this, I still made a point to thank the junior systems administrator for making the call, and getting security involved.

DETECTING SECURITY INCIDENTS

So now we've got a good handle on what constitutes a security incident, let's consider how we might become aware that a security incident has occurred, or is still occurring. Of course, it's worth remembering that every incident is different; they can materialise in a variety of ways depending on the technical and administrative controls in place. On this note, a particularly effective way to increase your value as a security incident handler is to invent new detection methods, especially if you're doing so to detect types of incident that are very specific to your organisation or industry. An example of this could be building an intrusion detection system signature for an industry-specific attacker or exploit.

Technical security incident detection

Technical controls are at the front line of incident detection and, depending on the size and structure of an organisation's security team, the incident responder may also be responsible for deploying them, or at least consulting on the controls and where they should be deployed.

Intrusion detection systems or intrusion prevention systems

There are plenty of spins out there on this well-established security technology. An IDS will alert you to activity that it believes to be indicative of an intrusion, whereas an intrusion prevention system (IPS) will go a step further and actually block the suspected intrusion. Given that an IPS reacts rather than alerts, some people question why IDS solutions are still deployed. Surely, it's better to do something than just yell about it?

It's a fair question, and one that has an answer in an area of focus that technology people don't always consider: the business. Remember, neither IDS nor IPS solutions are perfect – they often misclassify legitimate activity as malicious. Not such a big deal if you're just detecting, it's more of an annoyance than anything else, but if you're blocking the wrong thing you can break a critical business process. That doesn't do anything for the perception of the security team.

Intrusion detection or prevention systems are typically deployed either at the network level or directly on endpoints, like laptops or servers. You'll often see the abbreviations NIDS and HIDS used to demonstrate the differences: NIDS is network-based IDS, HIDS is host-based IDS.

The systems use signatures to match traffic patterns that appear malicious. These signatures are essentially a set of rules that must be met in order for the IDS/IPS to alert or block. For example, a rule might say that the traffic must be to the IP address 1.2.3.4, it must include an HTTP request for the file 'bad.php' and the request must be 12 kilobytes in size.

Alerts generated by a well-tuned IDS/IPS solution are critically important to the security incident handler and are often the first sign that something is awry. It is also important that new signatures are added and tuned as they become available to stay on top of new and emerging threats. In some organisations, a formal signature review board may meet to discuss which signatures need tuning or updating.

Log files

Lots of things can generate log files – firewalls, web servers, applications and operating systems, to name but a few examples. Given the breadth of coverage afforded by log files, it is no surprise that they can be a gold mine of critical information for detecting security incidents. There's just one problem. The sheer volume of data produced in log files makes them hard to handle, retain and mine for that valuable information. It simply isn't anything close to practical for someone to review every line in the many gigabytes or terabytes of log data generated by the typical organisation every day.

Thankfully, log aggregation tools, such as Splunk[2] and Sumologic[3] in the commercial world and the Elasticsearch[4] ecosystem in the open-source realm, exist to watch the

---

[2] Splunk (2018) *SIEM, AIOps, Application Management, Log Management, Machine Learning, and Compliance | Splunk*. Splunk Inc. Available from https://www.splunk.com/ [16 April 2018].

[3] Sumo Logic (2018) *Log Management & Security Analytics, Continuous Intelligence: Sumo Logic*. Sumo Logic. Available from https://www.sumologic.com/ [16 April 2018].

[4] Elastic (2018) *Open Source Search & Analytics · Elasticsearch | Elastic*. Elasticsearch BV. Available from https://www.elastic.co/ [6 April 2018].

logs and alert on specific conditions being met. These tools leverage log files proactively, but also require a significant investment to deploy and optimise.

If log files are used proactively they can provide an early warning of an incident in progress. More often than not, they are used reactively to gain additional context. Given this, it is critically important that log files are protected and stored in a separate system from the one that generated them. Remember, log files are a form of self-reporting, and if an attacker can manipulate or erase them before they are stored, they aren't going to be that useful. Log files can be valuable evidence, so need to be protected from tampering if they're to be used in a later forensic investigation.

Wire data

Wire-data tools, such as ExtraHop[5] (see Figure 1.2), Corvil[6] or ntop,[7] listen to network traffic as it flows across critical points, such as a core switch in a data centre. Traditionally these tools have been targeted at network engineering teams who need to keep an eye on network performance, but more frequently they are being marketed towards security teams.

Wire-data tools are similar in a way to a closed-circuit television camera (CCTV). They sit out of band, meaning they listen to the network by way of a monitor or span port, or even a dedicated network tap device, recording activity as it occurs in real time.

These factors make wire-data tools highly valuable for security incident handlers in detecting incidents identifiable by network traffic pattern changes.

Machine learning and anomaly detection

A relatively new trend is the application of machine learning to security incident detection. Machine learning is a field of computer science concerned with teaching computers to think for themselves, without being explicitly programmed how to think; this is typically achieved using mathematical algorithms.

In security incident detection, applying a machine learning algorithm to a vast array of network traffic data could yield the discovery of an anomaly in the data that might otherwise be impossible to detect. This is a growing field, but there is the potential for significant value to be found here for the security incident handler. Both the log aggregation suites and wire-data analytics platforms mentioned earlier are starting to include machine learning capabilities as part of their products.

Security incident and event management (SIEM)

All of these technical detection methods are incredibly powerful but must be harnessed properly to be effective. In a larger organisation, teams rarely have the opportunity to

---

[5] ExtraHop (2018) *ExtraHop: IT Operations & Wire Data Analytics Platform | ExtraHop*. Extrahop Networks. Available from https://www.extrahop.com/ [16 April 2018].
[6] Corvil (2018) *Network Analytics for IT Ops, Security & Digital Business – Corvil*. Corvil. Available from https://www.corvil.com/ [16 April 2018].
[7] ntop (2018) *ntop* – High Performance Network Monitoring Solutions based on Open Source and Commodity Hardware. ntop. Available from https://www.ntop.org/ [16 April 2018].

Figure 1.2 The ExtraHop wire-data analytics platform

review every IDS alert or every strange event in a log file. The solution, at least in part, is a SIEM tool.

A SIEM tool takes data from the various technical security controls across the organisation, correlates it, and spits the results out onto a (I'm sorry, I'm about to use an overloaded marketing term) single pane of glass display. Essentially, the goal of SIEM is to reduce the number of places the incident responder has to search for information relevant to a potential security incident.

As an example, if a log file entry for a known malicious IP address was detected at the same time as the wire-data system saw a connection to that address, we can be pretty sure that a conversation occurred with the malicious address.

SIEM tools, such as IBM's QRadar,[8] RSA's Netwitness[9] and AlienVault's open-source OSSIM[10] (see Figure 1.3), are extremely valuable, but only if deployed properly, and only if the incoming data quality has been validated. Remember: garbage in, garbage out. SIEM deployments always require the full support of the entire business to be successful, because they touch so many areas.

Non-technical security incident detection

Sometimes we come across security incidents in completely non-technical ways.

Someone reports an incident

'I think I got phished', or 'I double-clicked on this application and my files are now encrypted.' Two very common examples of user-reported security incidents.

End users in computer incidents are on the front line, and therefore well positioned to report anything that is suspect. A couple of things must be in place for them to do so. First, there must be a procedure for them to follow; it could just be calling the helpdesk, who in turn will have a procedure to escalate to the security team. Secondly, and most importantly, there must be a culture of trust within the organisation so that people are not afraid to report things, especially when a mistake has been made.

The police show up

Computers can be both victims of and accessories to a crime. The first you might hear that a security incident has occurred is if the police show up with a search warrant requesting the seizure of certain IT assets.

If a suspect has been using their work email address to send threatening emails, for example, the police may want to seize a copy of those emails and the suspect's laptop.

---

[8] IBM (2018) *IBM QRadar SIEM – Overview.* IBM. Available from https://www.ibm.com/us-en/marketplace/ibm-qradar-siem [16 April 2018].

[9] RSA (2018) *SIEM – Security Information and Event Management | RSA.* RSA Security LLC. Available from https://www.rsa.com/en-us/products/threat-detection-and-response/ siem-security-information-event-management [16 April 2018].

[10] AlienVault (2018) *OSSIM: The Open Source SIEM | AlienVault.* AlienVault Inc. Available from https://www.alienvault.com/products/ossim [16 April 2018].

Figure 1.3 AlienVault's OSSIM product

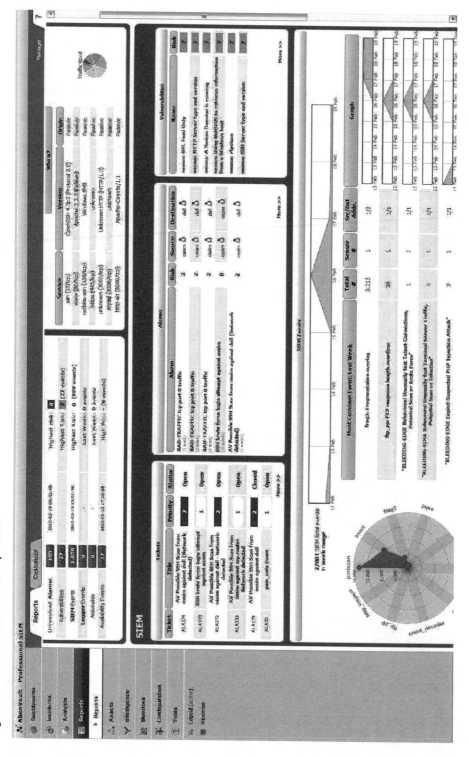

Human resources investigations

Human resources departments may discover or may suspect a security incident during disciplinary proceedings.

At this point the security team may become involved in helping to confirm the suspicion and preserve evidence.

Penetration test or audit findings

A penetration test is a simulated attack on a network or web application that an organisation orders up to test their security.

An audit is typically a review of administrative and technical controls in place at an organisation for the purposes of certifying compliance with a given standard. If a major flaw or something else unexpected turns up during either of these processes, then a security incident could be triggered.

For example, if during an audit it turns out that a systems administrator is running an illicit web hosting company from an old machine under their desk, that should be treated as a security incident.

WHY DO SECURITY INCIDENTS HAPPEN?

Security incidents happen daily and will continue to happen with such frequency so long as people use computers.

In the field of security incident response, we have two goals:

- reduce the overall number of security incidents;
- reduce the impact of security incidents when they do happen.

In order to achieve these goals it is important to understand some of the reasons that incidents happen in the first place.

Overly restrictive security controls

Sometimes in information security we can be our own worst enemy. Deploying a highly restrictive security control may sound great on paper, but it can do more harm than good. If a security control is deployed without proper understanding of the various business needs and processes that will be affected by the control, you can rest assured that people will fight it, or just work around it. The security team's relationship with the business leadership can also take a turn for the worse if they're perceived as being overzealous when deploying controls.

For example, if you prevent the sending of emails containing attachments from corporate email accounts, chances are people will send attachments from personal email accounts, which is worse.

Lack of a defined process or education

If you don't teach people how to do things securely, can you really blame them when they don't?

Security awareness training, and bespoke training for a given sensitive process, must be in place to ensure that people have read and fully understood security policies. Oh, and if your security awareness training is making your people sit through 150 PowerPoint slides, I've got bad news for you: that's not going to be effective training. People need to be engaged to really appreciate what they're being taught. Simply 'not knowing I was doing something wrong' can lead to a security incident.

Business pressures

In any job, there is always a certain degree of pressure. Pressure to meet deadlines, pressure to deploy a new feature in your software, pressure to let the boss install that video streaming application on their work laptop. Business pressures can lead to decisions that adversely impact security – for example, choosing to spend time installing shiny new software rather than spending time applying security patches to operating systems. This is where having strong leadership in security is critical. Without the support of the entire business, a security team can find themselves constantly swimming against the current.

Accidental exposure to the internet

As more and more organisations move their applications and workloads out of traditional and co-located data centres to cloud services, many information technology employees are having to reskill and understand a new way of doing things. As with anything new, when you start using it you're still learning, and more likely to make mistakes. When working with cloud providers, these mistakes could include accidentally exposing systems or services to the internet or allowing unauthenticated access to data. In recent years, many such incidents have been reported.

Failure to test

Early security involvement in application development is crucial, to ensure that potential vulnerabilities can be removed or mitigated before any code is ever produced. Unfortunately, factors such as a lack of application security specialists, a desire to build fast and ship often, and the pressure of delivering a product on a given timeline mean that sometimes vulnerabilities can go undetected for years. Then, even if they are eventually uncovered, a lack of support for a security programme, or those same pressures to deliver, can delay mitigation.

People are people

I may have mentioned this one once or twice. The vast majority of incidents are attributable to human factors. You may have the most secure network in the world, but if one of your employees stores sensitive information in their corporate email account, and subsequently gets phished, guess what? It's incident response time!

SUMMARY

In this chapter we've defined a security incident, introduced the different types of incident and discussed some ways that we may become aware of an incident. Finally, we touched on the reasons that security incidents can occur.

As you can tell from this opening chapter, the scope of the incident responder's role is significant, and can vary dramatically between different incidents. That said, we always work to the same goal: a well-executed response that allows us to get an organisation back on its feet, no matter what a specific incident may throw our way.

That well-executed response starts with a healthy chunk of planning and preparation, ideally conducted in the calmer waters of the time prior to an incident occurring. In our next chapter we'll look at how we can do just this, and be prepared to face those incidents with confidence and control.

2 BEFORE THE INCIDENT

There is an old phrase that many who've worked in the information security world will be very familiar with: 'No one is interested in security, until everyone is interested in security.' What this phrase is getting at is that people tend to pay more attention to security after a security incident has occurred. Unfortunately, there is more than a sliver of truth to this. I've known many folks, myself included, whose jobs were created thanks to additional funding made available following a security incident. I've even heard some security folks wish an incident upon their employer to advance their own security agenda, as extreme as that would be. As good, ethical security professionals, we will not adopt this mindset. Instead, we will work hard before the incident occurs to make sure all the pieces are in place for when we have to go into response mode. This is a much more satisfying, and healthy, way to go about things.

In this chapter we'll discuss the proactive technical and political steps that an incident responder should be taking prior to getting the phone call asking them to join the incident bridge. This includes building a playbook to refer to during the incident, and developing an understanding of the systems you're going to be working hard to defend.

BUILDING THE INCIDENT RESPONSE PLAYBOOK

If you're charged with leading your organisation through a security incident, your first task should be to compile an incident response playbook. This is usually an iterative process, and the first version of the playbook can be limited to a list of key contacts and a rough outline of the process to be followed in the event that a security incident is declared. However, the best playbooks are those compiled by an author, or team of authors, who have taken the time to really 'get to know' the business, its processes and its people.

The primary audience of the incident response playbook is of course the person, or people, charged with running the incident response. That said, it should be a document that can be made available to anyone in the organisation, especially members of other technical teams. You might even consider making the playbook available to customers or partners as part of a contractual agreement, or you might be required to do so. If you write a playbook with this in mind, it can actually become a differentiator for your company in the sales cycle. Vendor security reviews can make or break a sales deal, and one thing vendor due diligence teams like to see is a vendor who is prepared, in detail, to handle an incident. That said, I'd recommend removing any on-call contact information from a playbook given to a customer – if they have a direct number that they know someone will answer quickly, they will use it!

Review existing security policies

First, grab a coffee, and print and review all of the available organisational security policies. If you think back to the definition of a security incident from Chapter 1, you'll remember that the definition speaks to the violation of policies, so you'll need to review them to figure out what types of incident you might have to handle. If the organisation doesn't have any security policies, then return to the start, do not pass Go and do not collect £200; it's going to be incredibly difficult to build a playbook without them. The lack of even a single security policy would suggest that there is not enough overarching support for a security programme, and therefore you might need to be the one to seek out that support.

Once you do have security policies, and have confirmed that they're up to date, you'll be able to get a feel for:

- the types of incident you should be preparing for;
- what the organisation is most concerned about protecting.

On the second bullet point, if you have a security policy with 15 pages dedicated to rules about handling customer data, and only one page on laptop security, you can infer that customer data is the bigger concern.

Borrow from 'regular' incident management

Even if an organisation hasn't yet broached the topic of security incident management, many will have addressed handling non-security-related IT incidents. Things like network outages and software bugs that disrupt business operations are extremely damaging, and it has been long accepted that the fallout from them can be managed through a well-defined process.

Incident and change managers at organisations are usually battle hardened, able to navigate around the politics of an organisation, well connected, and now, as the person responsible for security incidents, your new best friends. A lot of the initial discovery work that goes into preparing the security incident response playbook is likely to have been completed by this person, or people, historically. Ask to review it and ingest as much of it as possible.

You can also review the tools and software that the incident manager or equivalent is using to track incidents, and alert teams that may be on call, to determine whether they will fit your security incident management needs. Many teams prefer to use a single notification system for all incident types, since this means they only have one source to monitor. In a security incident, it is important to have a reliable mechanism to get hold of the appropriate people quickly. This mechanism should be determined at this point in the planning phase. Even if it is ultimately decided to go in another direction, there are still likely to be good lessons about how the organisation prefers to handle incidents.

While it can be efficient to 'borrow' certain aspects of the incident management process, avoid an all-out pairing of incident management for both security and non-security incidents. The reason is that IT incident management processes, and the teams that execute them, typically like to get as many eyes on the issue as possible, usually a representative from each technology team. For example, if an application is running in a degraded state, the server team, the application team and the network team might all be immediately summoned to the incident bridge to get their respective takes on the situation.

Security incidents, by their very nature, can be sensitive affairs. If compromise of the HR database is suspected, affecting all staff at the company, having them all find out through an incident announcement while the incident is still occurring is clearly not the best approach. A dedicated, and protected, security incident phone bridge is an example of maintaining the separation between a 'regular' incident and a security incident.

Sometimes, as mentioned earlier, a regular incident can become a security incident. In this case, while you're busy getting to know the incident manager, a process for transitioning the state of the incident from one playbook to another, in either direction (suspected security incidents can also turn out to be 'regular' incidents), should be crafted.

Study business processes

Unless you're working for a specialised consultancy firm, most businesses are not in business to respond to security incidents, they usually have other things going on. As good incident responders putting together an incident response playbook, we should spend time really getting to understand the business. This doesn't just mean a high-level understanding of what the business does, but also digging a little deeper and understanding the nuts and bolts of critical business processes.

Now, what is a critical business process? Different people will define this in different ways – many people will likely attest that whatever process they're working on is critical! As the American business management author Patrick Lencioni once said, 'If everything is important, then nothing is important.'[11] This is especially true in the security realm; since resources and time are often constrained, we need to dedicate our energy to truly critical processes. From our perspective, a critical business process can be defined as:

- a process that if disrupted would cause significant financial impact to the business;
- a process that if compromised would cause significant damage to the business.

A compromised process could of course become a disrupted process, but not always. For example, in an incident where a payment process has been compromised by credit card stealing malware, it may continue to run undisturbed for months. Of course, the continued use of the payment process is in the best interests of the attacker, since cards need to flow through the system in order for their details to be stolen.

---

[11] Lencioni, P. (2012) *The Five Dysfunctions of a Team.* San Francisco: Jossey-Bass.

The best way to discover the business-critical processes is to spend time with various stakeholders in the business and the technical teams that support them. It's important to get multiple perspectives: someone in the weeds of a process might know more about what is critical from a technical perspective versus what is perceived to be critical at the business level. It's remarkable how many processes out there are critical yet hanging on by a thread and undocumented. Highlighting some of these, and helping to document them, can also do wonders for your value in an organisation, and elevate the perception of a security team.

Something to be avoided is having one person be responsible for a critical business process. As organisations move through their life cycle, from the start-up stage to initial public offering (IPO) or acquisition, critical components that one person set up years prior can carry on running for years. This becomes a major problem when that component breaks and the person is no longer with the company.

In the most extreme example of this that I can recall, I once was brought in to help an organisation who had a database containing critical data for a major customer. The database had been encrypted with the help of a hardware security module (HSM), which is a specialised piece of hardware that handles encryption keys. The problem? The encrypted database worked fine for years, until one day the hardware it was running on needed to be upgraded. This would require the database to be rebuilt, which in turn meant changes were needed to the HSM.

There was no documentation on how the HSM had been set up. Only one person had been involved in the installation, and tragically that person had been killed in a traffic accident shortly after the solution had been deployed but before the deployment had been fully documented. As much as we don't like to think about them, these things do happen.

After realising there was no documentation around this critical setup, the company should have held off on using it. They didn't, and as a result five years of critical data was trapped in their own data centre.

Data flow diagrams

A highly valuable resource both before and during a security incident is a data flow diagram, which shows how data moves through a process, and the components involved along the way (see the example in Figure 2.1). As you work through understanding a business process, putting together a data flow diagram can help both you and the team responsible for the process further your knowledge, and highlight ways in which a process could become compromised.

Even high-level data flow diagrams that lack technical detail are still useful. One thing that is true about working in information security is that no two days are the same, and frequently you'll be exposed to different areas of the business. Therefore, you cannot be expected to remember the full details of every process, and a data flow diagram serves as a helpful visual aide-memoire.

Figure 2.1 An example of a simple data flow diagram

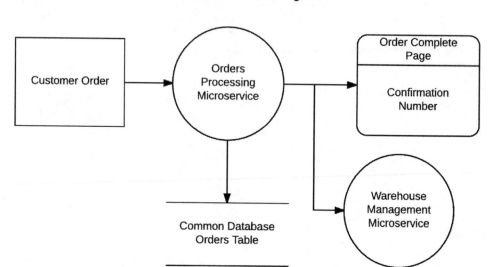

Orders - Data Flow Diagram

Assemble your team

Computer security incident response team (CSIRT), security incident response team (SIRT), incident response team (IRT), blue team, cybersecurity ninja response squad – whatever you decide to call it, you will want to recruit and list the members of the core team who will help you come incident time. The current contact information for each team member should be available at all times, either in the playbook or through some other redundant system. They should also be expected to contribute to the incident response playbook and be prepared to dedicate time to testing the contents of the playbook.

Every organisation is different, of course, but, generally speaking, good candidates for members of the team are:

- Security incident handler(s).

- Security team members, particularly those who are likely to be first responders in an incident response scenario (such as security operations centre analysts).

- A designated person to capture minutes and notes during the incident.

- The senior security executive, for example, the chief information security officer (CISO). The CISO might not be deeply involved in every security incident response, but should be aware of what is happening, and should be the single point of contact for other executives in the organisation.

- A network engineer. These folks have the power to help establish containment through firewall rules, route changes or wireless LAN reconfiguration.

- A systems administrator. The all-powerful systems administrator might be needed to provision or remove access during an incident to facilitate the response activities.

- Application development resources. In the event that the security incident focuses on one particular application, having a nominated 'security liaison' for that application is incredibly useful.

- An HR representative. If the incident involves the actions of an employee, deliberate or accidental, HR should be involved so that they might be prepared for any follow-up disciplinary proceedings that need to occur.

- A legal representative. Depending on the type of incident, it can be very useful to have someone with a legal eye watching over proceedings to make sure that any contractual or regulatory considerations are tracked.

- A facilities representative, to assist with any physical access requirements or threats to physical security.

- A corporate communications representative, to assist with any internal or external messaging that must be crafted in response to the incident.

In 2017, two major airlines experienced significant IT incidents that led to severe disruption for passengers. In January, it was Delta Air Lines who were forced to cancel hundreds of flights as a result of a systems outage at their primary data centre in the US state of Georgia. In May, British Airways experienced a similar outage at their Heathrow data centre, leading to days of cancelled flights.

In both instances, the root cause could be attributed to power issues in the data centre rather than any security incident. However, as both incidents played out, security was a recurring theme among commentators on social media.

Many members of the public theorised that the incidents were actually the results of an attack. Eventually, both companies had to explicitly deny this through their spokespeople. This is significant, as two or three years prior to these events, a security incident would likely not have been suggested as a theory so widely, or with such volume.

These examples go to show why it is important to have a member of the corporate communications team involved in the security incident response team. If the incident affects customers, you'll want to work with the corporate communications team from the start to craft the language provided to customers explaining the incident and its impact.

A disconnect between corporate communications and security teams in a time of crisis can make a bad situation a lot worse. Early involvement also has a secondary benefit. Often, corporate communications teams can learn of a security problem through a report made via social media. Educating the people who staff the corporate social media feeds to recognise and react to such a report is highly important. They will want to get the report to the security team, and have a response crafted in tandem, rather than responding directly and missing something critical.

Outline the process

At this point, you've determined what a security incident is, how you're going to alert your incident response team. Now comes figuring out what these people will actually do when they jump on the incident bridge, and documenting that in the playbook.

We're going to look at the incident response process in depth in the next chapter, so I won't go too deeply into the mechanics of it here. What I will say is that the incident response playbook is the place where you take the theoretical process and apply it very specifically to your organisation. For example, if a step in the process says 'Call the network on-call number', you'd actually print that number in your playbook.

Remember, the playbook is not a place to learn the ins and outs of incident response, it's a thing you grab in an emergency to remind yourself what to do. You don't want to be looking around for phone numbers, or who is on a given team. You'll want specific, actionable steps.

List third-party contacts

The playbook should include a list of key contacts at outside vendors who may have a role to play in your incident response process. Examples of these types of vendor include cloud vendor security contacts, co-located data centre contacts, internet service provider contacts, facilities contacts and payment processor contacts.

Making such a list is a great first step in preparation for an incident, but what is even better is actually having a proactive conversation and letting the people on the end of the phone know they are listed as a contact in your incident response playbook! This allows them to become familiar with you and your organisation, and allows both sides to discuss what information would need to be shared during an incident to facilitate the most expeditious conclusion.

TESTING THE PLAYBOOK

With the playbook crafted, it is preferable that the first time you run through it is not in response to a real incident. Practice makes perfect, and running through the playbook ahead of time gives you the opportunity to discover issues that can be subsequently remediated.

Peer review

The first stage in testing an incident response playbook is to submit it for peer review among other members of the organisation. A good audience for this review would be people who are listed as members of the incident response team. Submitting for peer review and asking for feedback helps to position the security incident response playbook as more than just another security document that must be obeyed. There is significant mileage to be had in collaborating on the document.

Peer review also affords colleagues the opportunity to review the plan before any other type of test, maximising the benefit of those subsequent opportunities.

Table-top exercise

This type of test involves bringing the incident response team together and running through the incident response playbook collectively. Unlike individual peer review, the table-top exercise will allow the incident handler to carefully review how the different parts of the plan slot together, and highlight opportunities for improvement in this regard.

During a table-top exercise, sometimes referred to as a walkthrough test, it is typical for more attention to be paid to the playbook itself than the type of incident that would cause the playbook to be necessary. For instance, you wouldn't get into specifics about what had triggered the security incident, just that a suspected incident had occurred and now you're in an incident response scenario. Frankly, incident specifics shouldn't matter at this point.

The playbook should be assessed for universal application against any security incident type. If you have the entire security incident response team together, concentrating overly on the incident type could also allow the exercise to get derailed as people nitpick at the details. This time should be used to assess the playbook, not your creativity in coming up with fictional security incidents.

Following the walkthrough test, make further changes to the playbook as required and submit it for peer review, then follow up with a second walkthrough test to see how the changes play out. Now, technically speaking, you can never overdo it when it comes to practice, but the reality is that if you're doing a walkthrough test every other week attendance is going to diminish, along with the effectiveness of the test.

Scenario-based testing

Unlike the walkthrough test, this type of test concentrates on specific incident types and how well the playbook stands up to them. Often, you'll run a scenario-based test in smaller groups, involving only the people who would be involved if the given scenario were to play out for real. For instance, there may be no need to involve HR in the response to a critical vulnerability being discovered in a piece of in-house-developed software, but they would need to be involved if an employee was suspected of embezzling funds.

Use creative licence in coming up with scenarios to be tested, but make them specific to your organisation and its processes. Some examples of scenarios to be tested include:

- A customer reports their own security incident that they think could be attributable to your organisation.
- Monitoring alarms are indicating unusual or erratic behaviour that cannot be attributed to faulty software or hardware.
- A sudden increase in traffic leaving the corporate network is noted.

- An unauthorised device is found on a production network.
- A government agency reports that they suspect the company has been breached.
- An employee is suspected of stealing confidential information.
- A user is phished, leading to the compromise of their corporate email account.

During a scenario-based test, the incident handler should note any omissions in the incident response playbook that are discovered as the scenario plays out.

Following the test, a debriefing should be conducted and feedback solicited on how well the playbook performed. Updates should be made based on the feedback as necessary.

Double-blind penetration tests

If you really want to put your playbook to the test in the most realistic way possible, then look no further than the double-blind penetration test. A penetration test is an exercise conducted by a trusted entity simulating the actions of a malicious attacker[12] for the purposes of validating the effectiveness of security controls, personnel and procedures. Often, in a penetration test scenario, teams at the customer organisation are briefed and know to expect the test, so as not to cause alarm. In a double-blind test, they are not briefed; the idea being that they will see the test as an attack, since they won't know any different.

Now, there are risks involved in such a test. The first is that people panic and make changes that adversely impact the business when they have no real need to do so. The counter to this is that if they are likely to behave in the same way in a real incident then surely it is better to find out in a somewhat controlled state. Secondly, people are busy, and if you suddenly drop an extra bunch of work on their plates by running a double-blind penetration test, it does nothing for that all-important perception of the security team. The best advice is to judge the culture of the organisation and get senior management buy-in before you engage in a double-blind test.

Double-blind penetration tests, if not executed carefully, can go awry. I once spent five hours on a phone call with a hosting provider abuse team because of what appeared to be a widespread phishing attack against a group of users of my organisation's product, when in actual fact it was a poorly designed double-blind test being conducted by one of our customers against their own users.

The customer inadvertently sent the phoney phishing email to another organisation, who also happened to be a customer of ours. With no context, that second organisation believed this was a significant phishing event and forwarded the evidence to us. We agreed, and began working with the hosting provider to get the phishing site removed. This process took hours, because we were pressing hard to figure out if the hosting provider could share with us the user IDs of any potential victims.

---

[12] You can learn more about penetration testing in BCS-CREST Penetration Testing Working Group (2019) *Penetration Testing: A Guide for Business and IT Management*, Swindon: BCS.

In the end, through the provider, we were able to figure out that the test was being conducted by a security consulting company, and through a mutual connection I was connected to the right person at that company to yell at.

INCIDENT PLANNING AND COMPLIANCE

Various information security compliance standards recognise the need for effective security incident response planning. Therefore, any activities you undertake when planning for a security incident should be aligned with these standards if they're applicable to your organisation.

Payment Card Industry Data Security Standard (PCI DSS)

Section 12.10 of the PCI DSS states that organisations should 'implement an incident response plan. Be prepared to respond immediately to a system breach.'[13]

ISO 27001

Appendix 16 of ISO 27001 contains seven controls specific to security incident management. The objective of these controls is defined as 'to ensure a consistent and effective approach to the management of information security incidents, including communication of security events and incidents'.[14]

NIST 800-53

Control IR-1 of NIST 800-53 states that an organisation should develop, document, and disseminate to its employees:

- 'An incident response policy that addresses purpose, scope, roles, responsibilities, management commitment, coordination among organizational entities, and compliance.'

- 'Procedures to facilitate the implementation of the incident response policy and associated incident response controls.'[15]

GDPR

The European Union General Data Protection Regulation (GDPR) has multiple articles that are relevant to incident response. One of the most substantial requirements for

---

[13] PCI Security Standards Council (2017) *Official PCI Security Standards Council Site – Verify PCI Compliance, Download Data Security and Credit Card Security Standards.* PCI Security Standards Council. Available from https://www.pcisecuritystandards.org/document_library?category=pcidss&document=pci_dss [16 April 2018].

[14] ISO/IEC JTC 1/SC 27 (2013) *ISO/IEC 27001:2013 – Information technology – Security techniques – Information security management systems – Requirements.* ISO. Available from https://www.iso.org/standard/54534.html [16 April 2018].

[15] Reprinted courtesy of the National Institute of Standards and Technology, US Department of Commerce. Not copyrightable in the United States. NIST (2017) *Security and Privacy Controls for Information Systems and Organizations.* NIST Computer Security Resource Center. Available from https://csrc.nist.gov/csrc/media/publications/sp/800-53/rev-5/draft/documents/sp800-53r5-draft.pdf [16 April 2018].

incident handlers under GDPR is the requirement under Article 33, which states that organisations must disclose breaches of GDPR-protected data within 72 hours. This is a really short amount of time compared to other similar standards, and a consideration that should be built into your incident response plan if applicable to your organisation.

FORENSIC READINESS

While you're running through the pre-incident planning phase, it is a good idea to visit the topic of forensic readiness. This is an early opportunity to tackle the challenge of balancing incident response and forensic requirements.

You are more likely to be given the go-ahead to transition an incident into a digital forensics investigation if you're prepared to do so, have the tools ready to roll and have covered the topic in your incident response playbook. The benefits of transitioning an incident in this way include developing a better understanding of the root cause of the incident, enhancing the ability to prevent a reoccurrence, and also identifying other incidents that may be related to the initial one.

In-house

If you plan on keeping forensic work in-house, then forensic readiness involves ensuring that the equipment required for a successful forensics investigation is in place, and that, perhaps most importantly, those who are likely to be called up to perform any investigation are fully trained and competent in performing digital forensics work.

Use of consultants

Not all forensic work need be conducted in-house. It is relatively common for organisations to retain third-party forensic professionals in the event that they are needed. In this scenario, forensic readiness would involve meeting with the retained professionals, and ensuring that they have been briefed on your organisation, your playbook and the types of forensic work they might be engaged on. This is all about saving time when they are needed in a real incident. Some forensic consultants even operate on a zero-cost retainer, meaning that there is no up-front cost for their services – you only pay for the services you use. The purpose of the zero-cost retainer is to ensure that all the legal agreements between the client and consultant, such as a non-disclosure agreement (NDA) and master services agreement (MSA), are signed prior to an incident.

Involvement of law enforcement

Provisions should also be made for the involvement of law enforcement in any digital forensics investigation that may spawn from a security incident. The decision to involve law enforcement, in my experience, is usually pretty black and white. Morally, and legally, you're expected to report a suspected crime. Sometimes there is resistance to law enforcement involvement when it is believed that involving law enforcement might exacerbate the impact of the incident without real benefit. For example, if your website is defaced by a suspect who lives in a jurisdiction where it is highly unlikely they'll ever be prosecuted, is it worth having law enforcement come in and potentially cause disruption while collecting forensic evidence?

Ultimately, this is usually a call that is deferred to the senior leadership and taken on the advice of the legal and security teams.

SUMMARY

In this chapter, we discussed the importance of planning for a security incident, and how doing so can give us a significant advantage when compared to acting on-the-fly during the panic of an incident. We talked through the process of creating an incident response playbook, assembling an incident response team and creating data flow diagrams for critical processes.

We then looked at testing that playbook in a variety of different ways, including as part of a table-top exercise, with scenario-based testing and through a double-blind penetration test. We linked the preparation and testing to various requirements in information security and compliance standards. Finally, we discussed the concept of forensic readiness, and how being prepared to invoke a forensics investigation from an incident will increase the likelihood of the transition being successful.

While the detail in everyone's incident response playbook and preparations will be different, and specific to their organisation, the core incident response process to be followed will be very similar for all of us. In the next chapter we'll break down the various phases in the incident response process.

3 THE INCIDENT RESPONSE PROCESS

During a security incident there will be panic, there will be confusion, there will be stress, and there may also be a degree of anger. Few situations lead to such an emotional display among information technology professionals as when they are faced with the prospect that someone uninvited found their way into their network, system or application. I've even heard it described by one developer, whose application was compromised by a Structured Query Language (SQL) injection attack, as 'a feeling similar to someone physically breaking into your home'.

As security incident handlers, we have a duty to remove the emotion from the situation, and keep the response occurring in the most orderly way possible. The security incident bridge is not a place for blame, it is a place for collaboration and teamwork of the highest order. Having a well-defined security incident response process is on the critical path to achieving these goals.

The process allows the incident to progress through a defined set of stages. While there may be some variation in the activities performed as part of each stage, depending on the nature of the incident, having these checkpoints along the way will remove the uncertainty that would otherwise compound the emotion. If people know there is a plan, they will work to it. If there is no plan, things get trickier.

There are four phases in the incident response process as defined by our old friend NIST SP 800-61:

- **Identification:** before you can respond to an incident, you must identify that a security incident is occurring.
- **Containment:** what actions can you take to ensure the incident doesn't get worse?
- **Eradication:** removing the source of the incident from the environment.
- **Recovery:** returning to 'business as normal'.

In this chapter we are going to break down each of these phases and look at some of the activities that fall under the umbrella of each.

Variations on the process

You should be aware that there are slight variations between varying security standards on the names of each phase, and even the total number of phases in the incident process.

That said, it is very easy to see where there is overlap between them. For example, in the ISO family of security standards, the incident response process is defined as five phases: prepare, identify, assess, respond and learn. In the ISO standard, pre-incident and post-incident activities are included in the process and are covered by the 'prepare' and 'learn' phases respectively. 'Identify' in the ISO standard of course aligns with the identification phase of NIST. Finally, 'assess' and 'respond' in the ISO standard overlap with 'containment', 'eradication' and 'recovery' in the NIST world.

As you can see from this example, if you're seeking to abide by a security standard that defines an incident response process, it will almost certainly align with the four phases of NIST 800-61. That is why I've chosen it as the model to follow in this book and, quite frankly, real-world experience has taught me that the more granular you try and make an incident response process, the more it serves to add additional confusion to an already stressful situation.

IDENTIFICATION

Being able to effectively identify or detect (to use an interchangeable term) a security incident is a challenge for many organisations. Incidents manifest in a number of different ways, and do so against a backdrop of constant noise and digital distractions that are part and parcel of doing business in today's connected economy. With only so many eyes to look at so many different places, incident identification is not a task solely for a security team, or even the wider IT team. All employees must be engaged in identification activities. A culture of trust must be instilled to ensure that as many people as possible are aware of the need to rapidly report suspected security incidents. Reports by vigilant employees remain one of the most common ways that a security incident is detected.

Reducing time to detect

Every year, American communications giant Verizon publishes its annual Data Breach Investigations Report (DBIR), which provides insight into various metrics regarding the security incidents it has reviewed over the preceding 12 months. Although it is of course a marketing tool for Verizon and their security services, it has been widely accepted as a good source of useful and compelling information regarding incidents and incident response. A reoccurring theme in the DBIR over the last few years is the vast difference between 'time to compromise' and 'time to detect'.[16] Time to compromise, meaning the time for an attacker to gain access to a system (and therefore the beginning of an incident), is typically measured in minutes, whereas time to detect is typically measured in months or even years. Obviously, that is a significant problem. With so long between compromise and identification, the impact of the incident becomes so much worse. The window of opportunity for those affected by an incident to take action to protect themselves diminishes the longer it goes undetected.

---

[16] Simon, R. (2017) 'Aha' Moments From the 'Verizon 2017 Data Breach Investigations Report'. McAfee Blogs. Available from https://securingtomorrow.mcafee.com/business/safeguard-data/aha-moments-verizon-2017-data-breach-investigations-report/ [17 April 2018].

In December 2016, the internet technology company Yahoo! disclosed a massive security incident involving the compromise of information regarding over one billion user accounts. The data stolen included the names, email addresses and passwords of Yahoo! users. As if that declaration wasn't bad enough, one of the most painful details of the incident was the fact that it was determined that the incident began in August 2013, meaning it had gone undetected for more than three years.

This incident came hot on the heels of another massive Yahoo! breach. Just three months earlier, the company had disclosed that a separate incident had led to the compromise of half a billion accounts, and similarly that incident had gone undetected for two years.

Although we may not be able to avoid all incidents, we should be able to significantly reduce the amount of time it takes us to detect and respond to them, and that is what the identification phase of the incident response process is all about.

Knowing where to look

Before you can start looking for a potential incident, you must first know where you should be looking. This might seem a bit remedial, but a surprising number of organisations do not maintain appropriate records of information technology assets. If you don't know what you have, how can you possibly keep an eye on it? This is where IT asset management (ITAM) comes in, a critical component of being able to identify a security incident. Good ITAM means an organisation is able to very quickly answer these types of questions:

- Which machines are in our environment?
- What is on this IP address?
- Which applications do we currently have in use?
- Which servers are publicly accessible?
- When was the operating system last patched?

IT asset management is typically an IT, rather than a security, function. That said, there are worse things that a security team can spend time on than helping to set up ITAM at an organisation, if needed.

If you do find yourself tasked with spinning up an ITAM programme for an organisation, it can be a pretty overwhelming request (particularly in larger organisations). The end goal should be to create a repository of data regarding technology assets that is good enough to be considered the 'single source of truth' for all technology assets owned by the company. Commonly, data relating to IT assets can be scattered around an organisation. Perhaps an executive brought their own laptop and charged it back to the company, or perhaps a development team purchased some test machines without going through IT. Ultimately, from an incident response perspective, it doesn't matter how a machine arrived; a compromised machine is a compromised machine, and the more we know about it before we have to respond to an incident involving it, the more effective we'll be during the response. Below you'll see an outline for a typical ITAM project.

1. Determine the scope of the ITAM project. For instance, does it include software, or just hardware? Adding software to an ITAM project can increase its complexity, but it also adds value as it allows us to track licence usage and, more importantly from our perspective, understand what software is expected to be on a given machine.

2. Identify all data that is relevant to establishing a complete ITAM list. This could be purchasing data, helpdesk support tickets, spreadsheets of various IT data that has been collected over the years, and support data from IT vendor websites.

3. Review and decide whether an ITAM tool will be used. Various products, such as Samanage,[17] Jamf[18] and ServiceNow Asset Management,[19] can greatly enhance the quality of ITAM data and automate the collection and maintenance of that data. Of course, these products are all commercial products, so consideration should be given to the costs of purchasing them.

4. Determine where the single source of truth will be (for example in a spreadsheet, database or specific ITAM application). Decide who will be responsible for maintaining the ITAM system once it has been established.

5. Normalise all existing data. For instance, one source might include serial numbers, whereas another might include model names and purchase dates. All should be combined into a single consistent format.

6. Validate the accuracy of the data. A great way to do this (I've found) is to use one of the all-time great network security tools, Nmap.[20] Nmap, or Network Mapper, is an open-source network scanning tool used for a variety of network fingerprinting and discovery tasks. What better tool to use to validate the accuracy of an ITAM list? By running an Nmap scan across a range of IP addresses, you can quickly determine if your ITAM data has any basis in reality. Nmap also includes service detection capabilities to add additional context to the hosts it discovers. Nmap is commonly run from the command line; a typical Nmap command with service detection would look like this: nmap –sV 192.168.0.1/24. This command would scan the entire 192.168.0.0 class C block with service detection. A note of caution, though: if you believe a network segment has IP-connected printers on it, be careful using Nmap – it can cause them to start printing pages and pages of binary data!

[17] Samanage (2018) Samanage Service Platform. Samanage Ltd. Available from https://www.samanage.com/ [20 April 2018].
[18] Jamf (2018) Mac, iPad, iPhone, and Apple TV management. Jamf. Available from https://www.jamf.com/ [20 April 2018].
[19] ServiceNow (2018) Asset Management Software | Asset Management Solutions | ServiceNow. ServiceNow. Available from https://www.servicenow.com/products/asset-management.html [20 April 2018].
[20] Nmap (2018) Nmap: the Network Mapper – Free Security Scanner. Nmap.org. Available from https://nmap.org/ [20 April 2018].

Once we, as security incident handlers, have knowledge of all the IT assets within our organisation, we can start to home in on ways to identify when any of those assets become subject to a potential security incident.

While performing an internal penetration test at a local government office in early 2010, I was surprised during a network scan to stumble upon a host that appeared to be running Windows NT 4.0. The operating system was released in 1996, and support had ended for it in 2004, some six years prior to my penetration testing engagement. This meant the host would have been left in an unpatched state for six years.

I sought the permission of the IT manager to exploit the host. He simply didn't believe that there was an NT 4.0 server on the network. Not only did he permit me to exploit it, he encouraged it, as he wanted to know exactly what it was doing! It wasn't connected to the domain, and he had no records of any passwords that would allow him to legitimately log in.

I used an exploit from the Metasploit framework and was able to get access to the server, albeit briefly. Unfortunately, the exploit caused the server to crash, so I lost all connectivity. The IT manager wasn't so worried, since he, quite rightly, wanted the thing gone from his network.

That was until about five minutes later, when another member of the IT department came running in. 'Hey, all the doors just failed open; no one shut down the NT 4.0 box that runs the door locks, did they?'

Sure enough, that NT 4.0 box was responsible for keeping all the door access card readers at the office operational. One IT employee knew this, but it wasn't documented or known to anyone else. Had that very soft target been compromised, it likely would never have been known about. I noted in my penetration test report that better IT asset management was needed, and of course that the NT 4.0 machine should be removed quickly from the network.

Knowing what to look for

Identification of a security incident is made significantly easier if you can define what is 'normal' in your environment. For example, if you know that a virtual machine should have 25 running processes on it, and one day it has 26, something has changed and that should be investigated. Similarly, if you know that Bill from marketing lives in Southampton, and one day his email account is accessed from the Ivory Coast, then that is a very clear deviation from normal.

It sounds easy, but defining normal is not always so clear-cut. Most organisations face two primary challenges when it comes to figuring out 'normal':

- Some systems have been around for so long that no one is quite sure what normal looks like any more.

- In some organisations normal changes so rapidly that by the time you've figured it out, it's no longer applicable.

On the first bullet above, consider that a machine has been compromised for two years, and a security team buys a tool to help baseline its network traffic profile. The malicious traffic used to persist the compromise is going to be part of that baseline. You'd have to wait for the box to be compromised a second time to see the shift in traffic. That's not ideal!

On the second bullet, consider a company using the Agile software development methodology. In this methodology, small incremental changes to software are continually released into the environment. Documentation of changes is considered less of a priority. Given this, it can be difficult to establish the normal behaviour of an application when compared to one developed using a traditional waterfall methodology.

In software development, the term 'waterfall' is used to describe a development methodology in which the development process flows through various stages in one direction (like a waterfall). Those stages include collecting requirements, design, writing, testing and fixing the code; and finally delivering the finished product. One stage must be completed and signed off before the next can begin. The sequential design of the model means that it doesn't lend itself to iteration and flexibility, since the later the development stage, the more difficult and more expensive it is to change the product being developed. However, some teams prefer waterfall for this exact reason, as it limits the possibility for deviation from the initial customer requirements.

To overcome these challenges in defining normal, the best approach is to spend time with the systems administrators, or the developers responsible for a given asset, and ask them to explain how they expect the system to behave. Where should it be connecting? Which type of log entries would indicate that something is awry? Then look for variations from that and ask them to come up with a reasonable explanation; if they can't, it's time to dig deeper. This activity should form part of your pre-incident planning and should be constantly revisited as systems change.

Don't fall into the trap of thinking you can only identify security incidents with tools marketed and sold specifically for security teams. If a team responsible for an application uses a custom app they've built to monitor it, ask for access and see what hooks you might be able to embed to help monitor for incidents.

Knowing when to look

Systems get introduced to an environment at different times, are configured by different people, and often aren't all on the same page when it comes to one of the most important questions you will ask during an incident response scenario: 'When did this all start?' If it takes more than a couple of seconds to answer, then you're at a significant disadvantage when you really don't need to be.

All devices, including network components, laptops and firewalls, should be reporting the same system time. This is critically important when it comes to correlating events across multiple sources of information during an incident. Having out-of-sync system clocks can also prevent you from identifying an incident. For example, if your firewall system clocks are five minutes off, perhaps your SIEM won't catch an important correlation between the firewall and a web server log.

The Network Time Protocol (NTP) is the solution to this problem. Nearly every operating system and device supports it. Nearly all security standards require you to use it, for the very same reasons listed above. An NTP client leverages a pool of NTP servers to obtain the correct time within a few milliseconds of universal coordinated time (UTC). The protocol, which uses User Datagram Protocol (UDP) packets, requests the current timestamp from an NTP server and uses an algorithm to factor in the network round trip time and figure out the current time with a high degree of accuracy.

Illuminating shadow IT

Shadow IT is a relatively new term, used to describe the phenomenon of IT users at an organisation electing to use tools and services that have not been officially sanctioned by said organisation.

A classic example: an employee uses Google Drive to store all their personal files at home, then elects to store all their work files in the same Google Drive account, despite the fact that a different cloud storage solution is mandated by the company. Convenient? Undoubtedly. The right thing to do? Not at all.

Of course, that's not to say there is anything wrong with the security of Google Drive. The problem in this example is that the personal Google Drive account falls out of the purview of the IT security team, who will be blind as to any attempt on company data stored there. Also, if that person leaves the company they get to take all the company data they've stored in their personal drive with them. Since the mission of security professionals is protecting company data, clearly this would put us at a significant disadvantage.

Given this, many companies actively seek out identifiers of shadow IT use, perhaps even blocking access to services that they know users might be tempted to access. Such identification can occur via monitoring of DNS queries to cloud service domains or by using wire-data analytics to look for patterns in network traffic to addresses known to be associated with those same cloud services. If shadow IT usage is discovered, this in itself should constitute a security incident and appropriate remediation should occur.

Building detections that fit

Once you've successfully identified the assets you must protect, how they should act when they're being normal, lined up all your system clocks, and blown all shadow IT out of the way, you're all set to start work on crafting detection mechanisms that will assist you in identifying an incident. Note, this flow of activities is cyclical. In any growing organisation new assets are added frequently, 'normal' changes at varying degrees of speed, and you'll play whack-a-mole with shadow IT and other similar threats constantly. All this while looking for incidents at the same time; hope you like being busy!

When we talk about detections that fit, we're talking about deploying appropriate measures to assist in the identification of a security incident in your given environment. If you're in charge of incident response at a company that runs the majority of its business from an infrastructure-as-a-service (IaaS) provider, a traditional network-based IDS designed for a data centre network probably shouldn't be at the top of your shopping list. If you have a mostly remote workforce who connect to a web portal that is the gateway to all your highly sensitive customer information, then focus your efforts on shoring up that web portal with better authentication and a mechanism for detecting abnormal usage.

Some of the most effective detection techniques are built right in to the business logic of an application. Working with a development team early in the software development life cycle is the absolute best way to make sure this happens.

For example, building fraudulent charge detection into an ecommerce application would be a significant value add, and would catch a type of incident that might blend in as perfectly normal if purely technical detection mechanisms like web server log file monitoring were used.

Technical detection

Let's take an in-depth look at some of the most common technical indicators of a security incident.

Network traffic monitoring

In security incidents that result in a data breach there is typically one factor in common: data gets exfiltrated over a network. The network is a busy place. It provides perfect cover for a stealthy attacker intent on subtly moving their hoard of compromised data from inside the victim environment to a location under their control, so that they can use it for whatever nefarious purpose they have in mind without the risk of losing access to it. They can be subtle, but they cannot be silent. Something has to move; when it does, we have one of the most effective technical identifiers of a security incident, when used properly.

Wire-data analytics tools frequently include dashboards that show multicoloured charts depicting real-time network activity. They're not just for show. Those dashboards can show unexplainable spikes in the volume of data passing between two hosts. They can show new protocols and ports suddenly bursting into life. They can break select protocols open and figure out how they are being used; DNS, for example, is present and permitted on every network in the world, but DNS can also be abused and leveraged for exfiltration. Wire-data tools might let you see a sudden increase in DNS requests for strange TXT records, a type of DNS record frequently used to exfiltrate information in plain sight.

Network flow records, such as those delivered by Cisco's Netflow technology, can also be used to identify conversations between IP addresses that may be of interest. Though more limited when compared to having full blown wire data, these records are hugely important if you can get them. A common comparison between Netflow and wire data is that Netflow is akin to telephone call logs, whereas wire data is a full copy of the entire conversation. Netflow records indicate the source and destination IP, protocol information and interface information for a given flow.

Firewalls sit at the ingress and egress of a network, and between network zones of differing security levels. They're the poster child for network security devices, and if an organisation is doing things right it would be very hard to have a conversation across a trusted network without going through at least one of them along the way. As such, firewalls see a lot of traffic, and some of the most relevant traffic from a security perspective. They don't always log by default, though, and when they do they can produce a non-trivial amount of log data. It's worth figuring out how to store and leverage that log data, because it can provide some very useful indicators of a security incident. You might see a series of short connections across a wide number of ports on the firewall, which would be indicative of a port scan in progress.

Operating systems come with multiple tools for reviewing active network connections. One such tool is netstat, a command-line utility that is commonly used by incident responders to check connections from a machine that may have become compromised. Netstat can accept various arguments at the command line that alter how it displays connection information. For example, 'netstat –a' shows all active and listening connections.

Log file monitoring

The log file entries on your web application server report that the majority of HTTP requests result in a '200 OK' response from the server. Then, all of a sudden, there are 100 lines of '500 Internal Server Error' responses. Of course, something could have broken within the architecture of the application, but it's also possible that malformed traffic was directed at your application by an attacker looking to exploit a potential weakness.

This is just one example of the tales that are told by log files, and is a great indicator of a potential security incident. As we've previously mentioned, the downside to log files is that there are just so many of them that it's hard to use them effectively. Log aggregation tools can be trained to identify log file entries that are relevant from a security perspective, and with some investment of time can become highly reliable sources.

Web server logs aren't the only type of logs, of course. Database query logs can provide a detailed audit trail of which person or system accessed a given row in a table and at what time. If the majority of your queries from a front-end application are 'SELECT' queries, and suddenly you're faced with a 'DROP TABLE' query that is flagged from a query log, that could be an indicator that an attacker has obtained control of the service account used by the front-end application and is trying to do some damage.

Authentication logs, showing who logged into a system and where they were located, can be critically important both from an investigative point of view and for highlighting real-time attempts to compromise an account.

Logs can even be applicable in the physical realm. Door badge access logs can play a key role in an information security incident. Was someone in the office with physical access to a system that was found to be infected with malware from a USB stick at the moment the malware was deployed?

Threat intelligence

An enhancement to log files and network monitoring data alike are threat intelligence feeds. There are numerous feeds out there, both free and commercial, including AlienVault's Open Threat Exchange,[21] the Facebook Threat Exchange[22] and ThreatConnect[23] (see Figure 3.1). Such feeds are used to deliver files containing IP addresses, domain names, hash values of known malicious files, and known compromised or spam-sending email addresses. Each of these types of information is known as an indicator of compromise (IoC) in this context.

An IP address in a firewall log might not initially appear to be of concern, but if a threat feed lists that IP address as a known command and control server for a botnet then that changes the situation dramatically. It's this addition of context that makes threat feeds so powerful.

When it comes to malicious files, such as a document containing malware, leveraging a threat feed with a cryptographically generated hash of that file can be a quick and easy way to prevent it ever reaching its target. Cryptographic hashes are generated by running the file through a hashing algorithm, such as SHA-256, and returning a fixed-sized value based on the contents of the file. If the same file is run through the same hashing algorithm twice, the resulting hash values will be the same. Hence, the hash can be used to verify that the malicious file seen by a threat researcher contributing to the threat feed is in fact the same file now being received by the customer of the feed.

SIEM

A security incident and event management tool is designed to be a place where all the alerts, network flow data, log files and threat feeds come together to show correlations between these disparate sources. Therefore, if it's doing its job properly, the SIEM tool should be the most reliable indicator of a security incident in progress in an organisation. Sometimes they aren't. They're complex tools that require significant investment to deploy and operate, but if you have one and it's working well then look after it forever and it will look after you.

These tools typically generate events based on given conditions, and assign a severity to the event. The severity of the event is what drives the response from the SIEM tool. Events deemed critical might trigger an SMS message to the on-call incident responder.

SIEM tools can also be used in an investigative mode to cross-check events that may be related to, but not the primary source of, a given incident.

---

[21] AlienVault (2018) *AlienVault – Open Threat Exchange*. AlienVault Inc. Available from https://otx.alienvault.com/ [20 April 2018].
[22] Facebook for Developers (2018) *Threat Exchange – Facebook for Developers*. Facebook. Available from https://developers. facebook.com/products/threat-exchange/ [20 April 2018].
[23] ThreatConnect (2018) *ThreatConnect | Security Operations and Analytics Platform*. ThreatConnect Inc. Available from https:// www.threatconnect.com/ [20 April 2018].

Figure 3.1 ThreatConnect's TC Analyze threat intelligence tool

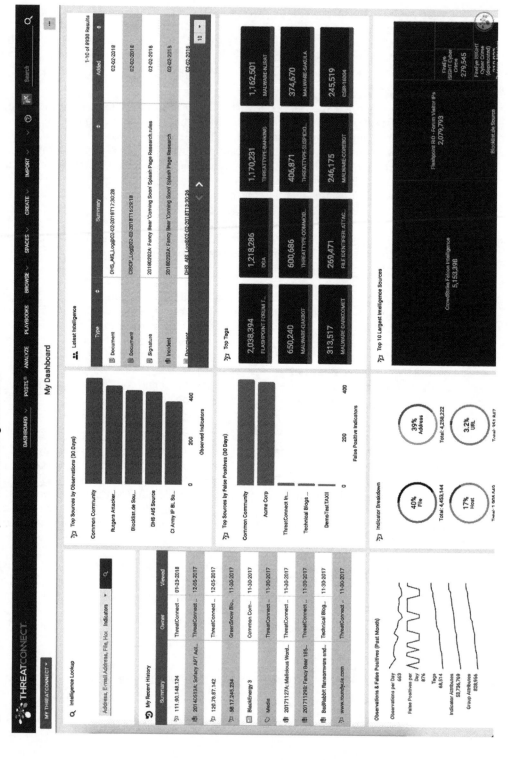

Antivirus software

The first line of defence against malware, antivirus software, is well known as a necessity, both in enterprise and consumer IT. Antivirus software primarily works by using a database of known 'signatures' of malicious software and comparing them to what is occurring in real time on a machine, for example by scanning a file that was just downloaded and checking it against the signature library or by studying a process in memory. Commonly used antivirus software products include Symantec Endpoint Protection,[24] Sophos[25] and AVG.[26]

Antivirus software for the most part is very effective, but sometimes it can't quite catch everything. So, whereas the default condition for antivirus software is to block a piece of malware, it might not always have enough information to do so comfortably. It might choose to quarantine a file, which means restricting access to the file and offering the user the chance to decide its fate. That might not be ideal if the user isn't sure of the risk and decides to go ahead and open the file anyway. Additionally, some antivirus products leverage behavioural detection techniques to determine whether a computer is infected; these techniques might result in false positives, or false negatives.

In all these cases, one thing is for sure: we don't want the antivirus software to operate in isolation. We want it to report back to a central server what it is seeing out there in the wild. If it does this, while it might not prevent an incident it will at least give us a very clear sign that one is occurring. Therefore, when selecting an antivirus vendor the incident responder should ensure that the software has the ability to send detection logs to a SIEM tool or another central repository.

File integrity monitoring

Widely known as FIM, file integrity monitoring also uses the same cryptographic hash comparison technique as the threat intelligence feeds discussed earlier. This time, though, instead of looking at malicious files, the technique is employed to make sure 'known good' files stay intact.

Imagine, for example, that a critical configuration file for a banking system should never be modified, and modification of the file might indicate that it had been tampered with. A FIM agent running on the banking system host would monitor the hash value of the file, and if the value changed it would alert a SIEM tool that a potential incident was in progress.

This technique can also be applied to operating system binaries, to flag when malicious versions of said binaries are introduced to a system. This is a common technique employed by rootkit-style viruses.

---

[24] Symantec (2018) *Endpoint Protection – Machine Learning Security | Symantec.* Symantec Corporation. Available from https://www.symantec.com/products/endpoint-protection [20 April 2018].

[25] Sophos (2018) *Endpoint Security: Next Gen Threat Prevention | Centralized Antivirus Protection, Malware and Web Threat Security | Sophos Endpoint Protection.* Sophos Ltd. Available from https://www.sophos.com/en-us/products/endpoint-antivirus.aspx [20 April 2018].

[26] AVG (2018) *AVG 2018 | FREE Antivirus & TuneUp for PC, Mac, Android.* AVG Technologies. Available from https://www.avg.com/en-us/homepage [20 April 2018].

FIM tools, such as Tripwire[27] and OSSEC,[28] should be able to alert, or log to a remote system where alerts can then be triggered. They can provide highly reliable indications that an incident is occurring.

Open-source intelligence (OSINT)

Not necessarily a technical detection method, but one that can be greatly accelerated by technology, OSINT is all about using information that is in the public domain to detect an incident. This could be something as simple as monitoring vendor reports of security problems that might affect your organisation. If a critical patch is required to fix a remote execution vulnerability in an operating system then you'll want to know about it as soon as the operating system vendor releases the patch.

More, shall we say, creative methods of using OSINT include monitoring social media for talk about security issues within your organisation, or plans to attack a given organisation. It sounds unlikely, but trust me, it's out there. Thanks to commercial social media monitoring tools, and the application programming interfaces (APIs) social media sites like Twitter provide, it can be mined for security incident indicators.

Listen to your people

As previously mentioned, one of the most common ways a security incident is discovered is through a report from an employee. People are the last line of defence. Therefore, we must build a culture that constantly reinforces the need for verification from a security team if an incident is suspected, or if something just plain doesn't look right. The flipside to this is that most of the reports you'll get will be false positives. You'll get the same user forwarding you every harmless marketing email they receive to report it as suspect. My advice on this is simple: take it. Take it a thousand times a day over the alternative, which is people not communicating with you at all because they are afraid to, or not sure how to. Be sure to respond to all reports, even false positives, acknowledging the fact that the employee took the time to reach out.

CONTAINMENT

Once an incident is identified, it is time to stop it from spreading. Containment activities vary based on the nature of the incident, but in all cases the ultimate goal is to stop a bad situation from getting worse. Let's take a look at some common incident scenarios and how they would be contained.

A device on the network becomes infected with malware

Isolation is key here; we want to get that host off the same network as our healthy machines and sensitive data, both to prevent the malware from spreading and to remove any avenues that an attacker may have to peruse our network at their leisure. There are many ways to achieve this, perhaps the simplest being physically remov-

---

[27] Tripwire (2018) *Tripwire File Integrity Manager*. Tripwire Inc. Available from https://www.tripwire.com/products/tripwire-file-integrity-manager/ [20 April 2018].

[28] OSSEC Project Team (2017) *Home — OSSEC*. OSSEC. Available from https://ossec.github.io/ [20 April 2018].

ing the network cable and disabling wireless networking on the device. This technique works well in small offices, where the most effective way to get to a machine is to run towards it; however, it doesn't scale well in global enterprises.

Other isolation techniques include remediation virtual local area networks (VLANs), which are special network segments that use access control lists to prevent hosts from talking to the internet, but still allow some connectivity to enable a helpdesk person or incident responder to get to the machine remotely and fix what ails it. Some network security products leverage the Simple Network Management Protocol (SNMP) to manipulate network switches and wireless LAN controllers in order to get devices into remediation VLANs. In some organisations, a remediation VLAN is the default VLAN, and you're only allowed to talk to others after you're given a clean bill of health. The class of products that does the scanning and VLAN manipulation is known as network access control (NAC).

In the case of virtual machines and containers you have even more flexibility when it comes to isolation. It is possible to remove virtual network connections containing the malware, yet maintain a console connection to the device.

A website is defaced

If someone is able to deface your website, it means they've managed to bypass some form of control that was supposed to stop them. Your goal is to figure out what that control was, before the site goes live again. If you use a content management system (CMS), perhaps a known vulnerability in the CMS was exploited, permitting the attacker to override data in the CMS. A SQL injection vulnerability may have been leveraged to manipulate the contents of an underlying database that serves content for the website. Perhaps the site administrator's password was compromised, or the compromise came from another server in the same network segment as the server hosting the website.

Whatever the cause of the defacement, the web server should be treated as fully compromised until either the operating system or the web server application can be confirmed as the cause. In this case, the best course of action is isolation. Of course, the downside to this is that your website will be offline while it is isolated, but in most cases, if websites are critically important to a business, they operate in redundant pools of load-balanced servers. In this case it might be possible that only one of the servers in the load balancer pool was compromised, and can simply be removed from the pool. Of course, if the application was compromised through the front door, that is, through the application itself, you'll need to fix all the servers running that application, otherwise the attacker could just repeat the attack against a fresh server in the pool.

An application is under a denial of service attack

Containment of a denial of service attack usually requires some pre-planning and a strategy. In a denial of service, an IP address or a URL will be targeted by an overwhelming amount of traffic, so the target either has to move to a location where it's not going to be targeted, or the attack traffic needs to be filtered out.

In the case of an attack against an IP address, an easy containment method is to move the service to a new IP address and, where applicable, update DNS records to point to the new address. Given that this is a relatively easy mitigation, it is more common for attackers to target DNS records directly. After all, you can't change an external domain name as easily as an IP address.

Given this, a more common technique for denial of service containment is traffic filtering or scrubbing. This method requires working with a provider who operates a 'scrubbing centre', which is essentially a bank of servers that analyse incoming traffic, dropping the attack traffic while allowing the legitimate traffic to pass through. These services typically work in an on-demand model whereby if an attack is detected routes to the target are changed to ensure traffic flows through the scrubbing centre before hitting the target site. The route changes usually occur through Border Gateway Protocol (BGP) route advertisements.

A critical vulnerability is detected in a web application

In this case, the goal of the containment phase is to ensure that no one can exploit the vulnerability in the time period between detection and remediation. This could involve disabling the component of the application where the vulnerability is present, or using an extra technical control to provide assurance while the fix is being developed.

A common example of this is virtual patching using a web application firewall (WAF); these work at layer seven of the Open Systems Interconnection (OSI) model, and therefore have access to, and filter based on the content of, HTTP traffic, as opposed to raw network traffic like traditional firewalls. Consider this example: a cross-site scripting vulnerability is discovered in a single page of a website, yet the fix will take a couple of days to properly develop, test and deploy. In this case, a WAF virtual patch to filter out characters and strings frequently associated with cross-site scripting attacks could be deployed in front of the vulnerable page to provide protection during those few days.

Virtual patching is a double-edged sword. If you deploy it, you should always make sure that there is no confusion about the fact that it is a temporary measure, and that a real fix should always be deployed as soon as possible.

Virtual patching via a WAF is a task that is worthy of its own documented process if it is to be relied upon as a containment mechanism on a regular basis. It's a task that falls within the realms of both the incident responder and the development team responsible for the underlying application. The goal of applying the virtual patch is of course to prevent a discovered vulnerability from being exploited, but it is just as important that the virtual patch does not disrupt legitimate traffic to the application. If it does, the business might be more inclined to reject the virtual patch in future incidents, and the incident responder will have one less containment technique available to them. Let's take a look at a typical virtual patching process.

- **Pre-incident preparation**. As with all things incident response, it is best practice for the first time we do something not to be in the midst of a real incident. Virtual patching is no exception. Time should be taken to examine the capabilities of the tools you have in place to apply the virtual patch, and practice runs against non-production systems should be conducted if at all possible. WAFs, load balancers, proxy servers and next-generation firewalls all have tremendous capabilities when it comes to crafting a virtual patch, but they're only effective if we know how to use them with complete confidence. Including virtual patching drills in scenario-based incident response planning is highly recommended.

- **Virtual patch request.** As the incident response evolves from identification to containment, the playbook should include a mechanism for requesting a virtual patch in applicable scenarios. The first part of this process is determining if a virtual patch is truly an option. There are two questions to be asked. First, does the equipment in a particular environment, or in front of a given application, even afford us the option of a virtual patch? It's no good jumping in to crafting a virtual patch only to then find out that WAF coverage doesn't extend to the application the virtual patch has been written for. Secondly, does the vulnerability we're going to virtual patch warrant the action in terms of both criticality and total time to patch in source code? A highly critical vulnerability that would take a long time to fix, perhaps due to requiring support from a third-party vendor, would be a prime candidate for a virtual patch.

- **Virtual patch development.** If we've decided that a virtual patch is the answer, it's time to craft it. As mentioned earlier, this is a task that should be completed by both the incident responder and the application developer. The incident responder will typically bring specialised knowledge of the virtual patching platform, and the application developer will understand what a legitimate request to the vulnerable component should look like as compared to a request that seeks to exploit the discovered vulnerability. Generally speaking there are two approaches that can be taken when creating the patch, blacklisting and whitelisting. Depending on the nature of the vulnerability, one or both of approaches can be used.

  - Blacklisting involves blocking 'known bad' requests and permitting all other requests that do not fall into this category. This approach works well if you're patching a vulnerability that is exploited with a very precise and easily detectable request body. For example, the 2014 Bash vulnerability CVE-2014-6271,[29] also known as Shellshock, was a significant vulnerability that was triggered using a very specific sequence of characters, namely '{ :; };'. Attackers leveraged various HTTP request elements to find servers vulnerable to Shellshock, and as a result any requests that contained that unusual sequence were highly likely to be exploit attempts. In this case, a blacklist approach was very effective.

  - The whitelisting approach works in reverse, blocking all requests except those that match a defined pattern. For instance, if a request parameter should only include a single digit, but instead includes a string of characters (which may be indicative of an attack), the request will be blocked. Whitelisting is effective when not all possible permutations of an attack string are known, or where the format of a legitimate request is highly predictable and therefore not likely to be inadvertently blocked.

---

[29] Us-cert.gov. (2017) GNU Bourne-Again Shell (Bash) 'Shellshock' Vulnerability (CVE-2014-6271, CVE-2014-7169, CVE-2014-7186, CVE-2014-7187, CVE-2014-6277 and CVE 2014-6278) | US-CERT. Available from https://www.us-cert.gov/ncas/alerts/TA14-268A [16 April 2018].

- **Virtual patch testing.** When we create a virtual patch, we're essentially running through a miniature development cycle. Just as we wouldn't put code directly into production, we shouldn't drop a virtual patch into a live environment without first testing it in a non-disruptive way. Good techniques for doing this involve using alert or detect-only modes on dedicated WAFs, or writing debug lines into the patch to log requests if using a device like a load balancer. If, after monitoring and testing the effectiveness of the patch by running through a series of legitimate and simulated attack requests (if possible), we're satisfied that the patch is performing as expected, it can be considered production ready.

- **Deployment, monitoring and removal.** The final stage in the process is to place the virtual patch into production with blocking enabled. The virtual patch should then be subjected to constant monitoring and, if needed, tuning and improvement. As said from the outset, virtual patches are meant to be a temporary containment measure, and ultimately the underlying issue should be addressed so that the virtual patch can be removed. The development effort to fix this issue should be tracked and monitored to ensure that it does not fall by the wayside. Once the application has been fixed and all parties are confident that the virtual patch is no longer required, it can be removed.

Customer data is leaked on the internet

Containment in this example would be a two-pronged effort. The first prong would be to begin outreach to the provider hosting the looted data to attempt to get it removed as soon as possible (perhaps with the help of a lawyer); secondly, identifying the source from which the data was most likely stolen will help to determine the next move. If the data is in the form of a database dump, and the database resides on only one server, then that server should become the focus of containment efforts.

Firewall rules could be used to limit the server's ability to communicate externally; access could be restricted to the server to prevent a malicious insider, who may have been the source, from touching the data again until an investigation is completed.

A user reports they've fallen for a phishing email

In this case, the most likely impact is either malware being installed or compromise of the user's credentials. To prevent the phisher from using the stolen credentials, containment would involve disabling the account until the credentials can be updated.

Additionally, email logs could be reviewed to ensure that no other employees were targeted by the same phishing email.

An employee has been terminated and is acting in a hostile way towards the company

A hostile termination is never pleasant, and what should be a somewhat routine HR procedure can develop into a security incident. The key to preventing a disgruntled ex-employee from doing harm to the company is ensuring that physical access credentials like door access cards are cancelled. Gaining physical possession of IT assets owned by the company but used by the former employee should be attempted if safe to do so, and technical access credentials should be disabled.

Controlling the rumour mill

Once an incident is confirmed, a heads-up to your public relations (PR) team to start monitoring for external and internal chatter will allow you to stay ahead of any rumours or misinformation that may start to circulate. Introducing them to what is suspected of occurring and having them start to craft internal messaging to control the narrative can prevent cycles being wasted to quash misinformation.

ERADICATION

Now it's time to remediate the issue that led to the security incident. This could involve reimaging a machine that became infected with malware, deploying a patch to address a software vulnerability, or resetting compromised credentials. As we enter this phase of the incident response process, we're in prime territory to experience the incident response versus digital forensics pressures that are a core theme in this book.

Digital forensics requires evidence preservation. As you can probably appreciate, eradication is the very opposite of preservation. We want to get rid of the bad things, and we'll likely be being pressured to do so as quickly as possible. Suppose you have isolated a compromised mission-critical server that costs the company £10,000 for every hour it is down, and are now ready to eradicate the avenue of compromise; suggesting you might take an hour or two to collect evidence for your upcoming forensics investigation before doing so might not sit well with everyone. They're going to want that thing fixed and back in business as soon as possible.

In response to this specific example, I'd suggest there is good reason to understand both how a mission-critical server became compromised in the first place and why it was not deployed in a redundant fashion. The business case for preservation would be that although we might lose an extra £10,000 today while we preserve evidence to figure out how this happened, we might not lose £20,000 the next two times this same incident occurs. Some people might buy it, others might not. You'll need to swap your incident responder's hat for a politician's hat to make the case. If you've already built up some trust in your organisation through some of the pre-incident work we've covered, trust me, this becomes an easier conversation to have and increases your chances of a favourable outcome.

I was contacted by an organisation who were dealing with a potential employee acceptable use policy violation. The employee had been let go after several reports of them accessing pornographic material while at work. The IT team at the company seized the employee's laptop immediately after termination. They were unsure if they wanted to back up the accusations with digital forensic evidence, due to concerns about the cost and whether or not management would want to foot the bill.

My advice was to keep secure possession of the laptop indefinitely, even if the management team ultimately decided not to pursue the forensics avenue. Three weeks passed before I heard from the company again. The management team had decided to pursue forensics, but there was an issue. The company had been short of laptops, and IT had been pressured to reissue the laptop that contained potential evidence; in doing so, they had reimaged the laptop. This obviously had an adverse impact on the evidence, and a reliable investigation was no longer possible.

A classic example of how business pressures can interfere with the digital forensics process.

Eradication methods

Let's look at some commonly used eradication methods.

- **Reimaging of a compromised system**. In the event that a machine, be it a laptop, desktop, server or virtual machine, becomes compromised for any reason, a complete reimage is considered the most reliable way of removing any lingering trace of the compromise. Many organisations have adopted this as a standard operating procedure and reimage machines in response to any sort of malware alert. The use of cloud storage for user-generated files and centrally deployable software packages can make this a more palatable approach for the end user. On the other hand, if a user has stored years of documents on a laptop, a complete reimage might not go down so well. In cases where data recovery is needed before a reimage, forensic acquisition of a compromised machine can serve a dual purpose. Not only can it allow for the recovery of important files (which can be scanned for malware before they are reintroduced to the reimaged machine), but it can also allow us to perform a forensic examination to determine in more detail how a machine became compromised in the first place.

- **Recovery of compromised data**. In the event that the integrity of data is compromised, backups are our friends. A common eradication technique is to restore data to the 'last known good' state, once all containment actions have been taken. Of course, backups have to be in place and have to be working to be usable. For this reason, frequent restore tests should be performed on critical systems.

- **Re-establishing access control.** In the event that credentials become compromised it is standard practice to reset them to prevent extended use of those credentials for malicious purposes. For user accounts this is typically a straightforward process, as password changes on those accounts are a routine task. In the case of shared accounts, service accounts or API keys, this can be more complex. The process involves identifying all sources where those credentials are stored before the change is made, to avoid unexpected downtime caused by older versions of stored credentials.

RECOVERY

In this phase, the environment is restored to a working state so that business operations may resume. Examples of this include restoring files encrypted by ransomware from backup, restoring network connectivity to isolated machines after they're confirmed clean, and removing a virtual patch after a real patch has been deployed.

The recovery phase also encompasses taking actions to prevent a repeat of the incident; for example, if an incident was caused by a missing firewall rule, confirming that the rule has been added. If malware was able to spread due to missing antivirus software, then ensure that antivirus software has been installed.

Now might also be a good time for your PR or communications teams to start crafting external messaging around the incident, with input from the security and legal teams of course.

Finally, it's time to thank everyone who participated in the incident response, and have them start to make notes on the things that they think could have been better, or how the process could have run more efficiently. Those notes will be very useful during the post-incident review, which we'll discuss in Chapter 5.

SUMMARY

In this chapter, we looked in depth at the four phases of the incident response process: identification, containment, eradication and recovery. We reviewed various tools and techniques we have available to help us achieve the objectives associated with each phase.

We noted the importance of establishing a baseline of normal activity, because many incidents can be identified by abnormal behaviour. We talked about various containment options available to us, taking an in-depth look at applying a virtual patch via a WAF. We studied effective eradication techniques, but noted the importance of balancing the need to eradicate with the need to preserve potential evidence. Finally, we talked through the final step in the process, recovering from the incident and getting things back in order.

While this chapter has been focused on all the things we should be doing during the response, it is just as important to be aware of the things that should be avoided. That's where our next chapter comes in, as we study the mistakes and missteps that could derail our response to a security incident.

4 THINGS TO AVOID DURING INCIDENT RESPONSE

We've obviously covered a lot of things an incident responder should be doing before and during an incident, but it is just as important to cover the things that should be avoided. Even the savviest incident response teams have found themselves falling into a trap in the heat of the moment. Some traps are self-inflicted, whereas others are left by a smart attacker deliberately seeking to redirect an incident response team. As a core theme of this book, we've talked about the often-conflicting needs of incident response and digital forensics, which actually brings us to the most important mistake to avoid during an incident: significantly limiting or damaging your ability to perform a more detailed forensic examination afterwards. In this chapter we'll discuss this challenge and various ways around it.

Other pitfalls to be avoided include spawning a fresh incident while responding to another. Some teams believe the fact that an incident is underway gives them carte blanche to abandon all change management best practices in the name of getting things back to an operational state. That is simply not true, and doing so can lead you deep into the woods without a trail of breadcrumbs to follow to get back to the point you started. Sometimes you need to roll back to move forwards!

Just as I started to write this chapter in September 2017, what will likely become the de facto case study of things to be avoided during an incident response had started to play out. Equifax, one of three major credit monitoring bureaus, disclosed that they had suffered an incident affecting at least 143 million Americans – that's a not insignificant percentage of the US population. From the moment Equifax disclosed the incident, they started to make mistakes.

First of all, Equifax disclosed that 40 days had passed from the discovery of the incident to the point of notification. The incident put social security numbers, credit card numbers and driver's licence numbers at risk: the trifecta as far as things criminals can use to commit identity theft and financial crimes are concerned, and they'd had plenty of time to do so. Now, to be clear, not detecting an incident for months or years is common, but knowing about an incident and taking more than a month to disclose it, all the while knowing the impact was so significant, rightly drew ire from the information security community and the public in general.

Secondly, a very broad description of the root cause of the incident was given. A 'website application vulnerability' could be a lot of things, and in this case, with so many people involved, many believed a more detailed description should have been given. Was this SQL injection? Was it a flaw in a piece of web server software?

Then, there was the website Equifax set up to handle the anticipated influx of traffic from consumers concerned about the safety of their personal information. The site was set up by a public relations firm on a domain that was newly registered, but which contained the word 'Equifax'. This alone was enough to quite rightly trigger multiple web security products to flag the site as a potential phishing destination. After all, it is common practice for a phisher to register a site with a similar domain name to the site they're trying to spoof – this is basic information security knowledge. To rub further salt into the wound, the site contained an information disclosure vulnerability that allowed cyber sleuths to quickly identify the disaster relations and PR firm behind the incident response.

If consumers were able to access the site set up by Equifax, they were prompted to enter the last six numbers of their social security number, along with their surname. At a time when consumer trust in you is zero, is it really wise to be asking for more personal information? The answer to that question is, of course, no. The site itself also gave conflicting information about whether or not a given person was included in the scope of the incident. People just want a straight answer in these situations; instead, they got more confusion.

If that wasn't bad enough, a few days into the incident actual phishing sites were set up looking to capitalise on the breach, and at one point Equifax's support personnel themselves started to direct angry consumers to those phishing sites. You really can't make this stuff up!

The final outcomes from this incident are still pending at the time of writing, but if the early response to the incident is anything to go by this could easily go down as the most disastrous computer security incident and response in history.

ERADICATION AND PRESERVATION

Eradication and preservation are two words at very much opposite ends of the spectrum, and two words that could be considered a core function of incident response and digital forensics respectively. As incident responders we must fight the desire to eradicate before we've adequately preserved, to avoid falling into our first trap: not giving ourselves the opportunity for a full forensics investigation. As discussed earlier when talking about forensic readiness, there are many benefits to completing a full forensics investigation in the aftermath of a security incident, and it is typically in the incident responder's interests to push for an investigation.

Create a forensics-ready environment

A golden rule of digital forensics is that you go into every investigation as if you'll have to defend your actions in a court of law. Incident responders, for the most part, don't go into every incident with this mindset, and even if they do they can be overruled by superiors who value getting the incident closed out as soon as possible, at the cost of any evidence. It is possible to tackle this challenge in a couple of ways. The first is to ensure that as many potential evidence items, or artefacts, to use the industry term, are duplicated off or moved away from the host that is generating them as quickly as possible, with real-time offloading being optimal. Additionally, offloaded artefacts should be stored in a completely separate system, with an enhanced level of security. For example, all log files on a web server should be streamed (another term for real-time offloading) to a logging platform that is protected by a network access control list and multifactor authentication. The reasons for this approach are twofold. First, we want to make sure that we get the logs off the host before they can be tampered with or disabled completely. Logs are, of course, self-reported data, and if an attacker has control over the reporter they can report whatever they like – a perfect way to cover their tracks or misdirect the incident responder. A log file stored only on a compromised host is a compromised log file. If you can offload a log file showing just indicators of the initial intrusion before the attacker has a chance to manipulate the logging, you're going to be in a much better spot than if you offloaded nothing. Secondly, we want to make it as hard as possible for an attacker to move laterally into our logging platform should they compromise a host on our network. A compromised logging platform is, quite frankly, the stuff of nightmares. If our logs aren't protected and isolated after they're offloaded, we're giving the attacker a helping hand by putting all the useful log data we'd use to catch them in one handy platform.

Modern-day logging platforms can be architected to collect data from hosts both inside and outside the corporate network, and if you have any remote workers this is a very important consideration. If you're working in a company that does most of its business in the cloud, without the need for a constant virtual private network (VPN) connection (which is becoming a much more common scenario), it's not going to be any good having log collectors only accessible with an internal corporate network IP address. Working with operations teams, IT teams and other members of the security team, incident responders should reduce the barriers to getting critical logs off systems in all situations.

Quality not quantity

The success of a logging platform is not going to be measured against how much data can be thrown into it, it's down to the value you can get out of it. If you have lots of logs, but if none of them contains actionable information, then you're going to be in pretty much the same position you would be without logs, except with a larger bill for storing all that data. Logs should include, at a minimum, a timestamp (recorded in UTC, for bonus points), identifying information such as IP addresses or hostnames, user accounts associated with the given action (where applicable) and details of the action taken to trigger the log entry.

In the case of web application log files, any load balancing or firewalling that may obscure the true client source IP should be factored into the log configuration. For instance, it is no good having a log file for an externally accessible web application accessed by thousands of clients that is full of only the internal IP addresses of a load balancer sitting in front of the application. In the HTTP realm, headers such as 'X-Forwarded-For' can be added to the request that can capture the true source address. The value of those headers will be lost if they aren't included in the log file.

When working with web application log files, especially in cases where the application has been compromised, there is significant value in extracting client IP addresses and examining them for trends. These trends, such as spikes in activity, could lead you to identify a particular IP address that is likely to be the source of the compromise. This is a useful piece of the puzzle in determining how exactly the application was compromised, and potentially who was responsible.

Over the years, I've found it hard to beat the grep Linux command line utility using a regular expression for achieving this objective. The grep utility can search through files, and if provided with the regular expression pattern for a valid IP address can extract those addresses with ease. An example of this is shown below.

```
grep -oE "\b((25[0-5]|2[0-4][0-9]|1[0-9][0-9]|[1-9]?[0-9])\.){3}(25[0-5]|2[0-4]
[0-9]|1[0-9][0-9]|[1-9]?[0-9])\b" web.log
```

This command will output a list containing each IP address in the log file (in this example, the filename is web.log). As this is a Linux command, we can pipe the output of this command into other utilities, such as sort and uniq, to very quickly determine which IP address in the log file is the noisiest, as shown below.

```
grep -oE "\b((25[0-5]|2[0-4][0-9]|1[0-9][0-9]|[1-9]?[0-9])\.){3}(25[0-5]|2[0-4]
[0-9]|1[0-9][0-9]|[1-9]?[0-9])\b" web.log | sort | uniq -c | sort -n -r
```

This command will return a list of all IP addresses in the log file, along with a count of the number of times that particular IP address has made an appearance. Thanks to the final sort command, the address with the most hits will be at the top of the list.

Sometimes log files can be compressed to save disk space. Not to fear, there are specific versions of grep that can run the same operation against compressed files without having to decompress them. These utilities, such as zgrep and zipgrep, take exactly the same arguments as the standard grep utility.

Retention

Once you've offloaded your logs, it's important to get a handle on how long you're going to retain them. Some organisations will be bound by regulatory requirements that dictate how long they retain logs. For example, PCI DSS, as of version 3.1, mandates a one-year retention period. Just like a CCTV camera that is always recording, logging platforms may store as much as they can on a given storage resource, such as a SAN array, before overwriting the oldest data first. Some organisations have been caught out by this. A new, particularly noisy, system may be introduced, causing a spike in logs that fills up the storage available to a logging platform. To counter this, older logs may be moved to cheaper, offline storage. If this route is taken, bear in mind that it's worth weighing up the financial savings of doing so versus the additional cost in lost time and tied up resources to restore those offline logs in the event of an incident.

Threat hunting

An up-and-coming area of information security with benefits for incident response has been dubbed 'threat hunting'. Threat hunting supports the idea of proactively sifting through a given host, or application, for indicators of malicious activities, for instance reviewing the active network connections from a host and the running processes on a host as a form of proactive triage. This makes a lot of sense, if you have the resources available to do it. A side effect of the emergence of threat hunting is that several commercial tools have popped up to support the activity. Examples of this include Cb Response by Carbon Black[30] (see Figure 4.1) and Falcon Insight by CrowdStrike.[31] Some tools, using an agent installed directly on the machine, continually track running processes, which libraries they're calling and what network connections they open, and offload this information to a central console. Forensics is literally built into the incident response workflow – wonderful! Given this, why doesn't everyone use such a tool? Unfortunately, these tools can be among the most expensive security products out there, they can have significant deployment times and require a dedicated team to use effectively. Therefore, they might not always be an option for a given organisation.

When considering the purchase of security tools to supplement incident response it is worth remembering that the full capabilities of any product, as pitched by a vendor, may never be fully utilised in a real-world environment. There are various factors behind this, one of the most common being deployment time. The longer a tool takes to fully deploy, the likelihood of a successful deployment diminishes. This is because other priorities surface, staff turnover occurs and business objectives change. Ask for references from other customers about typical deployment times and how they affected overall usage of the product.

First response

Another way of mitigating the loss of potential forensic evidence during an incident is to ensure that you have an effective first responder or forensic readiness training programme in place. The first person on the scene of a security incident is typically not a trained incident responder. It's more likely to be a helpdesk employee responding to a call from a user reporting that their machine has been infected with malware, or a database administrator who stumbles upon some strange entries in a transaction log, or even a security guard who notices that a USB drive has been left unattended in the car park of your building. In all these cases, the actions taken during first response can have a critical impact on the overall response, including any follow-up forensic work.

Clearly, we want our first responders to know who to call in the event of an incident to get the appropriate support they need, but we also want them to know what they shouldn't be doing. Under pressure from an executive who has malware on their

---

[30] Carbon Black (2018) *Cb Response | Incident Response & Threat Hunting | Carbon Black*. Carbon Black Inc. Available from https://www.carbonblack.com/products/cb-response/ [20 April 2018].

[31] CrowdStrike (2018) *Endpoint Detection & Response Solutions (EDR) – CrowdStrike*. CrowdStrike Inc. Available from https://www.crowdstrike.com/products/falcon-insight/ [20 April 2018].

Figure 4.1 Cb Response by Carbon Black, an example of a threat-hunting tool

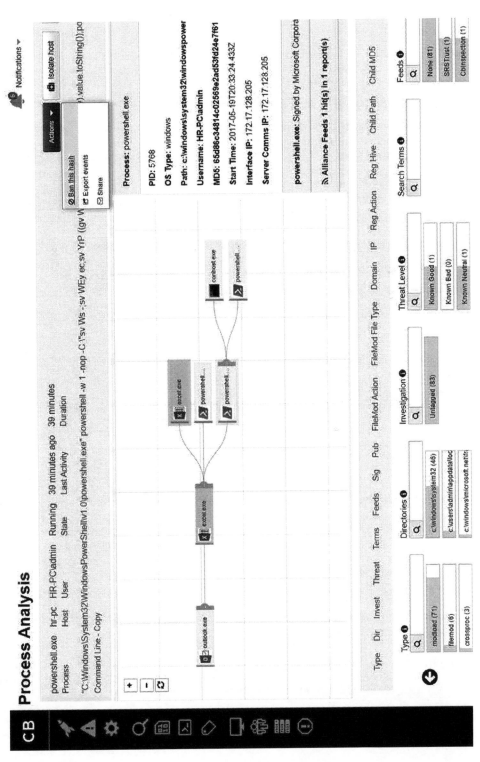

machine, the helpdesk engineer might attempt a quick fix and tell the executive that all is good. Wanting to leave the office on time, the database administrator might run through a rollback operation before anyone has the opportunity to notice the issue. In an attempt to reunite data with owner, the security guard might insert the USB drive into their machine to figure out who owned it. All very real scenarios that I can attest to personally having experienced!

The wonderful human desire to be helpful can be our biggest undoing in many a security situation. This is what most social engineering attacks depend on, for example. Given this, how do we teach our colleagues to slow down and think about the steps they're taking in the earliest stages of a security incident? A key rule of forensic preservation is to keep machines powered on until they can be imaged, yet, in the event of a strange pop-up on a machine, an understandable reaction is to slam the laptop closed or even power off the machine completely.

As someone who has run first responder training for 'non-technical' folks, I can attest that the reactions I've seen range from moderate interest to 'What did I do to deserve this torture?'. As information security folks who live and breathe this subject matter, it's hard to imagine that certain people couldn't be enthused by the topic of how to react in the event of a security incident, but trust me, it's not for everyone. I've found the best option is to reduce the takeaways to three or four key points. Let's review what they might be:

- Isolate by disconnecting from the network, rather than shutting down powered-on machines. Leave powered-off things powered off and unconnected.
- Take screenshots of indicators if possible.
- Jot down notes of the events that led to the suspected incident before you forget them.
- Contact the security team as soon as possible.

These actions, if applied to our example scenarios, would put us in relatively ideal starting positions. Our helpdesk engineer could isolate the infected machine and take screenshots of pop-ups that might help us to diagnose the nature of the malware, after writing down the steps that led to the infection. Our database administrator would contact the security team after recording the format of those strange log entries. Finally, our security guard would leave the disconnected USB drive disconnected, and notify the security team of the discovery. Straightforward, easy to understand, actionable steps that lead to forensic preservation while not adversely affecting the speed at which we're able to complete the incident response. For some more technical positions within an organisation you might consider adding a few more technical actions to the basic steps. In organisations with several branch offices, for example, it can be a smart idea to train at least one person in each office to perform forensic disk acquisitions, or to use a USB drive with a series of scripts coded in advance for offloading artefacts from a machine of interest. Anything to overcome the delays and communication problems that can become an issue across multiple time zones and languages.

Again, this sort of training sounds like a really simple thing to do, and it is. But, as is the case with a lot of information security activities, the basics are often overlooked. Do not undervalue the importance of first responder training, it really can make all the difference. Try not to confuse it with general security awareness training either. Both these types of training are important, but too much training in one session can have negative results. Try to split up the training into two different sessions, for example security awareness training within two weeks of hire, and first response for applicable employees a few months later.

AN INCIDENT FROM AN INCIDENT

When you have an incident on your hands you're typically dealing with a less than ideal situation. The last thing you'll want to do is make a bad situation worse, or multiply the number of bad situations you're having to deal with simultaneously. If you get into this state, it can be hard to determine if an indicator or behaviour playing out in front of you is cause or effect.

In an example of responding to an incident that spawned out of another, a security incident was declared after a fairly routine automated web application scan on one of our applications. A bot had attempted to insert some cross-site scripting code into a form field on the application. The form was set up to handle the code properly, and therefore the cross-site scripting bot was unable to find a vector in our application. All pretty standard, non-exciting stuff. At least it should have been.

Unfortunately, a less security savvy operations engineer saw the code the bot had tried to inject, and copied and pasted it into an internal messaging application to ask for advice on what the bot could be trying to do. The internal messaging application, unlike the externally facing application, was not set up to deflect cross-site scripting attacks properly. Thus, the cross-site scripting attack rendered in this app. The engineer had in fact brought the malicious code inside the organisation and affected about 300 people viewing that chat session.

Tracking changes

During the course of normal operations, with absolutely no incidents (security or otherwise) occurring, a change to an environment should be subject to review and scrutiny before it is deployed. As part of that review process, the team performing the change will explain why it is necessary, when they plan to make the change, the risk to the business associated with the change and how they plan to roll back in the event of the change not going as planned. The whole process is meticulous and well documented. After approval, changes are scheduled and another process kicks in to ensure that all stakeholders are aware of the status of the change, from the start of work to completion or rollback.

I was brought in to manage a suspected denial of service attack, the start of an exceptionally long and stressful incident. All of the external indicators showed that no attack was under way. Traffic profiles looked normal, except for the fact that a lot of legitimate connections were being dropped because the servers for a web application were overloaded. This was despite the fact there appeared to be plenty of capacity to handle the connections coming across the internet.

Internet service providers, a content delivery network and a cloud hosting company were all asked to verify the accuracy of our instrumentation; they, too, confirmed no evidence of a denial of service attack. So, what was going on?

It was time to dig into the change records and start to roll back all recent changes to see if we could determine whether something that had recently changed in the environment was now overloading the servers. Two weeks' worth of changes were reversed. By now, the war room was in its third day and was about 40 people strong. Two or three executives were in the room at all times. It was a very costly affair.

All of a sudden, the symptoms stopped. An air of disbelief fell across the room. A couple of people wanted to celebrate, but the majority were more annoyed that the problem had seemingly fixed itself. The room was silent as the various teams checked their monitoring, watching everything return to normal. Then, a lone voice broke the silence.

'Er, guys, last week during an incident I changed a setting on a load balancer to fix a problem, and I just remembered to change it back.' That setting, responsible for how the load balancer handled long-lived Transmission Control Protocol (TCP) connections, had effectively caused the load balancer to launch a denial of service attack on the servers behind it. That change had not been documented as it had been made in the midst of a different, much smaller, incident. Then, because of the weekend, it took a few days for the problem to manifest itself, by which time the detail of the undocumented change had been forgotten. This was undoubtedly the costliest incident spawned from an incident that I've ever seen first-hand.

Any change made during an incident should be reviewed, approved and recorded, without exception. Obviously, this will need to happen on the fly, rather than at the weekly change meeting, but it still needs to happen. The best option is to have the person making the change document it into a chat session that everyone working on the incident can see. If that person wants to concentrate more on performing the change than documenting it, then the documentation should be delegated to another team member.

Reducing security to fix a problem

Security review can and should be part of the standard change review process mentioned earlier. This review should also apply during an incident, otherwise an organisation may run into another classic scenario that frequently causes a security incident to spawn from a 'regular' incident. This scenario involves removing or reducing a security control to address a problem: it could be adding a firewall rule to permit a new traffic flow; it could be removing a WAF rule to improve application performance; it could be bypassing an intrusion prevention system that is believed to be a traffic bottleneck. Any change that is made resulting in a detrimental impact to security should always be raised with and approved by the security team.

You may be thinking that a security team would, or should, never approve a change that is detrimental to security, as that would swim in the face of their whole mission. That's a reasonable opinion, and one that a number of security professionals would agree with. However, it's not always the strongest position to hold in the grand scheme of things. You may have to concede a battle to win a war. Always remember, most companies aren't in business to be secure. Now, we all know they have to be secure to stay in business, but remember that not everyone will have that viewpoint at the top of their mind in the midst of a crisis. As good security professionals, we have to balance risk and reward. If we know that switching an IDS/IPS to IDS mode could fix a problem, the risk is that we lose a level of protection but the reward is that we maintain the same level of visibility in IDS mode, and enable the business to operate. In this scenario, the change might be approved with two conditions. The first is that if the change doesn't fix the problem, the IDS/IPS is switched back to IPS mode within an hour. The second condition is that an alternative IPS is tested and deployed to fill the void. Perhaps we switch from a host-based IPS to a network-based IPS, to spread the load.

Of course, if a change would place an organisation at an unacceptable level of risk, then by all means stick to your guns. You shouldn't have to abandon all professional pride at any point in your career. Politely reject the change and collaborate on a better solution.

Temporary is anything but

Sometimes a security-reducing change is positioned as a temporary fix. Be wary of this trap. 'Let's disable this until we can add more capacity', or 'Let's add this rule in the firewall to allow Bob to remote in and fix this', for example. I've become aware of temporary IT fixes that, if they were humans, would be old enough to drive a car by now. You have two choices when someone suggests a temporary fix: either accept it, assuming it doesn't increase risk significantly, and agree on a fixed rollback date (reminding the person making that change of the rollback date every day until it arrives, and enforcing the rollback if needed), or decline the suggestion and be collaborative in crafting an agreed solution that is acceptable in the long term.

THE BLAME GAME

The incident response process purposefully doesn't include a 'yell at the person who caused the incident' phase. This is because assigning blame while an incident is ongoing is actually something to be avoided. If someone made a mistake that led to an incident, as tempting as it can be to respond with anger, cooler heads must prevail. Anger during an incident is a waste of energy. The incident occurred, now it must be handled as best as possible. Things went wrong and we ended up at this point; we must now get to a better place.

Besides, you actually need the person who caused the incident to be on your team. If someone got duped by a phishing scam, they're most likely going to feel pretty bad about it. Directing anger at them will only compound their emotions, and might cause them to forget key details about what information was sent to the phisher, or worse, they might just walk out of the room. People who get ransomware on their systems, or who get phished or have their accounts compromised come from varied backgrounds and have different levels of technical skill, but all share one common trait: they're all victims. Victims of a criminal act, to be specific. This is always worth bearing in mind.

IT'S NOT OVER UNTIL IT'S OVER

Finally, we should always avoid calling an incident done before it truly is done. Sophisticated attackers can be some of the smartest computer scientists you'll ever meet. They know how you think, they read books like this one. Before the incident is declared over, the environment should be double and triple checked. Was an incident actually just the enumeration phase of a larger attack? Were we being distracted by a denial of service attack while data was being exfiltrated? Did that ransomware spread somewhere else before we could contain it? Do we need a third party to verify this? Did we apply the patch everywhere? All examples of questions to ask during the wind down of an incident. Before an incident responder moves on to post-incident activities, everyone involved in the incident response should have a say in declaring the incident over.

SUMMARY

In this chapter, we've looked at common mistakes that are made during the incident response process and how to avoid them. We discussed in depth the need to build an infrastructure that is forensics ready from the offset, so that we maximise our chances of preserving evidence even though we're taking steps to eradicate an incident. We mentioned the importance of first responder training in achieving this goal.

We also discussed how security incidents can spawn other incidents, because of the decisions that are made during the incident response process. Making changes that actually reduce security is one example of such a decision. We covered human interactions during the incident response process, and avoiding apportioning blame while an incident is still occurring. Finally, we talked about the risks of declaring too soon that an incident has been resolved. While we all strive for resolution as quickly as possible, it is incredibly important to ensure that we are absolutely sure all avenues have been checked, and checked again, prior to making the call.

An incident will have a conclusion, but even when we've arrived there our work is not yet complete. There are still activities to be completed following the incident to maximise our learning and prevent a reoccurrence of the same type of incident. In the next chapter, we'll take a look at these activities as we discuss the post-incident workflow.

5 AFTER THE INCIDENT

Despite the best efforts of an organisation, incidents can and will still happen. When they do happen, we must manage them well and do all we can to learn from them and ensure that they never happen again. There really should be no excuse for the same incident, or same type of incident, happening more than once. In the immediate aftermath of a security incident the mood will be sombre, that 'sick to your stomach' feeling associated with failure will be omnipresent for the people involved, and a lot of reflection and consideration of 'what ifs' will be occurring. Through the negativity, however, there is usually a renewed focus on security, and a momentum that should be harvested for maximum impact. Following a security incident, a security team can reach peak empowerment. This isn't ideal of course, but frequently it's the case. You can either complain about it or leverage it effectively.

To make the most of this momentum there are a series of activities that should be conducted. There are retrospective questions to be asked. In this chapter, we'll review them and discuss ways we can apply the lessons learned during an incident response to our organisation.

POST MORTEM

An incident is considered closed when the full incident response process has been completed, a decision has been made regarding any required additional forensic investigation and all notifications have been made internally and externally. As the incident handlers we should record relevant incident data, such as timelines, indicators, how the incident was detected, chat transcripts from the incident bridge and a list of actions taken during the incident response process.

Once an incident is closed it is time to plan a 'lessons learned' or post mortem meeting. I personally prefer the term post mortem, not because of the dark and dreary connotations of the name, but because such a meeting should include more than just the lessons learned. The nature, length or severity of an incident will typically play a role in determining how much of a gap will be left between the end of the incident and the meeting. In the case of a small, low-impact incident it wouldn't be unreasonable to hold a post mortem meeting on the same day, immediately after the incident is closed. On the other hand, following an incident with significant impact to the business, an enhanced level of complexity or which has been a particularly lengthy affair, it is worth taking a one- or two-day break before the formal post mortem. The break will give everyone involved in the incident the chance to clear their heads, collate relevant information and spend time individually reflecting on what transpired. No matter what the size of the incident, a post mortem should always be held. Another option is to hold several minor incident post mortems in one session. Encourage people to jot down questions, or issues that they would like to see addressed in the meeting. A maximum of two days between incident end and the meeting will reduce the likelihood of useful information being forgotten.

The meeting invitation should include the incident response team and other relevant stakeholders from the business. Just as people can get fired-up on the incident bridge, the post mortem might also fray a few tempers if not well managed. At the start of the meeting remind people that the goal of the post mortem is to leave with positive and productive conclusions that will ultimately lead to a more secure organisation. You cannot achieve this goal without collaboration.

When and what

The first point to be addressed is exactly what happened. From first response to closure, walk through the incident timeline. This is a key topic of conversation. Different players in the incident response may have joined the incident bridge at different times, and therefore, while having a general idea of what occurred, might not have been exposed to some specific details. Those details, when reviewed, may trigger a light bulb moment for that person, improving the overall understanding of the incident, or causing additional remediation actions to be conducted. Discuss the certainty within the team that the scope of the incident has been accurately understood. Having to go back and revise the size of an incident later is never ideal, especially when the incident is larger or has more impact than first thought.

In 2013, US retailer Target suffered a massive loss of credit card information in an incident attributable to specialised malware installed on their payment card terminals following a successful phishing attack on a third-party supplier.

The initial scoping performed by Target put the number of stolen credit card numbers at around 40 million. After further research and a post mortem the company revised the figure a few weeks later, identifying up to an additional 70 million credit cards. Having such a significant incident is bad, but having to revise notifications shortly after disclosing the incident is really unpleasant.

Drawing a timeline of the key moments in the incident response process is one of the best ways to identify areas for improvement and look for things that could have been missed during the response. Using a good old-fashioned whiteboard for this is particularly effective, as it promotes collaboration and changes can be made quickly as times are questioned and confirmed. Keep it legible, since a photograph of the whiteboard can be used to produce a cleaned-up electronic version of the timeline for the final incident report.

People and the process

At the end of any incident there is always one question that will be impossible to answer. When will the next incident occur? It could be the same day, it could be in a few days, it could be weeks, months, years or anything in between. The point is, whenever the next incident occurs, if there were deviations from the plan, or mistakes were made this time, how can we prevent them from happening again? I've heard it said that one positive from a security incident is that it provides the most realistic and thorough test possible for your incident response plan! It is true that some security standards even explicitly declare that the need for an incident response test is negated if the incident response process has been run against a real incident within the last 12 months. With this in mind, part of the post mortem should be dedicated to examination of the people and processes involved in the incident.

Everything from the first responder's actions to the steps taken to identify, contain, eradicate and recover should be subject to review, along with the internal and external communications around the incident. Not for the purpose of apportioning blame at this point (this is a topic we'll revisit shortly), but instead to highlight challenges, gaps or changes that need to be made to the incident response playbook. In the case of the first responder, perhaps they waited too long before raising the alarm, or maybe they didn't know how to raise the alarm properly? In the latter case, the onus wouldn't be on the first responder, it would be on the security team to improve education and awareness.

Misconduct

As incident responders, it is highly unlikely, and frankly should never be the case, that we'll be the folks to administer disciplinary actions to anyone who may be directly responsible for a security incident. In the event that an incident was caused by an employee violating a security policy it is understandable that we'll want to see some sort of action taken against that employee. There is little point in having policies if they're not going to be enforced by the organisation. The correct approach for the incident responder in this situation would be to consult with the HR team, provide evidence of the actions taken by the employee that violated policy, explain the severity of those actions and ask them to take appropriate steps to address the issue. Employment law and HR are largely outside the scope of this book, and topics that many incident responders are quite happy to keep as far away from their wheelhouse as possible. This is why an incident responder should be cautious with the language they use when discussing an incident with someone who violated policy. Leave such conversations to HR where possible.

Human resources teams can sometimes get a rough deal when it comes to how they're perceived in the corporate world, but trust me, as an incident responder it is worth building a strong partnership with them. Incidents come from the inside more frequently than the outside. If you're not the kind of person who enjoys conflict, which most of us aren't, having a good HR representative be the one to deliver bad news is very welcome. Earlier in this book it was emphasised that information security is a people business; well, you are reminded of that extremely quickly when you witness someone losing their job because of a security incident they caused and you investigated.

In the post mortem of an incident caused by an insider, the person may or may not be in the room. That would typically depend on their job role and the circumstances surrounding the incident. An incident caused by a database administrator making a mistake and deleting data is more likely to feature that person in the post mortem as compared to an incident involving a salesperson deliberately posting company secrets on a social media site. In either case, the post mortem should not become a forum for disciplining or condemning those people – it is a technical and scientific meeting, not a political one. Keep it that way: treat those folks as if they were any other non-human component of the timeline. This is one time that it's totally okay to treat people as mere assets!

Vendors as a vector

If, during the incident, it was determined that the actions of a subcontractor or vendor may be responsible then it will be prudent to have the person who maintains the relationship with that vendor in the post mortem meeting, along with legal counsel. Incidents involving vendors can get tricky because of the legal angle. It is no surprise that the affected organisation will want to seek restitution from the vendor that caused the problem.

In June 2012, Brighton and Sussex University Hospitals NHS Trust was fined £325,000 by the United Kingdom Information Commissioners Office (ICO) for an incident involving a third-party service provider, Sussex Health Informatics Service. The incident occurred in September 2010, when the service provider was tasked with securely destroying 1,000 hard disk drives containing sensitive medical data. The disks were all housed in a secure room, where they were to be destroyed.

The service provider, in turn, hired an individual subcontractor to do the work, but the job was never completed properly. Around a quarter of all the hard drives were removed from the secure room intact. Those drives found their way onto the online auction site eBay. Some of those disks were later purchased by a data recovery company, who reported to the ICO that they had found medical data, staff national insurance numbers and other sensitive information on the disks.

This is a classic example of an incident affecting an organisation but being caused by a sloppy vendor. It is often said that you can outsource the function, but you cannot outsource the risk.

Work with the legal team to ensure that the post mortem is used to collate all the information they will need to move forward with any claim.

Running the playbook

For any professional sporting event, in any given sport, the players spend the hours after the game reviewing footage of their performance and comparing it to their game plans and playbooks. The coaches will see which plays and set-pieces worked well, and which ones didn't. The point here is to discover which aspects of the game need to be improved, which should be dropped completely and which were the strongest, requiring the least rework. This is exactly what should happen in the post mortem of a security incident, except that in our case we're comparing the incident response to the incident response playbook. Were the appropriate people involved at the appropriate times? Did they follow the playbook? If not, was it because they simply forgot what to do, or was it because the playbook wasn't workable in this given scenario? If so, how do we make it workable? These are the types of questions that will ultimately go a long way towards streamlining the incident response playbook to fit the organisation perfectly. Mistakes happen; the least we can do is learn from them.

Even if the playbook was followed to a tee, and everything worked out reasonably well, it is still worth asking if it could be improved. Could time have been saved? Did we really need to do a given activity? Tweaks and changes to the playbook are completely acceptable, of course – it is a living document that moves in step with the organisation.

Control improvements

The final topic of the post mortem meeting should provide answers to the question 'How can we ensure this never happens again?' Those answers could include things like policy changes, deployment of new technical or administrative controls, or improving staff training. You may or may not have already implemented some of these things prior to the post mortem meeting. I'm sure we can all think back to an incident notification that includes verbiage like 'We're working with a leading cybersecurity company to improve our processes and deploy new equipment.' Well, if an organisation has stated such a thing, they should follow through.

We've touched on the fact that additional resources, including funding, may be thrown at a security team after an incident to fix the underlying cause of the incident. This is a double-edged sword. Most security teams fight hard for resources, so when they're given extra they have to take advantage of them. The counterpoint to this is that you can't just throw money at a security problem to make it go away. There are no magic tools that can make an organisation secure, despite what certain vendors will tell you. Security is a combination of people, processes and technology. If there are genuine needs for a product to fill a control gap, and you are given the means to obtain that product, do so, but set expectations that it is not going to be a silver bullet. Make it very clear that management support, and the support of the entire business, will be required to ensure the success of the new control.

After the post mortem

Following the conclusion of the post mortem meeting the incident responder should prepare an incident report including details of all the information discussed at the meeting. This report should be distributed to the executive level, and to anyone else within the business with a 'need to know' about the incident. It is going to be a sensitive document, so ensuring that it has the correct protective markings and is handled as such is of paramount importance. Once the pilot has landed the plane they don't relax – they have to taxi to the gate, which requires additional concentration. It's the same with the handling of an incident report. Loss or improper handling of an incident report could cause a new incident. If you've handled an incident well, don't fall down at the final hurdle: protect that document!

The structure of the report can be tailored to suit the organisation's needs, but should include an executive summary, the timeline of the incident, an explanation of how the incident occurred, what steps were taken to end the incident, both short and long term, and actions that were taken or are still pending to prevent a reoccurrence of the incident.

QUANTIFY THE IMPACT

A hugely important but often overlooked post-incident activity is figuring out how much the incident really cost the organisation financially. This isn't an exact science; it is non-trivial to measure things like the cost of the loss of future business as a direct result of reputation damage attributed to the incident. However, you can come up with a reasonably accurate figure by considering factors such as loss of productive time, lost sales due to downtime, and cost of third-party services.

Incident accountant

Before we talk about the formula involved in calculating incident cost it is worth noting that in some organisations the incident responder might not be the one to actually perform the calculation. The reason is that they might not be privy to all the required information – the salaries of the people involved, for example. In this case the incident responder will usually work with a person who does have the data required to fill in the blanks, typically someone in the finance or legal department. In either case the incident responder still has an important role in collecting all the cost information they can and pushing for the final calculation to be completed.

The reasons for quantifying the cost of an incident can include justifying the cost of a new control. If an incident cost a company three times as much to handle as the annual cost of a control that would have prevented the incident, with the cost data in front of a budget decision-maker it should be an easy call to deploy the control. You can, of course, make this point prior to any incident, but nothing is quite as effective as having the real numbers from an incident to back up what you're saying.

If a company has a cyber liability insurance policy, calculating the cost of an incident will form part of any claims made against that insurance. Depending on the amount being claimed, this will range from a self-assessment affair to a process lasting many months. In either case the input data will be the same, so should be collected in the same way.

Doing the maths

Let's look at an example incident and run through the costs involved, and how we might calculate them. In this case we'll simulate a ransomware incident at a company employing 1,000 people. In this incident a sales employee picked up some ransomware on their laptop which then spread to 100 other machines in the same VLAN. The ransomware also encrypted a shared drive on a network-attached storage (NAS) system, which fortunately was backed up to a cloud provider, but while it was unavailable for three hours 20 people from the accounting department were unable to work.

The incident response team for this incident consisted of a security incident responder, a network engineer, 10 IT support staff and one IT manager. Each machine was restored, but it was six hours before all 100 machines were reimaged and the incident considered closed.

The incident responders

The first cost centre to examine will be the incident responders. We had a total of 13 people engaged in the incident response. Depending on the spread of salaries in the given organisation we could either take an average or be more precise in our calculation. In this example, let's say we're dealing with an average salary of £40,000 per year. We'll also need to factor in the overheads associated with those employees to figure out the true cost. Overheads are things like holiday time, bonus, company car allowance, shares/equity, training costs and private medical insurance. Each organisation will have a specific overhead rate for their employees; typically it is salary multiplied by 1.3. In this example, £40,000 × 1.3 = £52,000.

The average salaried employee will work around 40 hours a week and is salaried for 52 weeks a year, so we can take this £52,000 figure and work out the hourly equivalent: £52,000 divided by 2,080 (the result of 40 × 52, or the total number of hours worked in a year) will be £25 per hour. We know that the incident lasted for about six hours, so to determine the total cost for 13 people at £25 per hour we calculate (13 × 25) × 6, giving £1,950.

Therefore, we can conclude that the cost of the incident responders in this incident was around £1,950.

Loss of productive time

This is another important calculation for a security incident: for how long were the people affected by the incident unable to work? In this example we're talking about those 120 people who were either directly affected by the ransomware or affected by the accounting file share being offline. Accuracy gets trickier here; without going around and asking those 120 people how many of them completely stopped work for the duration of the incident it is going to be hard to quantify accurately. Again, we can try and average it out using the facts we have available.

Let's assume that the 20 people in the accounting department were completely unable to work for the three hours their data was unavailable. We can use the same formula that we used to calculate the costs of the incident responders above. Suppose they have an average salary, including the overhead calculation, of £50,000; the loss of productive time for the accounting department would therefore be (24.04 × 20) × 3 or £1,442.40 in total.

Finally, we have the sales department. We know that 100 people were affected and would have experienced some loss of productive time. Let's assume an average salary, including overheads, of £30,000 for these folks. The cost per hour per affected person is £14.42. If we kept good records during the incident we should be able to work out how many people were affected for, say, an hour, versus the full six hours. One missing piece of information is how many people did other work activity, hence maintaining their productivity away from their laptops during the incident. In this case I'd actually recommend a quick internal electronic survey with a simple 'How many lost hours did you experience?' question. Ask them to enter a number between one and six. If you don't have that option, estimate. Let's assume in this case that 10 per cent of the sales people affected in any given hour of the incident were able to do some other work. Additionally, let's imagine that we have data that shows that the IT team were able to reimage around 20 machines an hour. Therefore, at the end of hour one, 72 sales people were affected. We arrive at 72 because IT fixed 20 machines out of 100, but we removed 10 per cent of the people from the 100 affected to factor in the 'other work' they were doing.

We can then work out the hour-by-hour cost based on the average salary calculation and the ever-decreasing number of people affected. When you get rid of those pesky remainders (in my experience, laptops and people only come in whole units!), you end up with something that looks like this:

- End of hour one: 72 sales people still affected, at a cost of £1,038.24 (72 × £14.42, the hourly cost we worked out earlier).

- End of hour two: 47 sales people still affected, at a cost of £677.74. (To get 47 people, we fixed 20 laptops and removed 10 per cent of the people affected who remained productive.)

- End of hour three: 25 sales people still affected, at a cost of £360.50.

- End of hour four: five sales people still affected, at a cost of £72.10.

- End of hour five: no sales people still affected – no cost.

You might be thinking at this point, what happened to hour six in this example? Well, remember the incident ran for six hours, but there is always going to be some time spent on identification and containment before we can start recovery. Therefore, only five of those hours were used for the purposes of recovery. We can add up each of the lines above to get total of £2,148.58 in loss of productive time for the sales department.

Our total figure for the loss of productive time, including the sales and accounting departments, is thus £1,442.40 + £2,148.58, which equals £3,590.98.

We can add the loss of productive time figure to the incident responder cost to get a total cost for this incident of £5,540.98. That figure, and this example, assumes that every-thing went pretty smoothly, no data was lost, and no one on the outside was affected by the incident. Therefore, it's relatively low. Incident costs escalate, and require additional factors to be examined, when you start to consider things like the cost of lost data, customer-facing downtime, reputational damage or legal fees.

If you have a customer-facing application, the team responsible for it should be aware of the downtime cost. There may also be service-level agreements (SLAs) in place that include penalties for downtime that need to be factored into the incident cost. In the cases of damage to reputation, or regulatory fines or lawsuits, honestly there are no hard and fast ways to calculate these. The best advice is to work with the business on a case-by-case basis and see which data points are available. In the case of damage to reputation, a good indicator might be customer retention after an incident. If customers desert an organisation, you can calculate the loss in revenue and factor that into the incident cost.

RSA are a giant in the world of information security. Every year the conference hosted by them draws in thousands of information security professionals. Yet, on 17 March 2011, they were forced, as so many other organisations have been, to sit down and pen a disclosure of a major security incident.

Two small groups of RSA employees were targeted by spear-phishing emails. An employee opened an email containing a malicious spreadsheet. That spreadsheet contained a zero-day exploit that targeted Adobe Flash. A remote access trojan named Poison Ivy was dropped into the network, and that provided the attackers with the hooks they needed to start digging around the RSA network.

What was stolen in the RSA incident has never been confirmed, but it is widely believed that sensitive data pertaining to RSA's multifactor authentication token product SecureID was looted, which in turn placed SecureID customers at risk.

RSA set aside $67 million to cover the costs associated with this incident.

FORENSICS

At the conclusion of an incident, some decisions will usually have been made about the level of digital forensic activity to be performed either during or following the response. In some cases, all the forensic work required, or permitted, will have been performed; in others, the forensic work might be ramping up.

Always be ready for more

The golden rule is to always assume that the forensic work performed as part of an incident will need to be reviewed in a courtroom for a variety of reasons, or that the incident might one day spring back to life and require additional forensic work. In either case you'll need the evidence collected during the incident, and records of what occurred during the response, to be retained.

Evidence should be stored securely, away from any of the systems affected by the incident. Agreement should be made as to how long the evidence should be retained. This is typically a joint decision between the security and legal teams. It is important to remember that not everyone involved in an incident will be at the same company forever. This is why, during the evidence retention process, you identify an area where more detail is needed and you collect it then and there. Do not wait – valuable insight might walk out the door.

SUMMARY

In this chapter we've talked through various post-incident activities that are critically important for the incident responder to complete to get the most benefit from a less than ideal situation. We looked at the post mortem meeting, including who should be involved, and when the meeting should take place.

We noted the importance of quantifying the true cost of an incident, which is a crucial calculation for business leadership to use in future risk management exercises, particularly when making a call on whether to pay for control improvements. Finally, we talked about steps that are necessary to lead the transition from security incident to digital forensics investigation.

While reading these chapters you've probably been thinking about your own processes, and the personnel you'd have available to you in an incident response scenario. Every organisation treats the business aspects of incident response differently. Some may choose to outsource elements of the process, whereas others will have dedicated internal teams. In the next chapter we'll look at these differences, and other aspects of the business side of incident response.

6 THE BUSINESS OF INCIDENT RESPONSE

Information security generally, and incident response specifically, have become topics of discussion not confined to an organisation's technical teams. You're just as likely to hear discussions around incidents, controls and policies in the board room and at shareholder meetings as you are in the IT director's office. Breaches are bad for business, and in a competitive landscape where you're constantly trying to find an edge, having a clean record when it comes to data security is hugely advantageous. This can be empowering for the information security professional, but for those of us who have come from primarily technical backgrounds it can also be daunting. It is for this reason that I wanted to put this chapter together, to shine a light on how information security, and incident response in particular, can be both a sales enabler and a differentiator for an organisation.

Secondly, I wanted to spend some time looking at the incident response services marketplace. Incident response has itself become a multi-billion-pound industry, with a crowded marketplace of vendors and suppliers all vying to get a piece of the action when a potential customer gets compromised. At a time when trust is so very important, how does the information security buyer know who exactly they can trust, and who they should avoid? It is well documented that there is an information security skills shortage, which begs the question 'How do I know I'm getting quality, highly skilled people to help me?' Let's spend some time in the business, and on the business!

REQUEST FOR PROPOSAL

Due diligence during the sales cycle is nothing new. For years, in big technology procurement deals it has become common for a prospective customer to pore over a vendor's service-level agreements and engage in legal tennis over contractual red lines. In the cloud era the depth and breadth of such activities has grown exponentially, with information security due diligence now a cornerstone for the entire due diligence programme.

> I received an inconspicuous instant message on the company instant messaging platform one Tuesday morning. My presence was being requested by a senior member of the information security team in a conference room on the other side of the building. At first I assumed that I was about to be briefed on a security incident, but a second message stated 'It's nothing to worry about.' A smiley face emoji may even have followed on a third line.

I made my way to the conference room where I found a large group of people. I recognised the face of the person who had summoned me, and perhaps one more senior person from my company that I'd met at a previous meeting, but the six or seven others around the table were new to me. They were introduced one by one, and it turned out that I was standing in front of the vendor security due diligence team for a prospect which, if signed, would become the biggest customer in the company's history. It was a big deal, quite literally.

On the spot, and with no preparation time whatsoever, I was asked to go into detail on a particular technical control, and then was grilled by the prospect's team on my understanding of that control. Needless to say, I was slightly terrified. One wrong answer could lead them to a line of questioning that might unravel the whole deal! I navigated the questions, and was eventually excused from the room. Later that day I suggested that the particular person who summoned me might in future give me a heads-up before placing me in such a situation again.

The deal actually did land, and several people received trophies commemorating being part of the team that reeled it in. I was not one of them, as is the plight of the information security professional.

When a prospect submits a request for proposal with the intention of making an information technology purchase they will usually include a vendor security assessment questionnaire. Many are based on controls found in security standards, like NIST or ISO, some are completely bespoke, and others are a mix of both. Nearly all of them are extremely long, which brings me to my first tip. Once you've answered one questionnaire, save the answers so that you'll have them on hand for the second, third and fourth that you'll be asked to fill in.

Leverage your strengths

A common question in a vendor security assessment questionnaire is 'How many security incidents has the vendor experienced in the last three years?', or something along those lines. Now, there might be different answers to this question depending on the person answering. One of the commonest reasons for this is because there is confusion or hesitation around what actually qualifies as an incident for this purpose. Earlier in the book an incident was defined as 'the act of violating an explicit or implied security policy', per the definition provided by NIST SP 800-61. This is a great definition and should make it reasonably easy to quantify the number of incidents that have occurred over the requested time period, or so you would think. Realistically, though, there are business pressures that might, shall we say, want to alter that figure.

For example, if I've had five cases of people in my company downloading pornography at work in violation of acceptable use policies during the period requested then by the NIST definition that would be five incidents, and therefore the answer on the questionnaire would also be 'five'. That would be a bad answer, at least without context. A better way to answer in this case would be to state, 'Over the past three years, we've detected and responded to five incidents of employees violating acceptable use policies. During each of these incidents, no customer data was placed at risk, and the employees involved were disciplined.' This way we're being perfectly truthful in regards to the number of incidents, we're showing our capability in terms of detecting and following up on those incidents, and we're explaining that although there were incidents, customer data was not at risk. We're answering the question, while minimising the risk of follow-up questions and the inherent slowdowns to the sales cycle that they can bring.

Suppose it is suggested to you that these kinds of acceptable use policy violations aren't even worth counting as incidents, and that by incidents the customer actually means 'data breaches'. Does the answer then change to zero incidents? No. Zero incidents is a terrible answer, because it could raise questions over your authenticity at worse, and your ability to detect incidents at best. One oft-forgotten secret of the vendor due diligence process is that you're allowed to reach out to the prospect and ask for clarification on a question. If you can independently verify that the prospect truly does mean 'breach' rather than incident, in this scenario you could answer with zero, but again provide context along the way. 'Following discussion with X around the nature of incidents that fall within the scope of this question, I can confirm that we've experienced no security incidents meeting these criteria' would be an ideal answer.

What if you really didn't have any incidents – should you be punished for a squeaky-clean record? Of course not, but just keep in mind that very few companies have experienced no security incidents, except for those who don't know that they've experienced one. If you're confident in your detection abilities, leverage them in the answer: 'While we have significant security monitoring capabilities in place, we're pleased to report that we did not record an event that qualifies as a security incident during the period.'

What happens if you did in fact suffer a security incident, and a pretty major one at that, during the period of interest to your prospect? Your strength is that you at least knew about the incident, and should have made improvements in response to it. Use this in your answer: 'We experienced a single security incident last year in which customer data was accessed by an unauthorised party; the incident was discovered within three hours, and steps were taken to eliminate the vulnerability that allowed the incident to occur.'

Incidents and events

A common mistake when questioned on the number of incidents that have occurred in an organisation is responding with the number of security events instead. There is a significant difference between an event and an incident. As per the NIST definition, an event is 'any observable occurrence in a system or network'.[32] Think about that for a second. The key word is 'any'. When a legitimate user logs in to a computer, that is a security event according to this definition. Every time there is an uncorrelated low-risk alert from an IDS, that would be considered an event. This can happen a few hundred times a day. In regards to these examples, if you were counting events as incidents you'd be rapidly running up the number of incidents to a meaningless very large number. Worse than saying you've had zero incidents is saying you've had half a billion. Not

---

[32] Reprinted courtesy of the National Institute of Standards and Technology, US Department of Commerce. Not copyrightable in the United States. Joint Task Force Transformation Initiative Interagency Working Group (2017) *Security and Privacy Controls for Information Systems and Organizations*. NIST. Available from https://csrc.nist.gov/csrc/media/publications/sp/800-53/rev-5/draft/documents/sp800-53r5-draft.pdf [20 April 2018].

so much because of the size of the number, but just because it suggests that there is no effective process in place for sorting through the event noise and discovering real incidents.

Other sales hooks

The involvement of a security or incident response representative in the sales process need not be limited to filling out security questionnaires. Potential customers frequently attempt to set their own contractual parameters around incident notifications, in which case the support and agreement of the incident responder is needed. For example, if you have a customer with a contractual requirement that requires notification of a suspected incident with a four-hour window, this should even be recorded in the incident response playbook since four hours can easily slip by during the response. It would be less than ideal if the first time the contractual requirement was noted was during an incident.

The sales cycle and contractual review period may also be a time when incident definitions are broached with a potential customer. Some may attempt to force their own definition of a security incident on the vendor, while others might have specific takes on what would qualify as a security incident based on the nature of the relationship with the vendor. An example of this would be if a customer had requirements around data jurisdiction, say, perhaps that their data may never be stored or accessed outside the United Kingdom, and any future storage or access of their data outside the United Kingdom would automatically qualify as an incident. In this case, the onus would be on the vendor to deploy appropriate controls to enforce the jurisdiction requirement, but controls sometimes fail. Perhaps during an outage, an on-call engineer from outside the UK performs a restore operation and in the heat of the moment views that customer's data. That would be an incident, and the security incident responder would need to be involved.

THE POWER OF PR

One core function of a PR team is to monitor external sources for noise around issues that may be detrimental to the brand they are promoting. This is a particularly useful function for a security team to either feed directly through their own tools or use for advance notice of a potential security incident. A classic example of this is when a post on social media indicates that there might be a security problem within a particular product or service.

Tavis Ormandy is a world-renowned vulnerability researcher working for Google's Project Zero initiative. Project Zero aims to uncover zero-day vulnerabilities, which are vulnerabilities in software that haven't previously been disclosed, and report them to the developer so they can be addressed. Project Zero gives developers a maximum of 90 days to address the vulnerability before they release details to the public.

On 18 February 2017, Ormandy tweeted 'Could someone from Cloudflare security urgently contact me?' Cloudflare is a content delivery and DDoS protection service provider. It turned out that Tavis's tweet was in relation to a significant vulnerability in the Cloudflare service, which some later dubbed Cloudbleed. The Cloudbleed vulnerability was so called because it was similar to the Heartbleed vulnerability that affected OpenSSL a few years prior, in that it allowed the potentially sensitive contents of uninitialised memory to be viewed by an attacker.

As Tavis described in his disclosure of the vulnerability a few days later, 'Seconds mattered here, emails to support on a Friday evening were not going to cut it. I don't have any Cloudflare contacts, so reached out for an urgent contact on Twitter, and quickly reached the right people.'

Proof, if any were needed that monitoring social media is a highly effective way to become aware of a security incident.

You can read the full disclosure from Tavis here: https://bugs.chromium.org/p/project-zero/issues/detail?id=1139

Social media is frequently used as an avenue for disclosures and complaints alike, since many know it'll quickly draw a response from the company in question, who'll want to route the conversation through less visible channels. A PR team should be trained in how to recognise a vulnerability disclosure, and quickly loop in the security team to ensure it receives appropriate attention. As a security researcher, there are few things more aggravating than a back and forth with a representative of a company who simply doesn't grasp the gravity of the vulnerability they are trying to disclose responsibly. Too much back and forth can lead to anger, which, depending on the person, can turn an attempted responsible disclosure into a very public and messy one. Having a formal, responsible disclosure policy publicly available for a security researcher to view can help to avoid this situation altogether. Such a policy may also be known as a 'bug bounty programme' if it includes incentives, such as a cash or other benefits that can be rewarded to a researcher for a detailed report disclosed responsibly. There is even an industry of commercial bug bounty programme operators that has sprung up in recent years.

Incident notification

Should the situation arise that an incident legally, contractually or morally requires that external parties be notified that something has happened, this should be a coordinated effort between the incident responder, PR and legal teams. You can do absolutely everything right when it comes to handling an incident. You can discover the root cause, shut things down within 10 minutes and prevent a full-blown disaster, only to see all that hard work blown away by a terribly worded or uncoordinated incident notification thrown together by someone acting in isolation.

There are many clichéd terms used in incident notifications that were great the first several thousand times they were used, but now only serve to anger and confuse an already angry and confused public. For example, don't suggest that an incident was down to a 'sophisticated actor' before you've done due diligence around that statement, because that kind of statement can come back to bite you in a very bad way.

In October 2015, UK-based ISP TalkTalk experienced the loss of several hundred thousand user records and bank account details in a security incident. The subsequent incident notification from the company declared that the company had experienced a 'significant and sustained cyber-attack'.

Fast-forward 12 months, to when a 17 year old was sentenced for using a readily available automated SQL injection scanning tool that led to the incident, and you can understand why the use of the term 'significant and sustained cyber-attack' in the notification was considered particularly grating.

In an incident notification, you should answer the following questions:

- What happened?
- How did you find out?
- When did this happen?
- What does this mean for customers?
- What should customers do to protect themselves?
- What are you doing about it?

Giving actionable advice that adequately describes the risk to the victim (victim is an important term here), without fluff and technical terminology, will go down much better than an over- or under-detailed, defensive-first write-up.

OSINT from the inside out

Social media is a rich source of OSINT, some of which may even originate from within your organisation. Although in some contexts it can be an ethically and legally questionable grey area, monitoring social media usage by employees, or alleged employees, can lead to valuable intelligence and indicators of pending security incidents. Now, to be very clear, this absolutely does not mean an organisation should be obtaining access to private conversations between employees on social media platforms through monitoring or any other means. That would be one of those questionable contexts, and is officially illegal in numerous jurisdictions. Instead, I'm referring solely to monitoring public posts being made by employees, some of which may or may not be anonymous.

Platforms like Glassdoor allow employees the opportunity to post anonymous reviews about their organisation. If one of those reviews suggests there is discontent in a particular department, the business should take steps to address that. Depending on the nature of the post, the security team may clearly also have an interest if the post is threatening in nature, or discloses proprietary information that would be a security incident and handled as such. Law enforcement may even need to be involved if the content is serious enough.

Open-source intelligence from social media is frequently used for other purposes in the business realm. Recruiters, of course, use public profiles on LinkedIn to find job candidates. They can even use analytic tools to look at profile updates that might suggest someone is getting ready for a job change. Security usage of social media that is similar in nature to this is considered quite appropriate, and organisations that don't leverage it are missing out on a valuable incident prediction resource.

MERGERS AND ACQUISITIONS

Should a company purchase another there will be plenty to consider for the information security team, and the security incident responder in particular. If you're the incident responder for the acquiring company, you might walk into the office one day to find the scope of your responsibilities has greatly increased, which is always a pleasant surprise! In mergers and acquisitions (M&A), there is usually a push to get the newly united companies in sync with one another quickly, and that typically involves bringing disparate IT systems together and connecting networks to aid the flow of information. All well and good, but doing so might actually lead to a security incident.

Trust, but verify

By joining networks with a newly acquired company, an organisation is placing itself at significant risk of inheriting the security problems that are embedded within that network. It is the information technology equivalent of jabbing yourself with a dirty needle. For this reason, security teams should be involved in any M&A activity as early as possible. A good place to start is a meeting with any existing security professionals at the acquired company, if there are any. A reassuring sign is if they're just as nervous about connecting their network to yours as you are to theirs. This shows they must have some pride around what becomes of the environment they've worked to protect for however long. Review policies, discuss controls, take a virtual tour of the network, whatever it takes to get a feeling for the health of the environment.

In the mad rush to get things talking to each other, suggest a gradual approach to getting things connected. Use a site-to-site VPN with very strict firewall rules to create a connected feel, but all the while maintaining a logical boundary between new and old.

Ultimately, as good security professionals our duty is to enable the business. Over time, those firewall rules will become less strict, and the site-to-site VPN will be replaced by permanent connectivity. Having a project plan in place that charts a timeline, and what remediation and risk management activities must be completed before those controls are relaxed, is a way to show that you're enabling, but also balancing risk appropriately.

ESCAPE THE TECHNICAL BUBBLE

One of the most effective things a security professional can do within an organisation is spending time learning about how it goes about its business. Many of us, myself included, have been guilty at some point in our careers of being a little over-focused on technical issues. Without taking a step back and observing exactly what the ultimate goal is, you can find yourself on a path to infinite frustration. This isn't a productive way to spend your time, and I've known more than one very highly skilled information security professional end up in a cycle of jumping around between jobs because their frustration limit had been reached. I get it – it's highly annoying when you find out that a business has skimped on a security control in the name of speed, politics or otherwise, but this comes with the territory of information security. A huge part of our job is to influence and instil a positive security culture, but you can't always do that effectively from behind a computer screen. This is very much a people business.

Listen and influence

At a great business, every employee should be able to understand to some extent the mission of the company, and how the company plans to accomplish that mission. This is a two-way street, and while the business is responsible for pushing out information and encouraging an employee to take the time to digest that information, the employee must actually be the one to take advantage of those opportunities.

As an incident responder, taking the time to listen to company leaders about the path the company is taking, meeting with and getting face-time with those in charge of the product roadmap and asking lots of questions is time well spent. You might feel as if you're always running behind the train, putting out fires and responding to incidents that really could have been avoided if you'd just known that a particular situation was on the horizon. Well, this is your opportunity to get in front of that train, so you can lay some track and influence the direction it takes. SIEM tools are great, but they can't influence people like you can, human!

INCIDENT RESPONSE SERVICE PROVIDERS

Depending on your situation, you might find yourself working for, or with, an incident response service provider. By now, we've all likely read a breach notification letter from a given incident, and typically one of the things they are quick to point out is that support from a 'leading cybersecurity forensic company' has been obtained. Now, this might sound a bit like marketing bumf, but there is real value in doing this, even if you have an in-house security team that is technically capable of handing the incident. An outside, fresh pair of eyes that have yet to be exposed to a particular environment may see things that otherwise may go unseen. For the highest level of effectiveness, engagement of an outside provider must not be seen, or positioned, as an indicator of failure on the part of an internal security team. Instead, it should be treated as part of a pre-approved plan to validate the work the security team has already conducted.

Unfortunately, it is the case that sometimes the business may not fully understand or appreciate the skills they have in-house, and force outside engagement on the internal security team. This is a situation that should be avoided, as it is only likely to lead to resentment and an ineffective investigation. To offset the risk of this situation arising, a security team should take time to select a favoured outside vendor and build their involvement into the incident response playbook. With so many service providers offering zero-cost retainers, it has never been easier to do this.

Selecting a service provider

The good news is that there is no shortage of incident response vendors out there, and with so many incidents occurring, many have the cash available to take you out to sporting events or fancy bars while you're deciding which one to sign up with. I say this in jest, but this is actually a very important point. There are lots of vendors who will try to woo you with things like this – it's all part of the sales process. Try not to fall for it; be professional and objective. There are three primary factors to consider when making an informed decision on what will more than likely turn out to be a very important call for your organisation.

Trust is the most important factor. Do you trust that the provider will supply professionals with adequate skills, qualifications and experience to help you in your time of need? Ask questions about experience in the field, the systems that investigators have worked on before, and the industries they've been exposed to. Of course, incident responders cannot go into fine detail about specific incidents they've worked, but they can absolutely give you high-level examples of the types of incident they have been exposed to.

Speed is important in an incident, and therefore your first consideration might be 'How soon could these people get here if I needed them?' Zero-cost retainers were mentioned earlier, which are great, but it is no secret that if you're on a zero-cost retainer with a forensic provider, you'll be bumped in favour of another customer who is paying a premium rate for priority service. This is one of the risk factors you must balance. Are a few hours going to make a difference to your company? If you're a payment processing company performing thousands of transactions a minute, then it probably will. On the other hand, if you're a graphic design studio you will likely have more leeway in the response time. You might be tempted to pick a provider with a local office for this reason, but always verify that the provider will send a responder from the same location. Forensic folks travel to incidents a lot, so can come from pretty much anywhere.

Finally, cost is another major consideration. Agree hourly rates and terms up front; the last thing you'll want to be doing is bartering over cost during an incident. Some service providers will charge additional travel costs, and equipment costs if forensics are needed. Make sure all these costs are documented and understood before signing up with the service provider.

Hit the ground running

After an incident response service provider has been selected it is worth spending time with them ahead of any incident to share information that will reduce the ramp-up time in the event they are needed. This could include information such as current network diagrams, IP address assignments, a copy of your incident response playbook and a list of computing assets.

Introducing other teams likely to be included in the incident response process in any preparatory work with the service provider can help to develop trust early on. As an outsider coming in to assist during an incident response it's not uncommon to have to spend some time winning over some of the people you're trying to help. Time spent mapping the politics of the organisation, getting appropriate access and convincing a given person that you know what you're doing is time that could be better used actually responding to the incident.

Many incident response service providers will actually insist on these types of session, and some will give them away for free. In my experience that is typically an indicator of a company being one of the better providers out there.

They work for you

A final reminder: any incident response service provider that you bring into your organisation is there because they are working for you. It is their job to fit into your processes, not the other way around. For the most seamless experience, an incident response service provider should be used as an extension to your internal security teams, and therefore they should report and document actions in the same way that you do. That said, they can only do this if you tell them how you'd like things reported and documented. Make sure that they have all the materials they need to do this ahead of time, and obtain a written agreement that these actions will be conducted as described.

SUMMARY

In this chapter we looked at various business considerations associated with incident response. We talked about the growing importance of the security team and incident responder in the sales cycle. We discussed the importance of having a solid relationship with a PR team to handle communications related to a security incident.

We covered mergers and acquisitions, and how these organisation changes can affect incident responders by altering the scope of their responsibility. Finally, we talked through the burgeoning incident response industry, and working effectively with third-party incident response service providers.

As we wrap up the incident response portion of this book, it's time to transition, as many incidents do, into the scientific world of digital forensics. In the next chapter we'll introduce the digital forensics investigative process. If you're primarily an incident responder you should of course read on. Incident responders can frequently transition to the role of first responder in a forensics investigation and, as we're about to find out, this can be the most important role in the process.

PART 2
DIGITAL FORENSICS

7 INTRODUCING THE DIGITAL FORENSICS INVESTIGATION

In the first part of this book we concentrated on incident response, which is a topic that allows for some variance and flexibility in approach even while still aligned to a published standard. As we shift to digital forensics in this part you'll notice that the approach is much more structured, as the audience of the process changes from others within the umbrella of an organisation to outsiders such as the legal and law enforcement professionals.

Often in an information technology career we're forced to make choices. Do I prefer network engineering or systems administration? Do I enjoy building apps or micro-services? Should I focus on security or data science? If you're fortunate enough to become a digital forensics professional then you all but eliminate the need to make these types of choice. Digital forensics is such a wide and varied field that one week you might be working on a case where the evidence lies within the packets and protocols on the network, only to find yourself carving through a desktop hard drive the next. It sounds like a cliché to say 'No two days are the same in this job', but trust me, it's the only area of technology in which I've found this statement to be completely true. To make things even better, when you wrap up an investigation and provide justice for a victim the satisfaction experienced is addictive. The majority of the satisfaction comes from the fact that you've used your technical skills to have a real, positive impact on actual human beings who have been victimised through technology, be that an individual, a group of people or an organisation. The rest of the satisfaction comes from the fact that you had to work hard and with meticulous accuracy to get there.

You will not find a textbook that walks you through, step by step, how to solve the case you're presented with on any given day. There are plenty of resources available for obtaining a general overview of the field, learning the best practices for handling various types of evidence and, of course, reviewing the laws and legal processes that must be followed in cases involving electronic evidence. The void between the generalities of the field and the specifics of a case that lands on your desk is a rich vein of satisfaction. It requires a mixture of technical skill and creativity to find it. Hit it in exactly right the spot and you'll love this work. If you're slightly off you might have to try again, and again, and frustration might start to creep in, which is of course understandable, but frustration leads to mistakes. This isn't a field that is forgiving of mistakes, but it is one in which there are communities of dedicated professionals who'll help you avoid them. The remaining chapters in this book will arm you with the forensics knowledge you need to feel comfortable in your creativity, which will ultimately allow you to drive an investigation to a successful conclusion.

THE INVESTIGATOR

A digital forensics investigation cannot happen without an investigator, or investigators. The job of the investigator is twofold: first they must be able to discover evidence, and secondly they must be able to accurately explain the relevance of the evidence they've discovered.

Who are these people, and what skills must they possess to be successful? A deep understanding of operating systems, file systems and networking protocols are a given, and have been since the inception of the field. More frequently, the scope of the forensics field has grown to encompass crimes committed against computers in addition to crimes committed using computers. Given this, an appreciation and understanding of the skills and techniques of a malicious hacker and other types of cybercriminal are of course highly recommended.[33] Criminal enterprises operate online with as much rigour and sophistication as any Silicon Valley tech company, so don't assume you'll be up against anything less. Finally, an awareness of the latest technologies and services leveraged by both consumers and businesses is critical for success. It is no good being equipped to deal with applications of technology that are two or three years behind a real-world implementation such as with the widespread adoption of cloud services and virtualisation technologies.

Not all of the skills required to be a successful digital forensic investigator are technical in nature. Interpersonal skills that can be used to help build relationships and trust between you, your clients and your victims can make all the difference in getting that little extra snippet of information that allows you to crack the case. During the incident response portion of this book it was emphasised how that is a people business; well, I think this is even more applicable in a digital forensics context. These investigations can become pretty intimate affairs; think of how much a person could learn about you if they had total access to your computers and other devices. Confidence in one's skills and ability is another key element. You don't have to be cocky, in fact this should be avoided at all costs, but you should be able to face down any scrutiny that might come your way, because it will. If you find yourself face to face with a defence lawyer it is pretty much a given that they'll try and poke holes in your skills, your background and your standards of work. They'll want to demonstrate that you're likely to have made a mistake in handling or during the processing of evidence.

This brings us on to our final point about investigators. You have to be ethically sound, and have a clean professional record. You can be the most technically gifted person in the world and follow the procedures to a tee, and yet still be called into question if there is something in your background that makes you seem unethical or untrustworthy. This could be a simple mistake, like posting pictures of yourself on social media, slumped over on the side of the street with a two-litre plastic bottle of clear cider in one hand and a hard drive in another. It could also be something more serious, like a criminal conviction. In either case, if you've got it in your past, be prepared for it to bite you in your future. Address such occurrences the best way you can now, so that they're not a problem later.

---

[33] Further information can be found in the BCS publication *Cyber Security: A Practitioners Guide* (www.bcs.org/books/cybersecurity).

Investigative roles

Not all investigations will be conducted by a single investigator – the sheer scale of a complex investigation may make that an impossible task. In such cases, where there are multiple investigators working in a team, each investigator might perform a specialised role.

First responder

A first responder typically travels to a client site and is charged with evidence identification and collection. First responders will use imaging tools to seize forensically sound disk images (more on these in our chapter on digital forensics tools), secure mobile devices or perform live acquisitions on servers and other devices that cannot be powered down.

Investigator/processor

Once the first responder has returned with the collected evidence, an investigator working in a processing role will be responsible for adding the evidence to a case file and launching the various processes that will hopefully uncover the vital artefacts needed to bring the investigation to a conclusion.

Forensic developers

In some investigations, specialised and new techniques need to be developed to meet an investigative requirement. Depending on the organisation, some (very lucky) forensic teams have specialised personnel to fulfil this role.

During my time working in incident response for a software-as-a-service provider in the financial space, I was frequently called upon to provide evidence for customers as part of their own investigations. After a handful of very similar requests, which each had to be performed and documented manually, I decided it was time to build a tool around those procedures to automate the process and save time. The tool essentially ran a series of database queries and collected selected log files used to prove data integrity. The end result was a single zip file containing the evidence, and a document that could be provided to the customer. An example of bespoke forensic tool development.

Lead investigator

A lead investigator is responsible for managing all elements of the investigation. If an investigation is large enough to warrant a lead investigator, the role will typically involve collating all discovered evidence from the various investigators working on the case, and providing an overarching professional opinion on what has been discovered.

No matter what role a person has on an investigation team, all must remember that they play a critical part in maintaining the integrity of the investigation. Therefore, all must be aware of the fundamental principles of digital forensics.

FORENSICS FUNDAMENTALS

Digital forensics is, of course, a branch of forensic science, and that's a fundamental truth that everyone entering into the field must remember at all times. The *Oxford English Dictionary* definition of forensics reads 'scientific tests or techniques used in connection with the detection of crime',[34] the key word in the definition being 'scientific'. The ultimate test of a scientific process is if it can be repeated by a third party and arrive at the same conclusion. In any investigation, in every action you take, always think to yourself, would I get the same result if I did this again, or did I manufacture this outcome? In the midst of an investigation, the pressure placed upon an investigator both internally and by outsiders may subconsciously put us on a path to taking actions to get the result we expect, when actually we must allow the process to return the correct result, be it expected or otherwise.

Another important word in the forensic definition is 'crime'. Sure, many investigations are conducted with the goal of proving that a suspect was responsible for a crime, but others aren't. In many cases, digital forensics investigations are conducted to prove that a suspect violated a corporate policy or committed some other form of misconduct. They might also be run in support of civil proceedings, rather than criminal. Given this, there might be the temptation to get sloppy, or feel as if, given that the burden of proof is lower in cases that aren't criminal, the process need not be as scientific. That simply doesn't cut it. Every single case, every single time, needs to be run as if it were a criminal investigation with the highest burden of proof, 'beyond a reasonable doubt'. If we always work to the highest standard, we can be confident when it comes to defending our work at all levels.

Chain of custody

The most important concept in any forensics investigation, not just one that happens to occur in the digital realm, is the chain of custody. This refers to the series of documents that track possession of evidence throughout an investigation. From the moment it is collected, through transfer, analysis, preservation and finally disposal, the location and custody of an evidence item must be documented with total accuracy. The reason is to avoid a situation that could undo an entire case: a claim that the evidence was planted, tampered with or spoiled. At all times a named individual should be responsible for ensuring that the evidence is secured in an appropriate location, and that any time it is moved, for any reason, those transactions are logged.

The chain of custody documentation can be supplemented with photographs showing the state of the evidence at the point of collection. This is especially important during acquisition of powered-on systems, which may have running programs and other relevant on-screen evidence.

Evidence should always be stored in a highly secured environment, where access is restricted. In a dedicated digital forensics lab there will most likely be a specific evidence storage area, protected by physical controls such as access cards, CCTV, and even

---

[34] Oxford Dictionaries | English (2018) *forensic | Definition of forensic in English by Oxford Dictionaries.* Oxford University Press. Available from https://en.oxforddictionaries.com/definition/forensic [23 April 2018].

an evidence clerk. In an organisation that doesn't have such a facility, the most common approach is for the security team to have a dedicated safety deposit box for the purpose of storing evidence.

In considering the location for the secure storage of evidence, remember that not all threats need be accredited to humans. Evidence should be stored in an area that is protected from environmental extremes, such as excessive heat or cold, the presence of water, or electromagnetic interference.

In 2010 I was managing a digital forensics facility in the UK. I'd just spent Christmas in the USA and was the first employee to return to the office after the break. I arrived early in the morning; as usual at that time of year, the office was very dark (the office itself had no windows, for security reasons).

Imagine my surprise when I put my foot inside the door only to be met by the unmistakable resistance of a significant amount of water. It had been extremely cold over the previous week, and a pipe had frozen and subsequently burst. The entire lower floor of the office was flooded. Thankfully, our lab was on a higher floor, and all the evidence was stored in a waterproof safe!

It took a couple of weeks to dry the place out and replace the carpet, but these are relatively minor issues when you consider what might have occurred if we'd lost our original sources of evidence and our forensic equipment. It just goes to show that it can happen anywhere, at any time, and for any reason.

Working on duplicates

Another fundamental tenet of digital forensics is that we always want to avoid working directly on the original evidence item. Forensically sound duplicates are our best friends – they allow us to limit our interaction with precious original evidence items. Through the use of write blockers and disk duplicators, specialised hardware tools that are discussed in the digital forensics tools chapter, we can make an exact replica of a hard drive which can then be subjected to analysis without the risk of losing or spoiling the only original copy we have. This is known as forensic acquisition, and is a luxury afforded to the digital forensics field that we must embrace when we can, because it is not always entirely possible.

Not all evidence data is stored neatly on a single hard drive. Sometimes it exists only in volatile memory and would be lost forever should a machine be powered down. Failure to acquire volatile evidence, which may in fact prove a suspect's innocence, would be seen as an investigative failure by any court. At other times, evidence can exist in a usable form only when a machine is operating, thanks to full-disk encryption technologies. In these cases we must weigh up the risk of losing valuable evidence versus the risk of altering certain data on the source device. In most cases, an investigator or first responder must proceed to perform a so-called live acquisition, with enough knowledge of the system and confidence in their technique to defend their actions and explain exactly what changes will have occurred because of them.

Proven tools and techniques

In any investigation, the investigator will have a variety of commercial and open-source tools available to them to facilitate the collection and analysis of digital evidence. Most commercial software suites, such as the so-called 'big two', AccessData's Forensic Toolkit[35] and OpenText's EnCase[36] product, will play up the fact that they are 'court approved' in their marketing speak. This isn't just hyperbole, there is substance to the fact that these tools will have been used in a court setting many times, and as a result it is harder to question their legal validity. Therefore, generally speaking, a safe assumption is that you'll have an easier time presenting a case that has been worked using one of these tools versus one handled in a lesser-known tool. That said, these tools don't always have a feature we need, or we might be faced with a new type of forensic challenge that they aren't equipped to handle. In such cases we shouldn't allow the lack of a boxed-up tool to be the difference between obtaining the evidence or letting it slip away. This is where the creativity of the investigator comes into play. The creation of a new tool or technique for unlocking evidence is by no means unprecedented, but the investigator responsible should be prepared to have the credibility of that tool or technique called into question. They should be able to expertly explain how the new tool or technique works, and submit the findings for peer review. Fortunately, in this community there is no shortage of folks who will be willing to jump in and validate what an investigator is proposing.

Document everything

Every single action an investigator takes during the course of an investigation must be documented. This is to ensure that the scientific integrity of your work remains intact. A totally different investigator should be able to work on the same evidence, run the same tests and come to the same conclusion that you did for your work to be considered admissible. Many purpose-built forensics tools, such as the aforementioned Forensic Toolkit and EnCase, maintain such an audit trail on your behalf, but even so the investigator is ultimately responsible for building a chronological list of actions performed on evidence.

Forensic challenges

It probably won't shock you to learn that not everyone who is in the business of committing a computer crime will leave evidence of such activity in a neat pile on their computer. I cannot personally think back to any case I've worked on where there was a 'crime' folder sitting on the desktop, full of all the evidence needed to definitively prove the suspect's involvement. It doesn't work like that. In some cases a suspect will actively take steps to beat the forensics investigation process, for example by using an anonymising network proxy service like TOR to hide internet activity, or through file or disk encryption. Many consumer devices have such features built in.

Disk encryption is a security feature that everyone has the right to use to protect data in the event that a device is lost or stolen. Anyone who has worked in information security

---

[35] AccessData (2018) *Forensic Toolkit*. AccessData. Available from https://accessdata.com/products-services/forensic-toolkit-ftk [23 April 2018].

[36] OpenText (2018) *EnCase Forensic Software – Top Digital Forensics & Investigations Solution*. OpenText Corp. Available from https://www.guidancesoftware.com/encase-forensic [23 April 2018].

will not question that. The flipside of the coin is that as forensics professionals it makes our job harder. Fortunately, we're typically creative types, so the challenge of working round such measures can actually be rather satisfying. Most full-disk encryption systems are based on complex mathematical algorithms that require significant computing power to break into. Unless you're working in intelligence or national security you probably won't have all the required CPU cycles to make that happen. Instead, you're more likely to have success using your creativity to sidestep the encryption. For example, the major weakness in full-disk encryption is typically the encryption password set by the user of the device. We all know how bad most passwords are. Therefore, in this specific example, a forensic investigator might build a password list based on knowledge of the suspect and attempt to use that to gain access to the encrypted data. Security works both ways; we cannot preach it to the good guys and not expect that bad ones will use it as well.

On the morning of 2 December 2015, a terrorist attack in the US city of San Bernardino saw 14 people killed and a further 22 injured in a mass shooting. There were two perpetrators, a husband and wife, both of whom were killed in a shootout with police a few hours after the attack. The victims were colleagues of the male shooter, Syed Rizwan Farook, who had gathered for a Christmas party.

The attack was, of course, horrific, but it will also be remembered for an issue raised during the subsequent investigation. The Federal Bureau of Investigation (FBI) were working to discover whether the shooters were linked to a larger terrorist cell, and as part of that investigation they seized a mobile phone belonging to Farook. The device, an iPhone 5C, had full device encryption enabled, along with a security feature that would wipe the device if an incorrect access PIN was entered multiple times. The FBI feared that this would destroy potential evidence. Apple, the manufacturers of the iPhone, had no way to bypass the security of the device and let the investigators in. This is, of course, how the feature is supposed to work, to protect the data on the device in the event that it falls into the wrong hands. In most cases, however, people using iPhones aren't hiding potential evidence of terrorist activity. This led to a conflict between Apple and the FBI.

Using a 1789 law, the All Writs Act, which allows United States Federal Courts the ability to request that private entities help federal law enforcement perform their duties, the FBI went to court. They wanted to force Apple to write new software and bypass the PIN locking security feature. Apple denied the request, stating that such an order would place the majority of their law-abiding customers at risk. A new order was sought by the FBI, this time with conditions allowing Apple greater control over the conditions of the request.

Ultimately the case was withdrawn in March 2016, during the back and forth between Apple and the FBI. The FBI used an undisclosed technique to gain access to the phone.

Public opinion on the issue was split, many agreeing that Apple shouldn't be compelled to bypass a key security (and, in this case, anti-forensics) feature that they'd built to protect consumers. Others believed that the company should do all it can to assist law enforcement, especially if it was to obtain evidence that could ultimately save lives.

ARRIVING AT AN INVESTIGATION

For a business, the decision to launch a digital forensics investigation is not one that is typically taken lightly. The out-of-pocket costs involved can be significant, and any investigation, even one completely outsourced, will require some input from one or more internal employees. This could be in the form of granting access to evidence, working with the investigator to understand the goal of the investigation or briefing executives on the current status of an investigation. If a company has an internal digital forensics team then the weight of cost in a decision to engage in a forensics investigation is usually less significant, but there are still other factors that may dissuade a company from going full steam ahead into one. The business benefit might not be considered worth it, or the company may already decide that they have enough evidence through other means to take action.

If a forensics investigation is instigated as part of, or following, a security incident, the investigator should be fully briefed on the nature of the incident as soon as possible. In some scenarios the investigator will have been part of the incident response team; in others, this will not be the case. Either way, the actions or inactions of the incident response team should form part of the scope of the investigation. If an incident response team was being proactive they might have preserved evidence for subsequent investigation. If not, the investigator cannot undo the actions of the incident response team, but they can account for them in their own work.

If you're primarily an incident responder, you should also be comfortable with the fundamental forensic principles in the previous section. If you can build them directly into your response playbook then you'll be setting yourself up for success down the line. Even if an incident ultimately doesn't require an investigation, it's still better to have potential evidence to discard than zero potential evidence.

INVESTIGATIVE PROCESS

The various types of digital forensics investigation were mentioned briefly a little earlier in this chapter. Criminal investigations are conducted to prove that a suspect committed a crime, either directly against a computer system or using a computer system as a means to commit another type of crime. Civil investigations are used to prove damages to a claimant (or plaintiff), and corporate investigations are used to prove that an employee violated a policy or committed an act of misconduct. The majority of forensics investigations will fall into one of these categories. Ultimately, this means that the findings of an investigation will be used to drive different outcomes. In a criminal case this could result in a custodial sentence or a monetary fine being levied against a suspect who is convicted. In a civil case, the outcome could involve a fine for the defendant. In a corporate investigation, the investigation could see someone lose their job.

A point that was also touched on earlier, but is worth reiterating because It is so important, is that we should always treat every investigation as if the outcome will need to be defended in a criminal court. This attitude must be engaged from the moment that the investigator is initially contacted to kick off the investigation.

Scoping

An important skill for any investigator, and one that must be honed to ensure that potential evidence is not lost in the earliest stages of an investigation, is scoping. When scoping an investigation the first question we're trying to answer is: 'Where could potential evidence of this crime be located?' The answer here could be as simple as on a single machine, but it's often the case that evidence can be scattered throughout many locations.

Locard's exchange principle[37] is a well-known forensic science concept which holds that a perpetrator of a crime will both bring something into a crime scene and subsequently leave with something from it. Dr Edmond Locard, a French forensic science pioneer who proposed the concept, did so with physical crimes in mind, but more often than not it also holds true in the digital realm.

The difference between physical and digital crime scenes, of course, is that a digital crime scene might be intangible to the investigator. As an example of this, consider that evidence of a digital crime conducted via the internet is spread across a massive array of disk drives physically located on the other side of the world. In such a case the investigator will be extremely unlikely to obtain access to that portion of the evidence, and instead would be better off focusing on other locations closer to home that might be more easily accessible.

This is a perfect example of why realistic scoping is important. In this case, the scope of the investigation might include log data held by a domestic ISP which, with appropriate legal backing, the ISP could be compelled to hand over. It could also include a work computer owned by the suspect's employer, which may also contain trace evidence of the crime. These two parts of the story might allow an investigator to reconstruct the entire crime without requiring the out-of-reach elements.

This brings us to some follow-up questions to be asked when scoping a digital crime scene:

- Is it safe for me to collect this evidence? Just because you can, it doesn't mean you should. Personal safety should be the first priority throughout the investigation. If evidence is stored in a location that could be dangerous if visited, then appropriate safeguards should be put in place or the location should be avoided altogether.

- Am I authorised to collect this evidence? For instance, do you have the appropriate legal authorisation, such as a search warrant, to seize the potential evidence? In a corporate investigation, is appropriate ownership of the device containing the evidence confirmed? Can you be certain that you're not attempting to seize a device that is actually owned by the suspect?

- Do I have the appropriate training and equipment to collect this evidence? There should be no shame in asking for support if you don't have all you need to collect the evidence. It is better to ask for help than run the risk of contaminating evidence by using inappropriate equipment.

---

[37] Locard, E. (1934) *Manuel de Technique Policière*. Paris: Payot.

Securing the physical scene

In the event that a digital crime features a physical scene, such as an office containing the suspect's laptop and other potential evidence sources, it is highly important that the first responder secures that scene upon arrival. Just as with a 'traditional' physical crime scene, there will always be the risk that evidence could become contaminated or damaged if the scene is not appropriately secured and controlled. We've all seen the crime scene tape used to block off streets after a crime has occurred to enable the white-suited investigators to comb the scene for vital forensic evidence. This same principle applies to computer-focused crime scenes.

Upon arrival at a location, prior to touching any equipment, the first responder should ensure that the scene is safe. This can involve confirming that the suspect, or their associates, are no longer present.

Powered-off devices

If a device is powered off then it should remain powered off. Clear photographs of any cables and connections should be taken. Depending on the requirements of the client, and the available equipment, the device may either be removed from the scene entirely or the hard drive might be imaged to forensically sterile media then and there. Personally, I've always opted to seize the entire device and perform the imaging offsite in a more controlled environment, but that isn't always an option.

Powered-on devices

In the case that a machine at a crime scene is running, the investigator should make attempts to collect any evidence that could be lost if the machine were to be powered off. This is known as **volatile evidence**. There are various tools and techniques for obtaining volatile evidence, to be discussed further in the chapters on live acquisitions and memory forensics.

In the event that an investigator has reasonable grounds to believe that a powered-on device is actively destroying data, they may decide that removing power to the device is the best course of action. In such a scenario, the investigator should record their reasons for this belief and be aware of the consequences of their actions, documenting both along the way.

Mobile devices

Essentially a tiny, powerful and well-connected personal computer, a mobile device can hold some of a person's most intimate data, and therefore can be a rich source of digital evidence. As these devices have become more complex, and more secure, the techniques and equipment needed to seize them has had to evolve just as fast as the devices. Given this, the investigator often has to relocate the device to a lab to perform forensic acquisition. The most important thing to remember is that mobile devices can be altered remotely, by way of the cellular and other wireless connectivity afforded to them. Therefore, the most important action to be taken when seizing a mobile device is eliminating the risk that these connections might be used to erase data. This is typically achieved by placing the device in an RF-shielded bag, which allows the device to remain powered on but become unreachable to the outside world.

Media

Storage devices that may contain evidence can also be found at a crime scene. Removable USB devices, CDs, DVDs and SD cards can all be imaged in a forensically sound manner, and should be included in the scope of evidence to be collected if discovered.

Sometimes, storage devices may not be present in the immediate vicinity of the primary computer. It has become more common to find network-attached storage devices or router-connected drives in homes and businesses. For this reason, the investigator should venture out to examine other locations around a crime scene, if they are authorised to do so.

Non-physical scenes

In the case that a digital crime occurs without a traditional physical scene, such as a remote attack against a web application hosted by a cloud service provider, the investigator's approach will be somewhat different. These types of investigation can require the cooperation of the cloud provider, and the investigator might need legal backing to ensure that such cooperation is forthcoming. We'll be discussing these types of investigation in depth in the chapter on cloud forensics.

Transportation

When transporting evidence from a crime scene great care should be taken to ensure its safety and security. This is an important part of maintaining the chain of custody and avoiding the worst-case scenario: evidence going missing. Having worked in corporate information security teams for a number of years, I'd need more than my 10 fingers to count the number of reports I've received of laptops being stolen from vehicles parked overnight. It is for this reason that due care and attention should be applied when transporting evidence. For instance, if you know you're going to be transporting evidence by way of an eight-hour drive, having a second person come along with you to provide cover during a bathroom or meal break would be highly recommended.

In some cases courier services may need to be used for practical reasons. When these situations arise it is the responsibility of the investigator to ensure that both the client and the courier are aware of the nature of the delivery, and that only specialised and appropriate courier services are used. You really don't want evidence items sitting idle in a warehouse under a pile of boxes because you selected the five-day super-saver shipping option! Instead, couriers that offer hand-carry services, where the package is never out of sight, or legal couriers that are trained in chain of custody procedures should be engaged.

Storage

Once our evidence is in the forensic lab, or other facility in which it will be examined, the investigator must still be careful during their interaction with it. Evidence should be stored securely, and removed from storage only during processing or analysis. Detailed logs of when the evidence was removed from storage, by whom, and for what purpose after it was transported from the scene are critical for the chain of custody.

Analysis

The bread and butter for any investigator is analysing the collected evidence and drawing conclusions based on that analysis. It shouldn't surprise you that the topic of analysis is enough to fill multiple chapters in this book. The analysis work performed by forensics examiners is, of course, typically used to help prove that a suspect committed a crime, but it also has other uses. Digital forensic work can also be used to prove or disprove an alibi in relation to another type of crime. For instance, the tracking data and call records from a mobile phone could prove that a person accused of murder was in the vicinity of the crime scene.

Forensic analysis can also be used to determine the authenticity of a file, in terms of who created it and when. Such work is particularly common in fraud examinations.

Proving that a suspect showed intent to commit a crime is another common use of forensic analysis. I'm sure we can all think back to a story involving a shooting or other type of violence where the news later reported that evidence was discovered showing that a suspect had visited a website containing related violent internet content.

The wide and varied application of digital forensics is one of the many reasons the field draws people from across the spectrum of the information technology industry and beyond.

Reporting

At the end of an investigation, an investigator will submit a report containing details of their findings to the client or other concerned parties. Accurate and detailed reporting is a key component in any investigation, and we'll look at it closely in the chapter on reporting and presenting your findings.

SUMMARY

In this chapter we've introduced some tried and true digital forensics fundamentals that all involved in an investigation, no matter their specific role, should practise with rigour. Speaking of investigative roles, we also covered the variety of functions that an individual or team of investigators can be called upon to perform. The actual role assigned to an investigator is typically dependent on the scale and complexity of an investigation.

We looked at the various factors, including cost and overall benefit to the business, that are considered when an organisation determines whether to begin an investigation. Finally we introduced the investigative process, which encompasses everything from initial scoping, through evidence collection, transportation, storage and analysis to reporting.

As we introduced the topic of digital forensics investigations we were reminded that digital forensics is a scientific process used to prove that a suspect committed a crime. Given this, digital forensics enjoys a relatively unique position as a technical topic that requires significant consideration of various legal elements. In the next chapter we'll introduce the laws applicable to the topic, and explain why investigators must also adopt a legal brain when handling and analysing evidence.

8 THE LAWS AND ETHICS OF DIGITAL FORENSICS

We always commence a digital forensics investigation with the assumption that we'll one day have to defend our work in a court of law. With that in mind, it should come as no surprise that we need to be cognisant of the laws applicable to our work as we go about the business of conducting an investigation. Information security in general has often found itself to be a field that draws interest from both technologists and legal professionals alike, but digital forensics unquestionably belongs slap bang in the middle of these two fields. Effective lawyers take the time to learn about the technical issues, and savvy technologists, including investigators, take the time to learn about the legalities.

In this chapter we'll examine various legal factors that come into play during a forensics investigation. We'll take a look at several specific pieces of legislation that may have direct or indirect impacts on an investigator as they go about their work. Finally, we'll look at the ethical standards required of an investigator.

CRIMES WITHOUT BORDERS

To throw in some additional legal complexity, digital crimes can easily bleed across international borders. Internet traffic flows don't yield to consider jurisdiction as they bounce from node to node. The need for stronger, more specific laws applicable to digital crimes is well recognised, and as a result a number of countries have taken great strides in implementing such laws. The challenge is actually enforcing them if the suspect is geographically located outside the victim's local jurisdiction. In the United States there is even some complexity within the nation's borders, as different states can have different laws. International cooperation in computer crime cases does occur, but not always. It's become almost a running joke in information security circles that many incidents and breaches are blamed on either Russian or Chinese actors by default, because cooperation with these countries on cybercrime issues is extremely limited, and there is more than a smidgen of evidence of state-sponsored online criminal activity originating from them. It is undoubtedly true that there are many attacks that originate from Russia and China; however, just seeing a Russian or Chinese IP address in a log file isn't enough to attribute an attack to one particular nation. Tools and techniques, or hacker tradecraft (to use an intelligence community term), are much better indicators to go on when looking to perform accurate attribution.

A recent example of the challenges and controversy that can be associated with the attribution of digital crimes is the 2014 Sony Pictures incident. The film studio was the target of a severely damaging attack that came to a head on the morning of Monday 24th November. That morning, several Sony Pictures employees found their workstations were completely unusable as wiper malware that had been installed previously was triggered. Data was lost, and an ominous message appeared on the screens of those devices.

The message warned Sony Pictures that a group calling themselves the Guardians of Peace were behind the attack. Initially the group demanded money and made it clear they had a significant volume of confidential Sony Pictures data, leaking some on the internet that day. Over the coming days the group continued to leak emails and unreleased films.

A few weeks after the start of the attack the narrative coming out of Sony and the FBI suggested that hackers working for the North Korean regime were suspected of being responsible for the attack in apparent retaliation for the upcoming Sony Pictures film *The Interview*. The film featured a plot in which two journalists are hired to assassinate the North Korean leader, Kim Jong-Un.

The FBI formally attributed the incident to North Korea on 17th December 2014, and based that attribution on analysis of the malware, the IP addresses used to launch the attack, and similarities of the incident with one that affected South Korean banks in 2013.

The FBI did not release detailed information about the indicators that had led them to this attribution, which led many information security professionals to question its validity. There were rumours that over 100 terabytes of data were stolen, which would have taken significant time to exfiltrate, and many questioned whether North Korea would have had the infrastructure to support this. Likewise, it is very uncommon for state-sponsored attackers to operate in such an overt fashion, such as with the ominous message on the workstations.

Given this, the industry pressed the FBI to release more details, something that hasn't happened to date. As a direct result of the attribution, US President Barack Obama issued an Executive Order applying additional financial sanctions on North Korea.

It is not just criminal law enforcement that should be aware of the challenges of reaching across borders. If you're involved in incident response or digital forensics for a company with global reach, you will likely run into challenges specific to the suspect's jurisdiction. In Europe, for instance, privacy laws are much stricter than in the United States – for example the European General Data Protection Regulation (GDPR), which levels the playing field across European Union member states and provides EU citizens with a published set of rights pertaining to their data. This can create hurdles that must be overcome during an investigation launched from the US, for example, against computers and employees residing in Europe.

I've been fortunate enough to work in both Europe and the United States, and throughout my career I've always been intrigued by the cultural differences when it comes to privacy expectations. In the United States it is not that difficult to find out where a person lives, which elections they voted in and who they live with; it's all public record. Conversely, in Europe this information is much more protected.

In one instance I recall rolling out a web content filtering system at a multinational company. The US portion of the rollout was completed with little drama, but once it was time to deploy in Europe the employees were not happy about the prospect of their website usage being monitored, and works councils became involved. In France, a works council is required for any company with 50 or more employees and it operates in a similar fashion to a trade union. This was not something I had been aware of at this point. Eventually the rollout was completed, but several changes had to be made to the deployment after works council approval.

Laws are closely intertwined with the second topic in this chapter, ethics. Tremendous trust is placed in a digital forensic investigator. In order to do the job, an investigator has to dive into a treasure trove of sensitive, compromising and deeply personal data. In order to have a long and successful digital forensics career, operating in an ethically sound matter is of the utmost importance.

LAWS APPLICABLE TO FORENSICS

There is a wide variety of crimes and situations that a digital forensics professional can become involved in investigating, and therefore a significant spread in terms of the legislation that can be applicable to their work. Given this, it would be impracticable to list every potential piece of applicable legislation in this book, but we can review some of the most common legislation that an investigator should keep in mind at all times.

United Kingdom

The UK has three legal systems that are in step with the geography of the country. English law applies to England and Wales, Scots law applies to Scotland, and Northern Ireland law applies to Northern Ireland. Plenty of legislation in the United Kingdom applies across all three legal systems; there may, however, be slight variances between them.

Computer Misuse Act 1990

The foundational legislation for all computer crime in the UK, the Computer Misuse Act applies across all three legal systems and frequently forms the basis for charging a suspect with a digital crime. Section 1 of the act deals with directly hacking into a computer. 'Unauthorised access to computer material', as it is referred to in the legislation, could also be invoked to cover obtaining access through credential theft, such as phishing. The legislation was updated in 2006 by way of the Police and Justice bill. That update increased the maximum custodial sentence for Section 1 offences from six months to two years in prison.

Section 2 of the Computer Misuse Act expands on Section 1 and covers intent to commit additional offences after obtaining unauthorised access to a machine, for example obtaining access to a server, stealing data or using that data to commit fraud. The maximum penalty for Section 2 offences is five years in prison.

In September 2016, 25-year-old Adam Penny was convicted under Section 2 of the Computer Misuse Act. He was sentenced to five years in prison after hacking into the website of a gold bullion dealer and stealing customer data. Using this customer data he was able to direct his accomplices to wait outside an address where a gold delivery was expected. The gold was intercepted, and subsequently sold on.

Penny was guilty under Section 1 for breaking into the website, and Section 2 for using that as a platform to facilitate the theft of gold.

Section 3 of the Computer Misuse Act covers 'unauthorised acts with the intent to impair operation'. At the time of writing, Section 3 was primarily concerned with the introduction of computer viruses to a system that would deliberately prevent a computer from operating properly, but in more recent times it has also been referenced in cases involving those suspected of launching denial of service attacks. Of course, you don't need access to a machine to perform those, hence the difference between Section 2 and Section 3 offences. Section 3 offences are punishable by a maximum 10-year jail sentence.

Section 3A of the Computer Misuse Act was introduced in 2006 and created a new offence targeting those who supply, offer to supply or obtain hacking tools and resources that could be used to commit Section 1 or Section 3 offences. These offences are punishable by way of a maximum two-year jail sentence. An example of a Section 3A offence would be operating a DDoS-for-hire service.

Police and Criminal Evidence Act 1984

Known as PACE, this act is a wide-ranging piece of legislation that provides the legislative framework for the police in England and Wales to combat crime. An equivalent act exists in Northern Ireland: the Police and Criminal Evidence (Northern Ireland) Order 1989. In Scotland, the majority of the PACE provisions are included in the Criminal Procedure (Scotland) Act 1995.

The Act is not computer specific, but it does cover the codes of practice to be followed by police officers during search and seizure activities. It also includes evidence collection and handling procedures, and rules for interviewing suspects – all topics that may very well form part of an investigation concerning a digital crime. If an officer fails to conform to the codes of practice contained within PACE during an investigation then evidence could be rendered inadmissible.

As digital forensic investigators our mostly likely exposure to PACE would be if we were working directly for, or as a contractor for, a police force during a criminal investigation where a digital forensics acquisition is required. Section 8 of PACE covers search warrants, a type of court order issued by a judge that gives a police officer the power to enter premises to search for evidence that a criminal act has occurred. Such a warrant can also include a provision allowing the officer to bring along a specifically authorised person, such as a civilian digital forensics expert, to assist in the search and seizure.

Regulation of Investigatory Powers Act 2000

Known as RIPA, the Regulation of Investigatory Powers Act was created in response to the challenges involved with performing surveillance and investigation in the internet era. The Act regulates the manner in which certain public entities, which can include intelligence and security services, as well as police forces, can perform certain surveillance functions, and from what level such functions need to be authorised.

As an example, RIPA enables intelligence services to demand that an internet service provider provide access to certain communications in secret for the purposes of detecting serious crime or protecting the economic well-being of the United Kingdom.

In the world of digital forensics, we may be exposed to RIPA if working for an organisation that is subject to an order issued by a public body under the provisions of RIPA, or if working for a public body that is able to issue such an order. For instance, if working in national security as a forensic investigator, a function may be to uncover evidence of a particular crime from some captured internet traffic.

Protection of Children Act 1978 and Sexual Offences Act 2003

The proliferation of sexual crimes, particularly those targeting children via the internet, is well documented. Child-pornography-related cases are unfortunately a relatively common type of case that digital forensic investigators may find themselves working on. In the United Kingdom, the Protection of Children Act 1978 covers the creation, possession and distribution of indecent images of children. A 1994 amendment to the act, by way of the Criminal Justice and Public Order Act, specifically called out images created by, or altered with, computers. The Act was again amended in 2003 through the Sexual Offences Act, which introduced more specific terminology and created a number of new types of offence. Importantly, the Sexual Offences Act altered the original 1978 definition of a child, from 'a person under the age of 16' to 'a person under the age of 18'. This legislation is of particular importance to investigators, as it compels us, or anyone else who becomes aware of a crime against a child, to report it to the police promptly.

Good Practice Guide for Digital Evidence

Though not a law, the UK Association of Chief Police Officers (ACPO) has published a document entitled *Good Practice Guide for Digital Evidence*, the latest version of which should always be close by for anyone working in the field.[38] The document is designed for law enforcement professionals who may be exposed to digital evidence during the course of their work, and contains the recommended practices to be followed at all times from both technological and legal perspectives. The *Good Practice Guide* is built around four key principles of digital evidence.

---

[38] Williams, J. (2012) *Good Practice Guide for Digital Evidence*. Association of Chief Police Officers. Available from http://library. college.police.uk/docs/acpo/digital-evidence-2012.pdf [30 April 2018].

- 'Principle 1: No action taken by law enforcement agencies, persons employed within those agencies or their agents should change data which may subsequently be relied upon in court.'

- 'Principle 2: In circumstances where a person finds it necessary to access original data, that person must be competent to do so and be able to give evidence to explain the relevance and implications of their actions.'

- 'Principle 3: An audit trail or other record of all processes applied to digital evidence should be created and preserved. An independent third party should be able to examine those processes and achieve the same result.'

- 'Principle 4: The person in charge of the investigation has overall responsibility for ensuring that the law and these principles are adhered to.'

These four general principles provide a solid foundation on which to conduct a digital forensics investigation.

United States

In the United States, laws concerning digital crimes exist at both the state and federal levels. The principal agency involved in investigating larger-scale computer crimes is the United States Secret Service, which is a federal law enforcement agency, and hence many of the higher-profile prosecutions are based on federal law.

Computer Fraud and Abuse Act

Enacted by the United States Congress in 1986, the Computer Fraud and Abuse Act (CFAA) was designed to address the gap between existing wire and mail fraud laws and the growing prevalence of computer crime. Although some laws specific to computer crime had been introduced two years prior through the Comprehensive Crime Control Act of 1984, the United States Congress and Senate continued to discuss the laws throughout 1985, before enacting the initial version of the CFAA in 1986. Since then, the CFAA has been amended multiple times.

A quirk of the law is that, technically speaking, the only computers covered by it are so-called 'protected computers'. Computers in this category are defined as being:

- 'Exclusively for the use of a financial institution or the United States Government, or any other computer, when the conduct constituting the offence affects the computer's use by or for the financial institution or the Government.'

- 'Used in or affecting interstate or foreign commerce or communication, including a computer located outside of the United States that is used in a manner that affects interstate or foreign commerce or communication of the United States.'[39]

---

[39] US House of Representatives (2017) *[USC07] 18 USC 1030: Fraud and related activity in connection with computers.* Office of the Law Revision Counsel. Available from http://uscode.house.gov/view.xhtml?req=granuleid:USC-prelim-title18-section1030&num=0&edition=prelim [20 April 2018].

This definition was introduced to quell federalism concerns (concerns that the federal government would infringe upon the rights of the individual states), by suggesting that only computers involved in interstate communications would be covered by the Act. However, in practice, any computer connected to the internet is likely to be communicating over state lines, given the geographical diversity of services on the internet, and as a result nearly all such computers and devices are covered by the CFAA.

The CFAA is similar to the Computer Misuse Act in the United Kingdom, in that it is used as the basis for prosecuting most computer crimes. The terminology used in the CFAA to describe what would be considered hacking is 'access without authorisation, or exceeding authorised access'. The CFAA contains penalties ranging between one and ten years depending on the nature of the crime. For second convictions under the CFAA, the length of a prison stay can range from 10 to 20 years.

Specific offences covered by the CFAA include:

- Obtaining national security information.
- Accessing a computer and obtaining information without authorisation, or in excess of authorisation.
- Trespassing in a Government computer.
- Accessing a computer to defraud and obtain value.
- Intentionally damaging by knowing transmission (of malicious code, or a given command etc.).
- Recklessly damaging by intentional access.
- Negligently causing damage and loss by intentional access.
- Trafficking in passwords.
- Extortion involving computers.

In addition to the custodial sentences afforded by the CFAA, it also contains provisions for victims of crime to bring civil cases in pursuit of financial compensation.

Electronic Communications Privacy Act (EPCA)

The ECPA is an important law as it is used to ensure protections are afforded to digital transmissions between computers. Title 1 of the law was an update to the Federal Wiretap Act of 1968, which is why ECPA is sometimes still referred to as the Wiretap Act. The 1968 law was of course designed primarily with telephone calls in mind, rather than internet traffic. The updated Wiretap Act prohibits interception, or attempted interception, of any wire, oral or electronic communication. As an example, a man-in-the-middle attack between two hosts on a network would be considered a violation of the ECPA.

As with any law, there are exceptions, and one that we've already touched on in this chapter is the use of technologies such as SSL proxies to monitor and filter web traffic for safety and security purposes. The Wiretap Act provides an exception which states that an employee of operators (of networks) and service providers can intercept communications 'in the normal course of his employment while engaged in any activity which is a necessary incident to the rendition of his service'. This can be used as a basis for the argument that corporate IT teams have every right to perform SSL decryption, and is usually supplemented with employees accepting that their transmissions may be monitored at work, through the signing of an acceptable use policy (AUP).

There are also exceptions for law enforcement officers to perform interceptions for the purpose of surveillance and investigation, but they are subject to a series of procedures, including obtaining a warrant to perform the interception. A judge can issue a warrant allowing a law enforcement officer to intercept communications for up to 30 days in exchange for evidence showing probable cause that an individual is planning or has already committed a crime.

Stored Communications Act

Title 2 of the ECPA is known as the Stored Communications Act (SCA) and provides protections for electronic transmissions that have reached their final destinations and therefore are no longer in transit. This covers items like emails stored on computers. The SCA protections are far less stringent than those in the ECPA for data in transit. One example of this lack of protection is the so-called 180-day rule. This rule states that data stored for more than 180 days is to be considered abandoned, and as a result requires less judicial review for a law enforcement officer to obtain it. Privacy advocates are critical of this rule because in 1986, when it was written, email services were very different from how they are today. In the mid-1980s emails were stored temporarily on servers before being transferred to a client computer. Today, with free services such as Outlook.com and Gmail, people often do not delete any emails, and they reside on the provider's server for years. Under the SCA, law enforcement can use the 180-day rule to obtain these messages.

To update this somewhat outdated aspect of the SCA, the Email Privacy Act has been proposed to afford additional protections to stored email messages. However, since it was first proposed in 2015, the bill has not yet made it into law.

Identity Theft Penalty Enhancement Act

A growing criminal activity around the world is identity theft, which involves illegally using the identity of another person to open lines of credit, make purchases and commit other types of fraud. Introduced in 2004, the Identity Theft Penalty Enhancement Act makes provisions for courts to deal with this relatively new crime. Custodial sentences of two years in prison are prescribed by the Act. There are also rules to prohibit a court from placing a person convicted of identity theft on probation.

Patriot Act

The Uniting and Strengthening America by Providing Appropriate Tools Required to Intercept and Obstruct Terrorism Act of 2001, to use its unabbreviated title, the Patriot Act was a law enacted a little after a month following the 11 September terrorist attacks against the United States.

The law is fairly wide-ranging, and provides a variety of provisions to reduce legal barriers for law enforcement and intelligence services to disrupt terrorist plots. In the immediate aftermath of the 11 September attacks there was widespread fear and concern that the intelligence services of the United States hadn't been able to detect and prevent the events that killed 2,977 innocent people. Of particular interest to us in the digital forensics field is Title 2, which is named 'Enhanced Surveillance Procedures'. This title updated sections of the ECPA, and effectively reduced the barriers for law enforcement professionals to obtain wiretap warrants for the purposes of performing surveillance on both US and non-US citizens. The law has caused some alarm among privacy advocates.

In 2015, the law was extended following the passage of the USA Freedom Act. However, as a result of the mass surveillance revelations made by leaker Edward Snowden, certain parts of the Patriot Act were eliminated, placing more restrictions on the National Security Agency's surveillance programmes.

CAN-SPAM

Everyone has received at least one spam email by now, and we all know how annoying they can be. The CAN-SPAM Act was signed into law in 2003 to address the increasing frustration and damage caused by unsolicited spam email. The law applies to all marketing email sent to US citizens and has several provisions for protecting recipients. Notably, there is a requirement that all marketing emails come with a visible and functional unsubscribe function.

There are also requirements applicable to the content of an email; for instance, the from and subject lines must be relevant, and the physical address of the sender must be included.

Finally, the Act placed technical restrictions on the sending of a message, laying out a number of rules, including the prohibition of open relays (servers that permit the sending of mail from any source), banning empty messages and false email headers.

Child pornography laws

In the United States, suspects in child pornography cases can be tried under both federal and state laws. At the federal level, the principal law concerning child pornography is known as the Child Protection and Obscenity Enforcement Act of 1988. The law lays out record-keeping requirements for producers of pornographic materials, under which they must keep track of the ages of models filmed during pornographic shoots.

There are also laws in the United States criminal code that explicitly prohibit the creation and handling of pornographic images of children, and additional laws specific to parents or guardians of minors (under the age of 18) who fail to protect them from becoming involved in the production of child pornography.

Best practices for seizing electronic evidence

Similar to the ACPO guidelines in the United Kingdom, the Secret Service in the United States provides guidance on best practices for seizing electronic evidence.[40] If you recall,

---

[40] US Department of Homeland Security (2017) *NCJRS Abstract – Best Practices for Seizing Electronic Evidence*. National Criminal Justice Reference Service. Available from https://www.ncjrs.gov/app/publications/abstract.aspx?id=239359 [30 April 2018].

the ACPO guidelines centre around four key principles. The US Secret Service guidelines feature eight golden rules:

- 'Officer safety – secure the scene and make it safe.'

- 'If you reasonably believe that the computer is involved in the crime you are investigating, take immediate steps to preserve the evidence.'

- 'Do you have a legal basis to seize the computer?'

- 'Do not access any computer files. If the computer is off, leave it off. If it is on, do not start searching through the computer.'

- 'If the computer is on, go to the appropriate sections in this guide on how to properly shut down the computer and prepare it for transportation as evidence.'

- 'If you reasonably believe that the computer is destroying evidence, immediately shut down the computer by pulling the power cord from the back of the computer.'

- 'If a camera is available, and the computer is on, take pictures of the computer screen. If the computer is off, take pictures of the computer, the location of the computer and any electronic media attached.'

- 'Do special legal considerations apply (doctor, attorney, clergy, psychiatrist, newspapers, publishers, etc.)?'

Europe

Within the European Union, a 2013 directive on cybercrime required member states to tackle larger-scale digital crimes through the use of specific laws and tough penalties. For the first time, the use of botnets in digital crimes was specifically called out in the directive.

GDPR

The General Data Protection Regulation took effect across Europe on 25 May 2018. As previously discussed during the incident response portion of the book, there are various articles in this legislation that apply directly to incident response, particularly around breach notification. From a digital forensics investigation perspective, there are elements of GDPR that apply not only directly to the case itself but also to the activities performed by the investigator.

The core of GDPR is about protecting the rights of individuals regarding how personal data about them is processed. Processing includes data collection, storage, transmission and disclosure. There are articles that describe the need for consent from an individual to process their personal data, and articles that frame the conditions under which a 'processor', such as a business, can keep personal data.

Article 25 of the legislation is entitled 'Data protection by design and by default', and describes how processors must demonstrably apply the most stringent privacy controls possible to end users of their products and services. Importantly, GDPR describes how the processor must continually show compliance with the legislation.

A frequent topic of conversation around GDPR is the severity of the sanctions that can be imposed for non-compliance. Fines can be imposed to the tune of 20 million euros or four per cent of an organisation's annual worldwide turnover, whichever is greater. That isn't a small amount of money. As an investigator working in Europe, cases that involve proving a client was compliant with GDPR at the time of an incident are likely to become more commonplace.

Investigators themselves should be aware of how GDPR applies to the work they are doing. If you're working on data collected by a processor as part of a case, which is highly likely, the investigator is also considered a processor. Just as we in the information security field preach good security practices, GDPR requires us to take a hard look at our own processes and procedures, to make sure they're up to scratch.

ETHICAL CONSIDERATIONS

Given the content and context of some of the laws just reviewed, you should have a very clear understanding of the sensitivity of the situations in which digital forensic investigators can find themselves. It is for this reason that we must act with integrity and in an ethical manner at all times.

Being an ethical professional

Ethics in this profession covers a large range of topics, from reasonably believing that you're competent to perform the given investigation, to acting within the confines of the law. Clearly, it is not a good situation to be using your technical skills for good by day, and then committing crimes with those same skills at night. Such activity could lead to serious questioning of your integrity as a person, and therefore call into question all of your previous work.

Various professional bodies that cover forensic science, computer security and everything in between have enacted various ethical standards to which members must subscribe. Examples of such organisations include the International Association of Computer Investigative Specialists (IACIS)[41] and the American Academy of Forensic Sciences.[42] Typically, such standards include provisions for ensuring that laws are followed, conflicts of interest are avoided and opinions are given without prejudice.

Sometimes it can be plainly obvious that a suspect is a bad person doing a bad thing, but without sufficient evidence to prove it we may find ourselves frustrated. It is in this scenario that our ethics might be tested. We must at all times show no bias and give opinions that are based solely on the evidence we have in front of us. Having worked with a number of law enforcement professionals, who frequently find themselves in similar ethical dilemmas, the most frequent advice I've received is to trust the process. If someone is guilty, but we can't prove it in this case, then we will be able to in the next case. It's not worth putting your professional integrity on the line to attempt to expedite the inevitable.

---

[41] https://www.iacis.com/
[42] https://www.aafs.org/

We're privileged to work in this field, we can help people, but only if we help ourselves first. Always, always act with integrity and morality and be ethical during any digital forensics investigation.

SUMMARY

In this chapter, we emphasised the importance of treating every investigation as if the actions taken during the investigation will need to be defended against scrutiny of the highest order in a criminal court. We discussed legal challenges unique to digital forensics investigations, including cases that span multiple jurisdictions.

We introduced a number of relevant pieces of legislation from the United Kingdom, United States and Europe that pertain to digital crimes and investigations. Finally, we talked about published frameworks for handling digital evidence, such as the ACPO *Good Practice Guide* and *Best Practices for Seizing Electronic Evidence*, as published by the United States Secret Service.

With this important context, in the next chapter we'll introduce the tools and techniques used to make sure that evidence is collected in accordance with the rules and regulations we've just discussed.

9 DIGITAL FORENSICS TOOLS

There are a variety of hardware and software products on the market, built specifically for digital forensic investigators, to aid in the investigative process. There are also a large number of open-source tools, freely available to download, and of course open for contribution. Depending on your situation, you might be able to obtain the most expensive tools, or you might not. Regardless of the tools in your arsenal, one thing is for sure: you have to know what they can and cannot do in a given forensics scenario. You also have to become intimately familiar with how the tools function, and what is occurring behind the scenes when a forensic tool processes evidence on your behalf. In explaining why this is important, I like to use the airline pilot analogy. An airline pilot flying a commercial jet uses a variety of different systems – hydraulic, electrical and navigational, to name but a few. The majority of the time those systems function without a problem, and in many cases they are autonomously managed by computer. However, in the event that a system on a plane has an issue, the pilot is required to know how the system functions so he or she can fix it, or work around the problem manually. The same is true of digital forensic investigators and their tools. The majority of the time they work well, but sometimes they might suffer from errors, or the investigator might be called upon to explain the process used by a given tool in detail. Digital forensics tools aid the investigator, and they are highly important, but they do not form opinions or testify in court. Those tasks still fall squarely on our plate. The relationship with your tools should be 'trust, but verify'. This is an important reminder, and something to always bear in mind when working with a forensics tool in an investigation, especially if that tool is new to you, or new on the market. Tools will either live permanently in our digital forensics lab or make the trip to a crime scene with us.

In this chapter we'll study a variety of hardware and software tools, specialised and non-specialised, that can be used during an investigation.

GRAB BAG

Information security incidents do not always occur during business hours, and digital forensics investigations do not always start at nine in the morning. Many who work in this field spend time on call, and can be dispatched to a crime scene at a moment's notice. This can come in the form of a telephone call that wakes you or pulls you away from a family gathering. Whatever the circumstances, when the call comes in you'll want to be ready to go, and that means having your first response tools in one easy-to-grab bag. During a first response our objectives are securing a scene and collecting evidence for later processing in the lab. Therefore, the grab bag typically contains tools that facilitate these objectives. Some of the tools are specialised in nature, others you can find at any DIY store.

The bag itself

It might seem a little self-explanatory, but still an important point to make, that the grab bag itself serves two purposes. One: to provide a single location for all your gear; two: to keep all that equipment safe and well organised. Personal preference or the preference of your employer will usually determine what type of bag is used. My personal preference is a hard-shell case with custom foam cut-outs for the equipment inside. This protects the equipment, with the added benefits of keeping things laid out neatly inside and looking really cool.

Screwdrivers

These are the universal keys to the innards of laptops, desktops, servers, portable hard disks, network attached storage devices and much more. You can never have too many screwdrivers to hand. Also, importantly, they should be stored with some order, so you can quickly find the right size. Finally, magnetically tipped screwdrivers are useful for clinging onto little computer screws, but remember that you will be working in the proximity of magnetic storage devices, so if you use them be extremely careful.

Pens and paper

We document everything, we sketch the layouts of crime scenes, and we might use a tablet or other device to do so. However, electronic devices always introduce the risk of unexpected issues. Pens and paper never run out of battery, never have software problems and are very important residents of your grab bag.

Chain of custody forms

That most important forensics principle, the chain of custody, starts from the first response. The process requires that chain of custody forms be filled in to track the evidence item, and who is in possession of it at all times. Have them ready to roll, so you're not scrambling to find a printer at a client site or, worse, a crime scene.

Write blockers

The mainstay of any forensic investigator's toolkit, the write blocker allows us to collect data from a suspect's hard disk drive while preventing anything from being written back to that drive. This is, of course, a key requirement in ensuring that we do not alter the content of our original evidence. Write blockers will be discussed in the level of detail they deserve in the forensic hardware section of this chapter.

Disk duplication equipment and sterile media

While write blockers are essential for any investigator, there will be differences in the disk duplication setups used by forensic investigators in the field. Budgets and types of investigation play a role in determining what equipment is available. Generally speaking, all investigators will carry some form of sterile media to store forensically acquired disk images. Sterile media refers to storage media that has been tested to ensure it is either completely empty of data, in the case of new drives, or has been overwritten to an approved standard, if dealing with drives that have been previously used. Sterile media usage is something of a holdover from the early days of digital forensics, when disks were imaged directly to other disks, rather than to a forensically sound disk image format on another disk. Nowadays, cryptographic hashes are used to determine the validity of a forensic disk image and disprove any claims of evidence spoliation. That said, it is still considered best practice to use sterile media, at the very least for the purposes of safeguarding the content of previously captured data, which may include sensitive material.

Forensic disk duplication devices come in many shapes and sizes and facilitate the most expeditious cloning of a hard disk, while preventing data from being written back to the source drive.

Digital camera

Photographing a crime scene should be standard practice; it is especially important in situations where computers at the scene are powered on, since we want to capture the state of the computer screen. Using a dedicated digital camera rather than the camera built into your mobile phone is strongly recommended. Why? There are a couple of reasons. The first is that not all crime scenes will be in locations where mobile phones are permitted – think of highly secured environments within aerospace companies, or government departments. Secondly, your phone goes with you everywhere. Your kids can get into them. Depending on the nature of the scene, you might not want anyone at home to see the photographs. If you arrive at a scene to find a pornographic image of a child on a suspect's screen then you'll need to take a picture for evidence, but it really has no business being on your phone.

Torch

Some scenes are poorly illuminated, and some jobs require a little extra light to be able to see properly to perform the task at hand. For most of us the torch we use most often is located on the back of our mobile phones, but for similar reasons to those made in regard to digital cameras, a standalone torch light is recommended.

Forensics laptop

A laptop to run software-based imaging, or even begin in-field triage, is a highly recommended addition to your grab bag. This shouldn't be the same laptop you use to buy groceries or check email. Having a clean laptop with a small set of special-ised tools, which can be reimaged prior to each use, is optimal. This reduces the risk of cross contamination between scenes, and will significantly reduce the likelihood of unexpected downtime of the machine due to performance-sucking productivity apps, or even malware introduced during the course of internet browsing.

Treating the laptop as a specialised tool rather than your day-to-day laptop will also mean that you can deploy it into a network at a crime scene to perform network-based forensics without putting your own data at risk.

Live CD/USB

A live CD or USB is a removable disk with an operating system image that can be booted on top of a computer's primary operating system for the purposes of performing an acquisition or otherwise reviewing the contents of a suspect machine. Live CDs can come in particularly useful in situations where devices cannot be removed from the scene, but may have specific hardware configurations that are important to preserve to expedite the processing of evidence. An example of this would be a server with Redundant Array of Inexpensive Disks (RAID) storage.

Live CDs can also contain 'known good' copies of common operating system utilities and binaries. When investigating a powered-on machine suspected of being infected with malware we cannot trust any self-reported information, such as the state of any active network connections. The malware might have modified the binaries used to report that information, to hide its presence.

Commonly used forensic live CD distributions include the e-fense Live Response[43] USB drive and DEFT,[44] a Linux distribution suitable for installation on a USB drive.

Cables

Network cables, USB cables, hard disk cables, mobile device cables and any other kind of cable you can think of a use for should be present in the forensic investigator's grab bag. I think it's fair to say that you can never have too many types of cable to hand.

Faraday bags

Also known as RF-shielded bags, these little pouches are used to block wireless signals and therefore remove a vector which could allow a suspect to remotely wipe a mobile device. With the increase in the number of cases focused on mobile devices, Faraday bags should maintain a steady presence in the grab bag.

FORENSIC HARDWARE

While we must maintain a balance between functionality and portability when selecting tools for our grab bags, we have much more freedom when selecting hardware to aid our investigations back at the digital forensics laboratory. Generally speaking, unless you're in a position where you act solely as a first responder you will be spending most of your time in front of your principal forensics machine back at the lab processing and analysing evidence.

---

[43] E-fense (2014) *e-fense: Cyber Security & Computer Forensics Software*. e-fense. Available from www.e-fense.com/live-response.php [30 April 2018].
[44] Deft (2017) *DEFT Linux – Computer Forensics live CD*. DEFT Association. Available from www.deftlinux.net [30 April 2018].

Forensic workstations

The purpose of a forensics workstation is to process evidence that has previously been collected at a crime scene. Processing, in this context, can be summarised as taking a forensically sound disk image and indexing the contents of that image for rapid searching and analysis by the investigator. It is not that uncommon these days for consumer PCs to feature hard disks with capacities measured in terabytes. That's a lot of data to process, and therefore forensic workstations tend to go big on memory, disk and CPU to handle it all. A typical configuration for a forensics workstation at the time of writing is as follows:

- Dual 12-core CPUs, each running at 2.2 GHz with a 30 MB cache
- 128 GB RAM
- 4 GB GPU
- Storage in the following layout:
  - 20 TB of magnetic storage, in a RAID 5 array (6 × 4 TB drives), for storage of forensically sound disk images.
  - Two 512 GB solid-state drives in a RAID 0 array for the case database.
  - One 512 GB solid-state drive for temporary storage.
  - One 512 GB solid-state drive for the case file.
  - One 512 GB solid-state drive for the machine's operating system.
- Write blockers and hot swappable disk bays built into the main tower of the PC.

As you can tell, that's a pretty serious configuration, but such a workstation will allow an investigator to work through the evidence as quickly as possible; in some cases, such as when dealing with terrorism or missing persons investigations, speed is highly important.

Digital forensics workstations can be purchased through suppliers who specialise in building the machines to a given specification, or can be built in-house by the lab. Given the power supply, disk and write blocker requirements, the majority of forensic workstations are usually built in the full-size tower form factor.

Another important consideration when building a forensic workstation is the type of monitors to be used. It is well known that most folks who work in information technology spend their entire careers determined to acquire as much screen real estate as possible (I used to work with one systems administrator who had six 22-inch monitors attached to his machine). Forensic investigators are no exception, and they actually have very good reason to obtain multiple high-quality computer monitors. Hours are spent in front of them, carefully going through each indexed element to flag potential evidence. Eyes get tired. There are often multiple windows within forensics investigation software that need to be placed side by side to get a full understanding of an evidence item, something that can only be achieved with multiple monitors. For these reasons, I'd consider two high-resolution, 27-inch monitors to be the bare minimum for a forensics workstation.

Write blockers

Earlier, the importance of write blockers was mentioned, and how these tools accompany the investigator into the field. Write blockers are typically portable, around the size of a mobile phone, for this reason. A write blocker usually supports one or more disk interface types, for example USB, SAS, IDE or SATA. The target disk is connected to the write blocker for acquisition using the appropriate interface and, in the case of most portable write blockers, by USB to the investigator's laptop. The write blocker allows read commands from the forensic laptop through to the target disk but blocks any write commands, preventing the investigator's laptop from modifying any of the data residing on the target disk. This is fundamentally important, of course, as it supports the fundamental digital forensics need of not altering the original evidence.

I was working in a remote office handling an incident that was slowly morphing into a forensics investigation, and required a write blocker to capture some evidence. Unfortunately, I didn't have one to hand, but I did have a contact in the area at a third-party forensics service whom I was able to reach. I asked to borrow a write blocker for a couple of hours, and my contact happily obliged. Arrangements were made for a junior investigator to drop the write blocker off at my location.

A couple of hours later I got a call that I had a package in the lobby, and ran down to collect it. It was the write blocker, or at least, it was supposed to be. The first thing that caught my eye was the fact this equipment had a bright yellow plastic shell. This was equipment manufactured by Tableau, and having worked with Tableau forensic equipment extensively in the past, I knew right away that there was something I needed to check. In the world of Tableau products, the yellow shell is used to indicate that the device is shipped in read–write bridge mode rather than the standard write-blocking mode. Tiny dip switches inside the device can be manipulated to change the mode, but in order to access those switches you need to open the plastic casing. I opened the casing and discovered that the device was still in the read–write mode. I made the change to write-blocking mode and went about my business.

When the time came to return the equipment I mentioned to the junior investigator that the device had been provided in read–write mode but was now in write-blocking mode. He turned increasingly pale, and left quickly. Needless to say, I think that device had been used previously under the assumption that it was configured as a write blocker. Knowing your equipment is incredibly important, and will help you avoid getting caught out by little pitfalls like this.

Write blockers also exist in non-portable forms, such as a 5.25-inch drive bay (the same size as a standard CD/DVD drive) found in a tower PC. In such a configuration, the write blocker will usually include more interface types in the single unit and be installed in a lab-based forensic workstation.

Disk duplicators

Like an extended version of a write blocker, a forensic disk duplicator allows the investigator to connect both source and destination drives to a single device. From that device, the entire disk acquisition process can be managed using the device's on-board firmware, usually by way of a built-in LCD screen. This can serve as an alternative to carrying a forensic laptop to perform acquisitions in the field. Disk duplicators typically feature the ability to clone a target disk to multiple destinations simultaneously; this can be useful if multiple investigators will be working on the case and each needs their own copy of the evidence, or simply to have a backup copy of a disk image (never a bad idea).

Given that disk duplicators have both read-only and read–write disk interfaces, the investigator must pay close attention to which interfaces they're using in connecting the source and destination disks. The nightmare scenario would be a mix-up between the sterile destination disk and the evidence on the suspect, or source, disk. Fortunately, most of these devices make it extremely clear which interfaces are which; however, double and triple checking is highly encouraged.

Like write blockers, there are both portable and non-portable forensic disk duplicators. The non-portable variety tend to look more like a traditional tower PC, and typically can write to multiple destination disks at once.

Media sterilisers

Using sterile media in the field was mentioned earlier. Essentially, this means ensuring that the destination disks we bring to use as targets for acquired forensic data have been certified as being devoid of any data that may previously have been on the disk. There are various software and hardware products that can handle this task. Before we discuss those products, there are a couple of important things to remember.

First, if using a brand-new disk, we of course do not expect data to be on the drive. In some cases a hard disk manufacturer may install small applications on the drive prior to shipping, usually if the disk is designed to be used as an external USB drive. We can validate the state of a new disk by connecting it to a write blocker and using a hex editor (a tool that will be discussed in the forensic software section of this chapter) to view its raw contents. Empty, brand-new disks will be full of zeros.

In the case of a previously used disk the hex editor will tell a different story. Instead of the zeros, we'll see all kinds of characters, representing the data currently stored on the drive. If that data represents a file system or disk image from a previously acquired target drive, then we'll be able to see the contents of those files. This brings us nicely to our second point.

These days, media sterilisation is considered more of a best practice than a hard requirement, but a best practice you really should be following. In the majority of cases, forensic examiners image to a file format known as an EnCase evidence file, or '.E01 file' (after its file extension). This file format is compressible without losing forensic integrity (lossless compression), meaning that we could take an image of a 60 GB disk and reduce it in size by a third. Cryptographic hashes are then used to compare the content of the disk with the content of the evidence file and validate that they are exactly the same. This is how we can prove the forensic integrity of the disk image.

When tools to image to the EnCase evidence file format were not available, forensic investigators would perform direct, disk-to-disk imaging. This used to be much more common than it is today. In such cases it was important to use sterile media to avoid the risk of being accused of having old data from a previous case cross-contaminating the evidence in the current case. Using a media sterilization technique on a disk prior to reusing it is a great way to avoid such a charge.

There are many media sterilization techniques, the most famous of which is probably the DoD 5220-22.M standard; this performs three passes over the disk, overwriting the old data in the following pattern:

- Writing a zero, and validating it.
- Writing a one, and validating it.
- Writing a random character, and validating it.

At the end of the process, the media can be considered sterile.

Sterilisation is for disks that will be reused. For disks that will not be reused, physical destruction is the best course of action.

Mobile device forensics

Specialised hardware kits for mobile device forensics are available. These kits usually come with a variety of cables and RF-shielded bags to facilitate data collection from different types of mobile device. This includes traditional mobile devices as well as Android and Apple iOS-based smartphones.

FORENSIC SOFTWARE

The majority of the 'magic' that occurs during a digital forensics investigation can be attributed to the various software tools that the investigator has at their disposal. I use the term 'magic' because, to many people outside the field, the fact that these tools can recover data thought to be long since deleted, and the level of detail that can be established regarding the usage of a device, is nothing short of magical. Modern-day forensic tools have been developed in response to the increasing complexity and prevalence of digital crimes, and can assist us greatly during an investigation by automating common tasks and drawing our attention to individual items extracted from raw data.

Investigative software suites

A digital forensic investigator will typically do most of their work in an investigative software suite. These tools are designed to handle the entire investigative process, from evidence acquisition to processing, analysis and finally reporting and presentation. There are two such suites available commercially that dominate the market and are sometimes referred to as 'the big two': AccessData's Forensic Toolkit (FTK) and Guidance Software's EnCase. These are both in regular use worldwide, in both the public and private sectors.

Most investigators will form a preference for one suite over another, but given that these tools are in direct competition with one another there is significant overlap in the features of both.

Collection

Through the use of lightweight imaging agents, both FTK and EnCase support the generation of forensically sound disk and memory images in a variety of different formats, including the de facto standard: EnCase evidence file format.

Processing

Both suites support the processing and parsing of collected disk images, or even of directly connected disks. During the processing phase the tools will perform tasks such as file carving, analysis of slack space, identification of encrypted files, and indexing and categorisation of the discovered files. Forensic processing is computing resource intensive, hence why the forensic workstation specification we looked at earlier was so powerful. The big two forensic software suites also support distributed processing across a cluster of servers, which is important for large investigations.

Decryption

With file- and disk-level encryption being used with increasing regularity to protect the confidentiality of data, forensic software suites have developed features to give investigators an edge. Both FTK and EnCase support various techniques for breaking common encryption schemes, including password word-list generation tools.

Analysis

Some of the most useful functionality of an investigative software suite is found in the user interface. These tools do a great job of presenting findings in a way that is extremely helpful for an investigator. Creation of thumbnails of images, sorting the results of keyword searches, and building graphical timelines of activity are just a few such features.

Reporting

Both FTK and EnCase support inline adding of evidence items to a forensic report directly from the investigative interfaces of the products. This reduces the time required to produce a report. Personally speaking, I don't think I've ever met a forensic investigator who wishes they could spend more time writing reports. Most of us enjoy spending time working on the case, so any feature that can help us out in this regard is most welcome!

There are, of course, challengers to the big two, other developers who are building creative products that provide more choice to the digital forensic investigator when selecting an investigative software suite. By all means, these should be reviewed when determining which suite to purchase, but in all cases, whichever tool is chosen should come with training to allow the investigator the opportunity to develop an understanding of the features of the product and how they fit into the investigative process.

eDiscovery suites

An abbreviation of 'electronic discovery', eDiscovery refers to any process used to electronically locate and store data that will be subsequently used in a legal case. eDiscovery software suites, such as AccessData's AD eDiscovery[45] and the Veritas eDiscovery Platform,[46] exist to support this on one machine or across multiple machines connected to a network. In a corporate environment, where a company may be required to provide copies of documents and other material based on selected keywords, such a suite is typically more accurate in obtaining more information than simply relying on employees to provide such data.

Cloud storage providers may also build eDiscovery tools directly into their product offerings.

Mobile device forensics

Just as with specialised hardware for mobile devices, there are specialised software suites for analysing the content extracted from those devices. Tools such as AccessData's Mobile Phone Examiner+[47] and Paraben's E3: DS[48] exist that can process traditional mobile phones and their proprietary data storage formats, along with Android and iOS. Such tools can discover call histories, text messages, stored photographs and other data that may contain extremely important evidence.

Hex editor

Being able to view and understand the fundamental binary data that forms a file is an important skill for a digital forensic investigator. A suspect may attempt to cover up their activity by changing a file extension, and hence the way the computer presents that file. Changing a file extension does not alter the content, however, and a hex editor can be used to review that content. Hex editors such as WinHex by X-Ways[49] or HxD[50] present the binary data in hexadecimal format, hence the name.

Hex editors are frequently used to look at a file's signature. File signatures are typically the first two to four bytes of a file, the value of which can be used to truly identify the type of a given file. For instance, the hexadecimal file signature of an executable is '4D 5A'.

Live CD distributions

Given that many computers these days don't even have optical disk drives, I should explain that the term 'live CD' can also refer to a bootable USB drive. In either case, the

[45] AccessData (2018) *AD eDiscovery | Industry Leading Legal Software.* AccessData. Available from https://accessdata.com/products-services/ADeDiscovery [30 April 2018].

[46] Veritas (2018) *eDiscovery Platform.* Veritas. Available from https://www.veritas.com/product/information-governance/ediscovery-platform [30 April 2018].

[47] AccessData (2018) *Mobile Collection.* AccessData. Available from https://accessdata.com/products-services/mobile-solutions [1 May 2018].

[48] Paraben (2018) *E3: DS.* Paraben Corporation. Available from https://www.paraben.com/products/e3-ds [1 May 2018].

[49] X-Ways (2018) *WinHex: Hex Editor & Disk Editor, Computer Forensics & Data Recovery Software.* X-Ways Software Technology AG. Available from https://www.x-ways.net/winhex/ [1 May 2018].

[50] Hörz, M. (2018) *HxD – Freeware Hex Editor and Disk Editor | mh-nexus.* Maël Hörz. Available from https://mh-nexus.de/en/hxd/ [1 May 2018].

end goal is the same: to collect volatile data from powered-on machines, all the while understanding the impact of directly interacting with the system being investigated.

Volatile data includes the contents of physical memory, the status of any active network connections, data pertaining to active user sessions, the contents of the computer screen, and other types of temporary file.

Live CD/USB distributions typically work using known good copies of operating system binaries, or custom software that has been written in such a way as to minimise the impact to the host operating system.

Network forensic tools

Not all evidence needs to be captured while stored on a hard disk; in some cases, particularly cases involving remote attacks or malware, we might want to pluck evidence directly off the wire. There are various software tools, both commercial and open source, that allow an investigator to perform packet captures, using a network interface to capture that data.

A couple of tools frequently used together for this purpose are tcpdump and Wireshark. Tcpdump is a Linux command line utility that can display the content of packets in real time, but also commit those packets to disk in the form of a PCAP file. A Windows port of tcpdump, called Windump, also exists.

Wireshark provides a graphical user interface that allows the exploration of captured packets. Packets can be filtered by protocol, source or destination, as well as a wide variety of other criteria. Both Wireshark and tcpdump are open-source tools, freely available to download. We'll discuss them in more detail in Chapter 11, which focuses on live acquisitions.

Open-source tools

It is important to note that it is entirely possible for an investigator to complete a digital forensics investigation using exclusively open-source software tools. There is an equivalent open-source application for almost all of the functionality found in the commercial forensic suites. For example, the Sleuth Kit is an open-source collection of command line utilities that can perform data recovery operations on hard disks, which when combined with another open-source tool, Autopsy, can offer very similar insights to a commercial investigative suite.

Given this, you might be wondering why anyone would consider a commercial tool if a freely available open-source tool can do the same job. There is always a trade-off between features, functionality, support, training and cost. If you are in the middle of an investigation and an open-source tool doesn't function in the way you expect, or stops working completely, who can you call to fix it? The answer is usually, no one – you have to work on the problem yourself, or engage with the community to help you fix the problem. The majority of open-source tool maintainers have day jobs and work on the tools in their spare time; you are not going to have a support SLA with them. This is an important consideration to factor in when relying on a given tool.

The answer usually lies somewhere in the middle. Most investigators, if given the option, will use a selection of tools from both the commercial and open-source realms. You don't have to pick one side or the other, and there is significant mileage in being aware of the capabilities of both.

SUMMARY

In this chapter we introduced the variety of tools, both hardware and software, specialised and non-specialised, that the forensic investigator will become familiar with as they go about the business of investigation.

We looked at the contents of a grab bag, carried by first responders heading to a crime scene, and we discussed the tools more likely to be found in a forensics lab, such as computers built to handle the load of processing a complex case, and the forensic software suites they run.

In the next chapter we'll look at how these tools are put to work, performing acquisitions and analysing collected evidence.

10 EVIDENCE ACQUISITION BASICS

Disks, file systems and stored data are the building blocks for the majority of digital forensics investigations. In this chapter we're going to look closely at how these mainstay sources of potential evidence are acquired, processed and analysed. A deep understanding of both file systems and disk geometry are crucial for a forensic investigator in analysing the evidence presented to them. In this chapter we'll look at these, and talk through performing basic digital forensics acquisitions.

If you're primarily in an incident response role, you should also become familiar with the contents of this chapter. You're likely to find yourself best placed to handle evidence acquisition as a first responder, even if you don't ultimately complete the entire investigation. The reality is that the opportunity to perform some of the tasks we're going to talk about can often be missed in the midst of an incident, but by being switched on and recognising when the opportunity to acquire evidence presents itself you can jump in and competently do the job. Remember, your work will be held to the same standard as the full-time investigator, so it is vital that acquisition is completed in accordance with published best practices.

THE HARD DISK DRIVE

If you pop the cover off a modern laptop or desktop computer you'll most likely find one of two types of disk drive: the traditional magnetic disk type that was first introduced in the mid-1950s, which remains in widespread use, or the increasingly popular and more modern solid-state drive. Though the term 'hard disk drive' technically refers only to the magnetic kind, you might hear it used to describe both interchangeably. The term 'solid-state drive', or SSD for short, is used to refer solely to drives using the newer solid-state technology. There are also hybrid drives that feature a mixture of the two technologies; these include a larger-capacity magnetic disk along with a smaller-capacity SSD cache, used to improve access times for the most commonly accessed files.

Magnetic disks

Traditional magnetic hard disks are remarkable pieces of engineering. They store data by creating extremely tiny magnetic fields on a thin magnetic coating applied to a spinning circular disk known as a platter. Modern disks contain multiple platters. The direction that the magnetic field is applied is used to differentiate between the binary numbers that ultimately make up all stored data, 0 and 1. The surface of each platter is magnetised using a write head, which is a very thin but highly magnetic piece of wire that floats just above the platter. When data is overwritten, the write head simply moves across the surface of the platter and writes directly over the top of the existing data. To keep data in order platters are divided into tracks, which are concentric circles that start at the centre of the platter and radiate out to the edge. Tracks are further divided into sectors, which are segments, or 'pie slices', to think of it another way.

For optimum performance a magnetic disk will start recording data on the first available sector, and then continue recording on the next closest free sector. This is to ensure that the read head doesn't have to jump around all over the place to access an entire file. However, through normal use it is common for chunks of files to become physically displaced across the disk. A cure for this is defragmenting the disk. This process reduces the time required to access a file by moving the fragmented 'blocks' of files closer together. Understanding this concept is important when analysing raw disk images.

Solid-state drives

Unlike their magnetic forefathers, solid-state drives feature no moving parts, which improves their reliability, reduces power consumption and makes them weigh less. They use the same type of storage that has been prevalent in USB or flash drives for many years: microscopic transistors that trap a small electrical charge. The presence, or lack, of an electrical charge is used to determine the presence of a binary 0 or 1. A fully charged transistor will not allow any more electricity to flow through it; the drive recognises this and returns a 0. An uncharged transistor allows current to pass through, which is interpreted as a 1. A brand new, completely unused drive features all transistors charged. Charge can remain in the transistor for years, meaning that the data the charge represents will remain on the device for just as long. The main benefit of this approach is that the time required to write data is reduced significantly when compared to magnetic drives. Transistors in solid-state drives can be charged in microseconds, whereas magnetic drive write heads take milliseconds to apply their magnetic fields.

Whereas a magnetic disk can theoretically be written to an infinite number of times, an SSD transistor has a comparatively short life expectancy. Typically, they can only be written to about 100,000 times before they are likely to fail. So, unlike the magnetic hard disk, which tries to keep blocks of a file as close to each other as possible, an SSD spreads the load across all the unused transistors in the drive randomly. This technique, known as wear levelling, avoids consistently storing charge in the same group of transistors, which would make them wear out faster. The computer's operating system is not aware of this process thanks to the SSD's on-board controller card. The controller presents the operating system with an abstracted list of hard drive sectors. To the host computer, and the forensic examiner's write blocker for that matter, the controller card will present the same abstracted list of sectors.

Both magnetic disk drives and solid-state drives can be acquired using our principal digital forensics tool, the trusty write blocker. Once images are acquired, the same software suites can be used to examine the drive contents regardless of its physical form factor.

Disk geometry

Understanding the fundamentals of how data is laid out on a hard disk is a crucial component of an investigator's overall understanding when analysing that acquired data later.

Sectors

Sectors are the smallest physical unit of storage on the hard disk. Traditionally a sector is used to store 512 bytes of data; however, in recent years a new standard of 4,096 bytes per sector has emerged. This new standard is known as the 'advanced format'.

Clusters or allocation units

A cluster is the smallest logical unit of storage on a disk, and is made up of multiple sectors. For example, a 4 kB cluster, the default size in many configurations, could be made up of eight 512-byte sectors or a single 4,096-byte advanced format sector. Clusters need not be made up of contiguous sectors.

Slack space

Only one file can be assigned to a given cluster on a disk. Clusters are, of course, fixed in size, whereas file sizes can vary greatly. This means that, more often than not, there is a difference between the number of clusters assigned to a file and the amount of storage that the file actually needs. For instance, on a disk with 4 kB clusters, a 3 kB file would be assigned a single 4 kB cluster. The term 'slack space', or 'file slack', refers to the unused portion of that cluster. In this example, that would mean 1 kB of slack space in the cluster.

Slack space can have significant value to a digital forensic investigator, which is why it is a highly important concept to understand. Consider the following: a user saves a document that is 8 kB in size; the document is assigned two 4 kB clusters. There is therefore no file slack in this case, as the file size aligns perfectly with the combined size of the two clusters. The user subsequently deletes that file, which causes the operating system to mark those two clusters as unused, but crucially the operating system doesn't delete the actual contents of the clusters. A new document is saved. This time the file is 6 kB in size, and it is assigned to the same two 4 kB clusters as the old document. Those two clusters now contain the 6 kB of the new document, and 2 kB of the old one as file slack.

The file fragments found in slack space can hold many secrets thought long since deleted, and can therefore be a valuable source of forensic evidence. When you acquire a forensically sound image of a hard disk drive, you will acquire the contents of the slack space alongside those files that are fully intact. Forensics suites allow you to filter slack space and explore the fragments found there, if you know you're looking for a file that has been deleted by a suspect.

Slack space became famous around the world in July 2016, when then FBI Director James Comey gave a televised update on the status of the FBI investigation into former US Secretary of State Hillary Clinton's usage of a personal email server. The investigation was focused on the fact that Secretary Clinton was accused of storing classified information on a non-government-approved server.

During his remarks, Comey noted how one email server that had formed part of the investigation had been forensically examined. This particular server had been decommissioned three years prior, a process that resulted in the email server software being removed. This meant that emails couldn't be viewed in their 'natural' state, but could be reconstructed from slack space.

On removing the email server software, Comey stated, 'Doing that didn't remove the e-mail content, but it was like removing the frame from a huge finished jigsaw puzzle and dumping the pieces on the floor. The effect was that millions of e-mail fragments end up unsorted in the server's unused, or slack space. We searched through all of it to see what was there, and what parts of the puzzle could be put back together.'[51]

Hard disk interfaces

In order to connect a hard disk to a write blocker to acquire it, you must first identify the type of hard disk interface present on the target disk. The interface is used to pass data and control signals to the disk. The majority of hard drives that are encountered in modern-day investigations use the Serial ATA interface, known as SATA. Occasionally, older drives that use Parallel ATA (PATA), also known as Integrated Drive Electronics (IDE), may make an appearance. In the case of servers, the Serial Attached Small Computer System Interface (SCSI), or SAS, interface is commonly used.

SATA

The most commonly used disk interface these days, the SATA interface, was first introduced at the start of the 21st century and has been through multiple revisions ever since. The most notable change in each major revision is the data transfer speed. The very first version of SATA supported data transfer rates of 1.5 Gb per second. This transfer rate increased to 16 Gb per second as of version 3.2, introduced in 2013. SATA interfaces are found on both magnetic and solid-state drives.

SATA disks feature both power and data connectors that are typically positioned next to each other. The data connector has 7 pins, and the power connector has 15. This is a significant reduction when compared with the older PATA connector. One of the most annoying aspects of working with PATA drives was the ease with which the pins could be accidentally bent or, worse, snapped. Both the desktop-sized 3.5-inch SATA drive and the laptop-sized 2.5-inch SATA drive use the same connector, which means only one type of SATA write blocker is needed to acquire both form factors.

SAS

Disks with the Serial Attached SCSI interface are commonly found in rackmount servers. SAS was introduced in 2004 and superseded the classic parallel SCSI (pronounced 'scuzzy') interface. SAS drives are used in servers for a few reasons. First, they're more reliable than SATA drives, and secondly, they allow for faster read and write times. In

---

[51] Federal Bureau of Investigation (2016) *Statement by FBI Director James B. Comey on the Investigation of Secretary Hillary Clinton's Use of a Personal E-Mail System.* FBI National Press Office. Available from https://www.fbi.gov/news/pressrel/press-releases/statement-by-fbi-director-james-b-comey-on-the-investigation-of-secretary-hillary-clinton2019s-use-of-a-personal-e-mail-system [1 May 2018].

addition, SAS allows more disks to be connected to a single device when compared to the classic SCSI, or even SATA, interfaces, and with longer cables – perfect for building high-availability RAID arrays. Several manufacturers produce SAS-specific write blockers.

PATA/IDE

Older, but still very much out there, Parallel ATA or IDE was the hard disk interface technology used throughout the 1990s. Easily spotted by the wide ribbon cables that connect the disks to a PC's motherboard, PATA drives have extremely limited capabilities by today's standards. Only two devices could be connected to a single PATA controller, in a master and slave configuration, and data transfer was limited to 133 Mb/s in the most recent version of the interface.

PATA disks typically feature 40 pins on their connectors, which, as mentioned previously, are easily bent or damaged. Therefore, caution should be used when connecting a PATA drive to a write blocker – repairing these is not a pleasant task, by any means.

You should always have sufficient confidence in your abilities when it comes to using write-blocking equipment, acquiring disks and performing any type of investigative work using forensic tools. The first time you use a new piece of equipment, or tool, ideally won't be in the midst of a real investigation. As with anything in life, practice makes perfect. Fortunately, the internet has you covered. It is very easy to get your hands on several resources to help you practise acquiring and analysing hard disk drives.

Many sites and organisations offer pre-made forensic disk images for forensic training purposes; these image files usually contain evidence that has been planted to encourage you to solve a given fictional case.

Here are just a few:

- The Computer Forensic Reference Data Set Project (https://www.cfreds. nist.gov/)
- Linux LEO – The Law Enforcement and Forensic Examiner's Introduction to Linux (http://linuxleo.com/)
- Digital Corpora scenarios (http://digitalcorpora.org/corpora/scenarios)
- DFRWS Forensic Challenge (http://www.dfrws.org/dfrws-forensic-challenge)

Images and challenges are a great way to hone your skills and test your equipment in a realistic scenario. Of course, once you're at the stage of having a disk image to work with you're already past the point of actually creating that image, which is just as important to practise.

If you're anything like me, you'll probably have piles of old hard disks in some cupboard that you've collected over the years as computers have come and gone from your life. Using these old disks is a great way to practise acquiring disk images, as they're often smaller in capacity and may feature different file systems, operating system versions and hardware interfaces.

If you don't have old disks to spare, a great tip is to head to any online auction site and look for used hard drives. They're cheap, easy to buy in a job lot of five or ten, and are rarely erased properly. I have performed research on many second-hand hard disks from various sources, and I can assure you they provide very interesting practice subjects. Unlike your own disks, having no clue what you're about to come across on the disk also adds to the realism of your practice activity.

REMOVABLE MEDIA

A digital forensic investigator would be remiss not to consider that potential evidence may be located on removable storage media, especially when such media is located in or around the crime scene. Removable media is, of course, physically easier to hide, and is frequently used to transfer data between computers.

USB

The Universal Serial Bus (USB) was developed in the mid-1990s to solve a problem. Lots of PCs were being built, and lots of external devices for those PCs were being built, but there wasn't really a common standard defining how they should connect. USB was the solution, and it paved the way for a wide variety of devices that use USB to hit the market. Of particular interest to us as forensics examiners are USB mass storage devices such as flash drives that use solid-state technology, or magnetic hard disks that are packaged to reside outside the computer.

Specially designed USB write blockers allow for the forensic acquisition of USB mass storage devices. These are particularly useful when dealing with external hard disks, since even though these disks usually feature a SATA interface 'under the hood', getting at that interface can often involve damaging the plastic chassis of the external disk, which is something to be avoided.

Optical disks

Though they are gradually being dropped in favour of flash-based storage, it is not uncommon to see optical storage disks still in use throughout offices and in residential settings, particularly to facilitate the sharing of digital media files such as photographs, music and video. Data is recorded to an optical disk by way of a laser. The laser etches a microscopic bump, known as a pit, which represents the binary data being recorded, into a reflective material on the underside of the disk in a spiral pattern. This etching process is commonly referred to as 'burning'. A laser is also used to read the disk. The etched pits do not reflect the laser light; this is detected and a binary 0 registered. Areas of the reflective disk surface without pits are known as lands; they do return a reflection, which is detected to register a binary 1.

The three primary types of optical storage disk in use today are:

- Compact disc (CD), which typically features a 700 MB capacity;
- Digital versatile disc (DVD), which typically features a 4.7 GB capacity but can store up to 17.08 GB in certain configurations;
- Blu-ray disc (BD), which can store up to 50 GB.

The majority of optical drives used to access optical disks are read only, so they inherit write-blocking characteristics out of the box. However, all three of the formats above can be purchased as write once, or can be fully rewritable. To complement this, there are disk drives widely known as burners that can be used to record to a given format of disk. Therefore, the forensic investigator should be aware of both the hardware used to read a given disk and the writable characteristics of the disk if it is being acquired as evidence.

Memory cards

There are multiple flavours of memory cards with varying storage capacities based on flash storage technology. Some are standards based, such as the popular Secure Digital (SD) card, whereas others are proprietary, such as the Sony Memory Stick. The majority of digital cameras and camcorders record to some form of memory card. Therefore, images and video relevant to an investigation, including those previously deleted, may be located on them. Of course, memory cards can also be used to transfer any other type of data.

Write blockers specifically for memory cards are available, and should be used when acquiring a forensically sound image of any memory card, regardless of type. Such write blockers typically support multiple media types. For example, the Forensic Card Reader manufactured by UltraBlock supports the following commonly used memory card formats:

- Smart Media;
- xD;
- Compact Flash;
- SD;
- MMC (MultiMediaCard);
- MicroSD;
- Memory Stick.

PROCESSING DISK IMAGES

Once an investigator has acquired a disk image and has taken it back to the lab, it's time to load the image up for processing in a dedicated forensic suite or other tool. Processing involves taking the raw disk data and extracting from it the various artefacts contained within. A typical disk image will contain a basic file system, operating system components, applications and many user- and system-generated files, all of which may contain valuable evidence. There is a lot of information to be unlocked.

Forensics software suites are designed to sift through as much of this information as quickly as possible, to make the investigator's job of finding information and evidence relevant to their case go as smoothly as possible.

During the processing phase the case file is built, which includes metadata regarding the contents of the disk image being processed. For example, an index is built that allows for faster keyword searches against the contents of the disk. Without this index, each keyword search would have to be run across the contents of the entire disk, which if you have many terabytes of data is going to take a non-trivial amount of time.

Forensics suites generally allow you to choose which activities are to be performed during processing, for example including file carving (a topic discussed later in this chapter) in the processing job, or creating thumbnails of discovered images. As a general rule, the more tasks you want to complete during processing, the longer it will take.

Once the processing phase is complete, the investigator will be able to interact with a graphical overview of all the discovered artefacts.

FILE SYSTEMS

The system for organising and retrieving data stored on any type of storage media is known as a file system. For digital forensic investigators, knowledge of both the general characteristics of any file system and specialised knowledge of the more common types of file system in use are core competencies.

File system functions

In today's world there are many flavours of file system in use, each with their own variances in how they go about doing the job of organising files. Some of the most important functions in any file system are listed below.

Mapping files to a physical disk location

The file system is responsible for keeping track of where a file is physically located on a given disk, so the user can both access and update the data in that file. Conversely, the file system must store data about unused disk locations, so it knows where to place new files.

Supporting user-facing file and folder structures

We're all familiar with filenames, and storing files in folders (or directories). This is another important function of the file system.

Storing file information

In addition to actually storing the file itself, the file system stores information about the file. In other words, it is creating data about data, which is known as metadata. Examples of file system metadata include file creation time, file access time and file modification time, which are all of extreme importance during forensics investigations.

Protecting information

Using file system access permissions, control can be afforded over a user's ability to access or modify a given file. The file system can also be a layer where file- or folder-level encryption is applied.

Commonly used file systems

While there is no shortage of file systems that could be in use on a given system, as a forensic investigator in the field you are most likely to encounter one of the following file systems. Therefore, time should be taken to fully understand the properties of each.

NTFS

The New Technology File System was developed by Microsoft for use in its Windows NT family of operating systems. It remains the most commonly used file system on Windows servers and desktop machines.

NTFS uses a single table, known as the master file table (MFT), to keep track of all file and directory locations on a given volume. The MFT is also used to store file metadata, such as timestamps and permissions settings. On any NTFS volume there is a backup copy of the MFT to be used in the event that the primary MFT becomes corrupted. The MFT is considered the most important aspect of NTFS for forensic investigators to understand, since it plays a key role in how forensic investigation suites display acquired evidence.

Linux machines can also use NTFS by way of a driver. Apple macOS machines can read NTFS devices, but do not support writing to them by default.

FAT

Before NTFS, the File Allocation Table or FAT family of file systems reigned supreme as the default file system of Microsoft Windows. The name comes from a statically allocated index table used to keep track of the clusters assigned to a file. FAT went through three major revisions, mostly to accommodate ever increasing disk sizes. While it is not the default in Windows any more, the FAT file system lives on and is frequently used on removable USB drives and memory cards. Therefore, all modern operating systems support it, and you are still very likely to come across it during an investigation.

APFS

The Apple File System is the new default file system on Apple's range of computing products, from watchOS to macOS. It debuted in March 2017 with the release of iOS 10.3 for iPhone, and hit Apple laptops and desktops in September 2017 with the release of macOS 10.13, also known as High Sierra.

APFS is designed to better support two technologies increasingly prevalent in personal computers: solid-state drives and encryption. As a result, there is native support for full-disk encryption, and support for the SSD TRIM command. The TRIM command is used to proactively inform an SSD when blocks of data are no longer in use, and therefore can be wiped, to reduce future wipe time.

APFS also aims to make more efficient use of storage space on a disk by using techniques like cloning during file copies. For example, if a file is copied in an APFS file system, no actual data duplication occurs. Instead, the file system uses metadata to make a note of the copy, but still points to the original file. In the event that either version of the file (the copy or the original) is changed, a new version of the file is created and new storage space is allocated; this technique is known as copy-on-write.

HFS+

Between 1998 and 2017, HFS+ (also known as Mac OS Extended) was the default file system in Apple products. Therefore, it is still highly prevalent, and the most likely type of Apple file system an investigator will encounter. The file system uses a catalogue file to store file and folder metadata in a B-tree storage system.

Of particular interest to the forensic investigator working on HFS+ is the fact that the file system supports journaling, and this has been enabled by default since 2003. Journaling is a mechanism in which changes to a disk are first committed to a journal file, which acts as a buffer to ensure that all disk update transactions are fully completed. In an event such as the rapid removal of a USB storage device the transactions may not be fully completed, and the file system may become corrupt. The journal file will keep track of all uncommitted transactions, which can include chunks of files that were not fully saved. Imagine a suspect quickly trying to hide a removable storage device, for example.

XFS

Linux distributions come in all shapes and sizes, but the most commonly used have adopted XFS as their default file system in recent years. XFS has been around since 1993, when it was first created by Silicon Graphics, Inc. In 2001 it made its way to the Linux platform, but it wasn't until a few years ago that its use became widespread.

XFS features include metadata-based journaling, which helps the file system to remain consistent in the event of a system crash. It also makes use of a classic Unix file system data structure, the inode. Inodes can be found in most Unix file systems, and store information attributes about a file and where on the disk the file is stored.

File systems and acquisition tools

Regardless of the form factor of the media, or the file system in use, a forensically sound disk image will be an identical copy of the raw contents of the drive. The file system and the individual files will be preserved for analysis. In some cases the investigative suite an investigator uses might not fully support processing the file system of the acquired disk, which makes for a more challenging investigation, but not one that we should give up on by any means. We'll discuss strategies for dealing with such a scenario shortly.

OPERATING SYSTEMS

When a suspect engages with a computer, they do so in the same manner as any other user, via an operating system. The operating system is responsible for managing the hardware and software resources available to the computer. The core functions of an operating system, such as executing programs, managing memory, providing networking functions and presenting a graphical user interface (GUI), should be well understood by a digital forensic investigator. Determining the operating system in use on a suspect's machine, either by observation prior to imaging or by reviewing the contents of an acquired image, helps to point the investigator towards operating-system-specific artefacts that contain evidence.

Microsoft Windows

Since it is the dominant desktop and laptop operating system, investigating evidence generated by Microsoft Windows is a familiar concept to both digital forensic investigators and incident responders alike. Remember, the default file system in use by Windows is NTFS, which is well supported by all the major forensics suites. Once evidence is processed by a forensics suite, areas of interest or specific types of file will be presented for enhanced review. Some examples of Windows-specific evidence locations are shown below.

The file system

Microsoft Windows uses a letter-based system to label connected storage volumes. Most people who have used a Windows system will be very familiar with the 'C:\' drive, which typically represents the system volume. In each volume you'll find various types of file that are present on the computer. Of course, depending on the nature of the investigation, you'll be able to select the types of file that are of most interest.

The page file

Also known as the swap file, the page file is used by Windows as a form of virtual memory. Used to supplement random access memory (RAM), the page file contains chunks of memory that have been swapped to the hard drive so that the memory items currently in use can reside in the faster physical RAM. This makes the page file an interesting prospect for forensic investigators. For example, some applications may store passwords in memory in cleartext; if those passwords are swapped to the page file and the computer is shut down, they may very well still be there. There are a variety of page file parsing tools out there.

Event logs

The Windows platform features a standardised file format for recording different types of event, to overcome the problems associated with multiple applications having proprietary logging formats. Since the launch of Windows Vista, that format, known as .evtx, has used an XML-based structure to record multiple details of any given event. There are a multitude of different applications designed to parse .evtx files and home in on specific event types, including open-source tools and native Microsoft Windows tools, and this functionality is built in as a feature of the majority of forensic investigation suites.

For a forensic investigator a common usage of Windows event logs is to look for specific security-related events of interest, such as a user logging on to, or logging off, a computer. In such a scenario the investigator would likely use a tool to parse the raw .evtx file for a relevant log event. Event IDs are used to indicate the type of recorded event; Windows event ID 4624 represents a successful log on, and 4634 represents a user logging off.

Registry

The Windows registry is a database of various operating-system- and application-specific settings that can provide tremendous insight for a forensic investigator. The registry also stores user-specific settings, primarily for the purpose of improving the user's experience with the operating system, but in doing so it reveals how the user is using the operating system to an investigator.

One example of the value of the Windows registry would be the way in which it keeps records of all devices connected to the computer. This includes USB storage devices, the usage of which is recorded in great detail. The HKLM\SYSTEM\CurrentControlSet\Enum\USBSTOR registry key contains a record of the serial number of each USB device, along with timestamps displaying the first and last time that a device was attached: absolutely wonderful information for determining if a given device should be included in the scope of evidence.

A user doesn't typically interact directly with the Windows registry; instead, the applications they're using, or the operating system, will make changes on their behalf. It is entirely possible, however, for a user to manually modify registry keys. A built-in Windows utility, regedit.exe, makes this possible. It is also possible to delete registry keys entirely, so a savvy suspect aiming to cover their tracks might attempt to do this. In such cases it might still be possible to recover the deleted registry key; the registry database is just another binary file subject to the same rules of slack space as anything else.

Prefetch files

Each time an application is run on a Windows system, a so-called prefetch file is created to facilitate faster load times for that application. It does this by storing chunks of the various files an application needs to load into a single file, which means the operating system only has to look in one place. The prefetch file also contains metadata that is relevant for a forensic investigator. A prefetch file can tell you how and when an application was first run, when it was last run, how many times it has been run and from which volume it was run. Prefetch files are typically located in 'C:\Windows\prefetch', and have a .pf file extension.

Apple macOS

Once considered by many to be a platform reserved for the creative industries, Apple's macOS (formerly known as Mac OS X) platform has seen a significant increase in popularity in recent years. These days you're just as likely to find a Mac on the desk of a car dealer as you are a digital designer.

File system structure

The modern-day macOS is Unix based, and as a result the file system is laid out using Unix standards. All connected volumes fall under a root directory, represented as a single slash, '/'. In the top level of the volume the operating system places a selection of directories that form the core data layout.

Of particular interest to us would be the /Users directory, which contains home directories for all users on the computer. Evidence in user-generated files will typically be found here. Because it is Unix based, macOS also treats all connected disks as if they were files. For example, an attached USB drive would appear under the /Volumes directory.

Plists

Throughout a macOS system you'll find lots of files with the extension '.plist'. These are property list files, and are raw XML or binary-encoded files used by macOS (or iOS) to store various strings related to a given application. Sometimes these can be user specific, and therefore have relevance to an investigation. Utilities for converting binary plist files back to XML, such as 'plutil', are frequently used in the hunt for evidence.

Swap

macOS generates swap files for the same purpose that Microsoft Windows generates the page file. Rather than a single file, macOS can generate up to 10 different swap files, depending on need. These swap files can be found in the '/private/var/vm' directory. This directory also contains a 'sleepimage' file, which is used to dump a copy of the RAM contents if the computer is put to sleep: something to be aware of, since this could provide a source of otherwise volatile evidence.

System logs

Again, thanks to that Unix foundation on which it was built, macOS produces a variety of log files in the Unix format. These log files are found in '/private/var/log' and include a system log for generic system messages, and a secure log for keeping track of authentication events on the machine.

Linux

Primarily, but by no means exclusively, used on servers, Linux-based operating systems can be found in a variety of different scenarios. There are various Linux distributions, of course, each with their own different system utilities and nuances, but all of them have a few things in common.

Filesystem Hierarchy Standard (FHS)

This standard defines the conventions used by Linux distributions when laying out a file system. Linux uses a hierarchical file system, in which everything falls under the root, or '/', directory, even if the computer uses more than one physical disk drive. For the first level under the root directory, the FHS defines a series of directory names and provides a description of what types of file should be stored in them. The result is that even if you've never worked with a particular Linux distribution before you'll still be able to navigate around the file system and know where to look for particular evidence items. The first-level directories include:

- /bin, used to store essential Linux command binaries;
- /boot, used for boot loader files;
- /dev, where raw device files are stored (remember, Linux treats storage devices as files);
- /etc, used to store system-wide configuration files;
- /home, which contains user home directories, and is the most likely place you'll find user-generated evidence;
- /lib, which contains shared libraries;
- /media, designed to be used for mount points for removable storage media;
- /mnt, typically used to temporarily mount file systems;
- /opt, for optionally installed software;
- /proc, a virtual file system that is used to store process and kernel information (we'll discuss this more as we look at live acquisitions);
- /root, the home directory of the root account (the superuser on a Linux system);
- /run, used to store real-time variable information such as which users are currently logged in;
- /sbin, used for system binaries;
- /sys, used to store information about device drivers;
- /tmp, a temporary file space that is not preserved between reboots;
- /usr, used for multi-user utilities and applications;
- /var, used to store variable files, in other words things that change during normal operation. For the forensic investigator, /var/log is a favoured location since it is used to store system and application log files.

/etc/shadow

The shadow file is used to store encrypted passwords for users of the Linux system; it also lists the username for each account on the system. These two pieces of information may prove useful to an investigator wishing to uncover passwords used by a suspect. A well-regarded open-source password cracking tool, John the Ripper, is frequently used against shadow files.

Bash history

A list of shell commands previously executed by a user will normally be present in a file called '.bash_history', which is typically found in the user's home directory. This is very useful for determining the type of activity a user was conducting, if they were indeed using the shell. In investigations that focus on servers, without an installed GUI, this is usually a valuable source of information.

Logs

Unlike Windows, log files on Linux systems tend to be stored in a standard text format, which means they can be parsed without special tools. Most logs are located in the /var/log/ directory, and include a mixture of system-level and application-level event data. Some examples of logs that may be of interest to an investigator include:

- /var/log/secure, which includes system-wide authentication events;
- /var/log/apache2/access.log, which includes information regarding access events on the Apache web server platform. For instance, each time a user address accesses a web page, information such as source IP, user agent string and the page accessed is recorded in this log file.

FILES

Ultimately, the majority of evidence discovered during any investigation will come from user-generated files, or artefacts recorded by the system regarding user activity. The file systems and operating systems in use may be the same between thousands of computers, but the user-generated content on them will of course be very different. An understanding of both operating system and file system lets us know where we should start to look, but once we've arrived there it is up to our own ingenuity, technical skills and investigative brain to figure out the rest. This is what makes digital forensics the exciting and rewarding field that it is.

Cryptographic hashing of files

When a file is processed for forensic analysis a cryptographic hash of the file content is recorded. A hash is a mathematically derived representation of the data contained within the file, returned to a fixed length. Typically this is done using the MD5, SHA-1 or SHA-256 hashing algorithms in most modern forensics suites. The purpose of hashing a file is to prove that the content of the file hasn't changed from original source to forensic image. Changing a filename will not alter the hash value of a file, but changing the content will.

Known file filters

To help us cut through the noise when working with many thousands of files on a computer, a tool called a known file filter can help us get a head start. Known file filters compare the cryptographic hashes of files collected from the suspect's machine with a large database of known benign operating system files. This allows us to very quickly discard files that are not going to be of any interest to the investigation.

Known file filters can also be used the other way around, to look for files that **are** of significant interest to us. An example of this would be a service called PhotoDNA, which was developed by Microsoft to provide hashing of known pornographic images containing children. Many cloud service providers such as Dropbox, Google and Facebook use PhotoDNA in their products to flag such images and take action.

Carving

File systems keep files nice and organised, but what happens when either the file system has become corrupted or a file has been deleted and is no longer referenced in the file system? The answer is file carving, a core function of the digital forensics profession.

File carving involves using tools to scour through the raw data on a disk and carve out either full files or fragments of files. The process works by looking for file header values, known as magic numbers, that match a known value for a given type of file. For instance, the hexadecimal value FFD8 is present in the file header for a JPEG image file. Therefore, if we find an FFD8 in the raw data of a forensic image, it's likely that at least some of the data that follows will form a JPEG image.

File carving tools use a variety of different techniques in the quest to accurately determine the start and end of a discovered file. Files can, of course, be fragmented across various physical locations on a disk, and without the file system information to tie them together the task of reassembly can be complex. Both free open-source and highly expensive commercial carving tools exist. Both can work, but typically with a paid-for offering you are paying for the quality and intelligence of the carving model and algorithms. File carving functions are also built into all commercial forensic investigation software suites.

Internet browsers

Some of the most sought-after user-generated artefacts are those created by internet browsing activity. With so many digital crimes involving the internet, it should be no surprise that a suspect's browsing habits might be of interest to an investigator. All operating systems come bundled with a browser, but the user is free to download and use whichever browser they'd like.

Knowing where a particular type of browser stores artefacts such as user histories, cookies and bookmarks will assist the investigator greatly when it comes to building a timeline of internet activity.

- Microsoft Internet Explorer uses a database file called 'index.dat' to store web history information in a format known as MS IE Cache File Format. These database files can be examined with specialised tools.

- Mozilla Firefox and Google Chrome use a series of SQLite databases to record things like form submission history, web browser activity, cookies and downloaded files. SQLite is a format that can be explored with relative ease.

- Apple Safari uses a macOS .plist file to store history under a user's home directory.

ANALYSIS OF ARTEFACTS

While acquiring disk images, and waiting for them to process, are critical parts of the investigative process, the majority of the enjoyment of digital forensics is contained within the analysis phase of the investigation. Here, leveraging our tools, creativity and skill, we can piece together the various evidence items that will allow us to build a solid case. While the differences between the tools an investigator might use for a given case mean it's hard to describe a single analysis workflow, I will attempt to describe a typical one below.

Knowing where to start

Earlier, we discussed the importance of only investigating in response to a very specific allegation and avoiding the generic 'we think this guy is bad, please find something that we can fire him for' scenario. The reasons behind this become very clear when we arrive at the analysis phase of the investigation. Without a starting point it is very difficult to start. Analysis of digital evidence usually starts with a specific timeframe, or file or topic that can be explored via a keyword search. Merely looking through hundreds of files for evidence of something generically defined as 'wrong' or 'bad' isn't an enjoyable way to spend your time, and isn't an effective use of digital forensics tools.

Leveraging the user interface

Forensics suites present us with a number of screens for interacting with evidence at different levels. They're smart enough to know that we'll want to be able to sort emails by sender, or by date received. They'll present files in native formats, or allow us to explore them using a hexadecimal viewer so we can find hidden details that might not otherwise be apparent.

Focusing on relevant items

Normally, artefacts are filtered in and out using the forensics tool, so that only files created, accessed or modified during the timeframe of interest remain. Then, features like known file filters are used to further narrow down the selection. It's all about minimising noise and distractions and finding relevant data. Once an artefact has been found that could be of interest, the investigator will bookmark it. Bookmarks, as you'd probably expect, make it a simple task to go back to those artefacts of interest, so you don't have to go through the entire filtering process once again.

Using timestamps forensics suites can build visual timelines of file usage, which make understanding a suspect's actions on a machine a much simpler task.

In addition to keyword searches, regular-expression-based searches can be used to home in on data that matches a particular pattern – for instance, finding any documents containing credit card numbers. Similarly, features such as explicit image detection look for files that contain pixels matching flesh tones, which would be of interest in an investigation involving pornography.

Overcoming challenges

During the analysis phase the investigator might also come across files that are encrypted. Many forensics suites have built in decryption features, such as rainbow tables and wordlist generators that are used to attempt discovery of encryption keys for those files. Truth be told, if someone has taken the time to encrypt a file, and it falls within the scope of an investigation, it is likely to be worthy of our time to investigate.

From time to time, a forensics suite alone might not be enough to fully analyse the file in question. Therefore, all suites allow the option to export the file for analysis in third-party tools. For example, if you have a proprietary file format that requires a special viewer, it may need to be exported and examined. Here, the cryptographic hashing that occurs during the processing phase is used to validate that the file exported from the forensics suite is exactly the same as the source file.

Preparing to report

At the end of the analysis phase, the investigator will typically export the bookmarks they've made using reporting features. The reports generated by a forensics tool are then typically included in the final report produced at the end of the case.

SUMMARY

In this chapter we've studied the bread and butter evidence sources that we'll work with during an investigation. Evidence collected from hard disks, removable media and file systems often forms the foundation of an investigator's case. Therefore, it is vital that any investigator understands each of them deeply.

Secondly, we looked at the user- and machine-generated artefacts found on those disks, such as files, internet histories and event logs, that can lead us to vital clues in determining what has occurred.

It is true that offline or powered-down acquisition of these sources is ideal; however, this might not always be possible. Therefore, in the next chapter we'll take a look at factors that may influence the decision to perform a live, or powered-on, acquisition.

11 CAPTURING A MOVING TARGET

The nature of many security incidents, and the digital forensics investigations that are associated with them, often places a first responder in a challenging position. There are frequently factors that force our hand and require the first responder to interact directly with a system containing potential evidence. This situation runs contrary to the fundamental forensic principle that actions taken by the digital forensics professional should not alter or affect the data stored on the suspect machine. It is impossible to use any sort of live capture tool without having some sort of impact on a machine. It is, however, possible to do so in such a way that the first responder is fully aware of the impacts of doing so. This is the standard we must adhere to in this situation.

Loading live capture tools on a system will inevitably cause changes to memory state, as system resources are consumed to perform the capture operation. Therefore, one of the most important decisions a first responder should make is the order in which they elect to capture data in a live acquisition. We'll want to capture things that are less likely to persist first.

Live evidence might not be confined to a computer or other single device. In some cases, directly capturing network traffic from the wire or plucking it from the airwaves will be a necessary course of action. This requires more specialised tools, techniques and an appreciation of packets and protocols. In this chapter we'll review the factors that can play into the decision to perform a live acquisition, the tools that are used to do so and how a first responder should protect themselves from accusations of evidence spoliation arising from their actions.

INCIDENT RESPONSE AND DIGITAL FORENSICS

Before we kick off, an important point: this chapter highlights a key topic at the intersection between the two disciplines that are the focus of this book. A good incident response playbook will make provisions for live acquisition of potential evidence in support of any future investigation. If well planned and executed, it can happen almost seamlessly, with minimal impact on the time needed to enter the incident recovery phase. The goal of any first responder should be to ensure that they are trained, equipped and trusted enough to deliver on this objective.

LIVE ACQUISITION DRIVERS

'Always on' is an expression widely used in information technology circles to describe services that are constantly available. The time when personal internet connectivity was 'on demand' has long since passed in the majority of the world's developed countries. Now, broadband connectivity that runs over dedicated infrastructure, the prevalence of wireless networks and the reduced cost of getting connected mean that an always-on service is the expectation rather than the exception. For us in the forensics field, this means that digital evidence is rarely static. As machines and networks churn away, they can distribute evidence across multiple locations, and bear witness to the creation and demise of volatile evidence. This always-on state is the principal driver of a decision to lead a live acquisition and, while it can be seen as a hindrance to an investigation, it can also be extremely helpful.

Business pressures

While there are numerous technical drivers for a live acquisition, one of the most frequently encountered might be entirely non-technical in nature. Businesses run 24 hours a day, seven days a week. Any unexpected downtime to critical systems can be highly disruptive and costly. A first responder who arrives at a client site to ask for a file server to be powered down to facilitate a powered-off forensics acquisition might be ushered out of the room, even though it might be the most defensible strategy. On the other hand, if the first responder recognises that they might not be able to collect evidence using any technique other than a live acquisition, they are more likely to be accommodated in the incident response process.

Forward-thinking companies should consider forensic acquisition requirements when architecting critical systems, particularly those that store user-generated files. An outage to support a forensic investigation, or eDiscovery, is materially no different than any other kind of unplanned outage. It seems strange that 'we can't tolerate any downtime' is used as an argument against forensic acquisition, yet those systems deemed so critical are not built to be highly available or resilient. Unfortunately this is a common reality, and one that we must work around rather than complain about. In any information security role, complaining is not a strategy.

Having driven around 300 miles to respond to an urgent request for forensics assistance, I found myself in front of a CEO who was furious. He suspected an employee of having shared commercial secrets with a competitor and, to use his own words, would stop at nothing to see them prosecuted. I was told that anything I needed to get the job done would be accommodated.

Having scoped the investigation I requested access to a server that I believed would hold the evidence. Initially, given the support of the CEO and the desire to prosecute, I recommended that a powered-off acquisition take place to ensure that unquestionable forensic integrity was maintained. It just so happened that this server ran a key application for the company. As a result, the IT team were hesitant to shut down the server, even after hours. The CEO was consulted and, once IT explained the situation, his tune changed. 'Anything I needed' transitioned into 'what is the minimum level of disruption we can get away with?'. Ultimately, a live acquisition was performed. A classic example of how quickly things can change when business needs are factored into an investigation.

Full-disk encryption

The rise of encryption as both a legitimate security measure and an anti-forensics technique is an increasingly common factor in the decision to go with a live acquisition. The primary objective of using encryption is to maintain confidentiality of data should it fall into the wrong hands. For instance, encrypting the data stored on a laptop hard drive is considered a pretty standard defence against loss of data occurring as a result of the physical theft of the laptop. Viewed in an encrypted state, and without a valid encryption key, any image of a disk or file is of little use to an investigator. There are different types of encryption, and understanding the nature of the encryption technology in use on a given device is key to devising a strategy to successfully acquire evidence. As it happens, a powered-on machine might afford us our best chance when attempting to work around encryption.

Full-disk encryption works by encrypting the entire contents of a hard drive with the exception of a small portion of the disk that contains information required to boot the operating system. In cases where full-disk encryption is used, a user will typically be asked to provide a key or password to 'unlock' the volume and boot into the operating system. Device drivers provided by the encryption software present the disk as a decrypted volume to the operating system, then encrypt data on the fly as it is committed to the physical disk. The entire file system, including metadata, is encrypted in this approach. Any image of a disk with full-disk encryption that is acquired offline will be unusable as evidence, since the contents of the image will bear no resemblance to the operating system and files the suspect had been interacting with in the logical volume. That is, unless we can acquire a key.

In a corporate environment, it should be possible with a centrally managed full-disk encryption solution for an IT administrator to decrypt a hard drive by way of a backup key (sometimes called an escrow key), or a challenge/response recovery mechanism. If this is the case, the investigator can use traditional powered-off imaging techniques and the disk encryption software's recovery feature together to produce a decrypted version of the disk image. However, it is always recommended that, if a machine is powered on and is known to have full-disk encryption in place, a live acquisition is attempted first. This will allow the investigator to acquire a copy of the decrypted, logical contents of the drive. During a live acquisition the contents of a disk will be changing as temporary files are written and other system files change as the operating system and applications run. This is not ideal from a forensic integrity perspective, but it is better than the alternative.

In cases where a full-disk encryption backup key is not known, or not accessible, a live acquisition affords the investigator the best opportunity to access the decrypted contents of a drive. Again, not ideal by any stretch, but having a logical image to scour for evidence is better than nothing. Also, remember that people make mistakes. It's not uncommon to find that someone has stored a copy of their password or key in a file on the volume that the key or password is used to encrypt, so there is a possibility of using that to later perform a powered-off acquisition. All live acquisitions are, of course, dependent on the machine being powered on or in a standby mode. Standby modes conveniently, for both the user and us, bypass the boot-up process and therefore persist the mounted volume.

Another option is extracting the full-disk encryption key from the computer's RAM. This can be done in a couple of ways depending on the investigator's level of access to the machine: either by using a memory capture tool, if the investigator has access to a valid user session (the preferred way), or by performing what is known as a 'cold boot attack'. A cold boot attack relies on the fact that volatile data can persist in RAM for a few minutes even after a reboot, so it is theoretically possible for an investigator to pull the plug (to mitigate an orderly dismounting of an encrypted volume), boot a machine into a live CD/USB distribution and use a memory capture tool from there. The chances of success using this technique vary, and there is always the risk of corruption to the file system whenever power is abruptly removed from any machine.

RAID

The 'redundant array of independent (or inexpensive) disks' is a regular inhabitant of many a server, and even some desktop configurations. It works by taking multiple physical disks and connecting them to a special controller card that presents them to the machine as if they were one single disk. Different RAID configurations, or levels (to use the appropriate vernacular), are available depending on the number of disks and the level of redundancy required.

- RAID 0: Data is striped across two or more disks with zero fault tolerance.
- RAID 1: Data is mirrored (an exact copy is made) between two disks. If one of the disks in the pair fails, the other can be used to recover the data.
- RAID 5: This requires at least three disks, onto which data is striped; parity information (which is required to rebuild in the event that a drive fails) is distributed across all of the disks in the array. A RAID 5 array can survive the loss of one disk.

Whatever the RAID configuration, one thing is for sure: when a forensic investigator walks up to a machine with a RAID array, unless they're accompanied by someone who knows the configuration, they have no way to tell what level RAID has been implemented. In the case of a RAID 1 array RAID might not be the biggest issue, since there are essentially two copies of the same disk present. However, in a configuration like RAID 0 or 5, where data is striped over multiple disks, reliable forensic examination will be extremely difficult since files will be fragmented between physical disks.

A live acquisition might be considered in such a situation, either by using live acquisition tools on the host operating system or by booting into a live CD/USB-based forensics tool and mounting the array as read only. Acquiring the RAID array from the perspective of the operating system eliminates the challenges associated with having to rebuild the array offline, as the operating system sees the array as a single volume. Also, as discussed earlier, if someone has taken the time to fit out a machine with a RAID array for redundancy, there is a good chance they're going to expect that machine to be always on, which may be the final nail in the coffin for any powered-off acquisition.

That said, powered-off acquisition of a RAID array is entirely possible. Specialist software tools, such as OSForensics[52] and RAID Reconstructor,[53] exist to detect and rebuild RAID arrays from images of individual disks in an array; however, they might not always support every configuration, or every RAID controller driver. The best advice in making the decision on live versus offline acquisition of a RAID array is to learn as much about the array configuration as possible. If you have a comfortable level of knowledge about the array configuration and the hardware and drivers used, and the situation is better suited to an offline acquisition, then by all means go for it.

Fileless malware

Generally speaking, malware is smart. Fileless malware is extremely smart. One of the problems malware creators face in getting their product onto a machine is evading detection technologies, such as antivirus software. These products typically work by examining the content of a file as it is written to disk and comparing it to a known database of malicious file signatures.

Fileless malware aims to avoid these detections by, as you can probably guess, not using any files. It works by leveraging native operating system programs and functions to pull its payload into RAM and operating solely from volatile memory. Nothing is written to disk, and nothing can be compared to a file signature database.

Faced with a machine that appears to be infected, but with no evidence of malware on the disk or in the antivirus logs, fileless malware should be a consideration for the first responder. A live acquisition of memory using a memory capture tool could be one of the only ways to capture the malware in action and fully understand what it is doing.

Fileless malware isn't the only volatile evidence that can be present in RAM, of course. In the next chapter we'll delve into this in detail.

Virtual machines

Essentially an emulation of a machine running within a machine, virtual machines (VMs) have become a standard in many organisations as they strive to reduce costs, build scalability into their systems and increase fault tolerance. A special platform known as a hypervisor is required to run and manage VMs, and there are both open-source and commercial hypervisor offerings available. The nature of virtual machines is that they can often be found moving freely between different physical hardware resources, which from a forensics perspective might sound pretty daunting, but in practice – it isn't all that bad.

Virtual machines, regardless of the type of hypervisor, have one thing in common: they all need to be backed by a disk image, which is a file that represents an entire raw

---

[52] OSForensics (2018) *OSForensics – Rebuild RAID. Rebuild a RAID array from a set of member disk images.* PassMark Software. Available from https://www.osforensics.com/rebuild-raid.html [3 May 2018].
[53] Runtime Software (2018) *RAID Reconstructor – Recover Data from a Broken RAID Array.* Runtime Software. Available from https://www.runtime.org/raid.htm [3 May 2018].

physical disk. In the event that a forensic investigator finds themselves having to work with a VM in an investigation, the very fact that the disk is already an image file can be very advantageous. By their very nature, all forensic collections of VM drive images happen by way of a live acquisition, unless of course they are included in a wider powered-off imaging of the hypervisor's storage.

Once the investigator has located the virtual machine to be acquired using the hypervisor management software, they can determine the path to the machine's disk image(s) (typically a .vmdk format file). Most hypervisors feature a function called 'snapshotting' which allows the VM disk image to be frozen in time. For instance, if a snapshot is triggered in VMware ESXi, a commonly used commercial hypervisor platform, a new copy of the disk image is created, writes are prevented on the original copy and the new image gets promoted to being the primary image in use. Essentially this is a software-based write blocker built right in to the platform.

This is perfect for incident response; the cost in terms of time and hardware when it comes to creating a snapshot for deeper examination is minimal. Of course, we need to stay on top of things to ensure that this step is completed – the flexibility of VMs means it can be just as quick to recreate the VM from scratch, disregarding any potential evidence.

LIVE ACQUISITION TECHNIQUE

To perform a live acquisition, regardless of the tools we're actually using, there are essentially two steps that are taken. First we will introduce our live acquisition utilities to the target system, and secondly we'll output the evidence we're acquiring to a storage location outside the target system for subsequent analysis.

A very common live acquisition setup involves inserting in our suspect machine a removable USB device that has been preloaded with our chosen toolset; this completes step one. The second step would be to select an available location for the image we acquire using those tools. That may well be the same USB device that we're running the tools from, if creating a forensic image file, or a second USB mass storage device if performing a direct disk-to-disk copy.

A variation on this could be the installation of a forensic agent on the target machine as step one, and the creation of the image to a network drive for step two. This technique is more likely to be used in an enterprise setting, where the security and/or IT teams have full control over the target system and are on the same local area network, making remote copying of data more likely to succeed. If remote copy performance is an issue, it is also possible using this technique to acquire selected pieces of data such as running processes (more on this in the next chapter), which alone could provide sufficient evidence for the investigator.

ORDER OF VOLATILITY

In the world of volatile evidence, some sources are more volatile than others. In 2002, the Internet Engineering Task Force (IETF) published *Guidelines for Evidence Collection and Archiving* (RFC 3227), which included a section entitled 'Order of Volatility'.[54] This section lists the order in which digital forensic evidence should be acquired, based on its volatility.

CPU registers and cache

This is the most volatile source on this list, so volatile in fact that in reality it is rarely ever captured as part of an investigation; it is included here for completeness. Data can reside in these locations for mere nanoseconds. A CPU register is a temporary storage area within the CPU that is designed to accept and transfer data extremely quickly. A CPU cache is memory used by the CPU to reduce the load on a machine's main memory. Debugging tools like IDA[55] can be used to set breakpoints to slow down and review the contents of CPU registers at a more manageable pace.

Routing table, ARP cache, process table, kernel statistics, memory

The second entry in the order of volatility is wide-ranging and encapsulates the majority of evidence locations we'll include in our live acquisition strategy. The routing table and Address Resolution Protocol (ARP) cache are both networking-related items and can contain details about the hosts a machine has been communicating with. Since both of these locations are dynamically updated during the course of normal operations, capturing them as soon as possible after an incident is important.

Routing table

A typical routing table includes the following information:

- destination IP addresses or networks;
- the gateway IP address, or interface name if a directly connected resource;
- the metric, or cost, associated with the route – this enables the most efficient route to be selected;
- the outgoing interface the machine will use when forwarding a packet.

Command line utilities are typically used to obtain the routing table. For instance, on Windows the command 'route print' will bring up the table. On Linux and Mac the command 'netstat -rn' will display it. Separate routing tables will be displayed for IPv4 and IPv6 if applicable.

ARP cache

The Address Resolution Protocol is used to map IP addresses to Ethernet hardware addresses, known as media access control (MAC) addresses. The ARP cache on a machine is used to store those mappings, which are dynamically updated by the protocol. A man-in-the-middle attack is a frequent example of an attack that takes advantage of manipulating the ARP cache on a machine. Using spoofed ARP packets an attacker

---

[54] Brezinski, D. and Killalea, T. (2002) *Guidelines for Evidence Collection and Archiving*. IETF. Available from https://www.ietf. org/rfc/rfc3227.txt [3 May 2018].
[55] Hex-Rays (2017) *IDA: About*. Hex-Rays SA. Available from https://www.hex-rays.com/products/ida/ [3 May 2018].

can flood a host and alter the IP address mapping, redirecting traffic through their own machine. This is a big problem if a cleartext protocol such as FTP is used, since the traffic could now be silently sniffed by the attacker. If such an attack is suspected, this could be one of the drivers for a prompt acquisition of the ARP cache since if an attacker stopped their spoofing attack the cache would reset with no trace.

On Windows, Mac and Linux, the ARP cache can be viewed using the 'arp -a' command.

Process table

The process table displays which applications and services are running at a given moment on a machine, who is running them, how long they've been running and how much memory they're using. This information can be vital in determining exactly what is occurring on a machine at the point of acquisition.

To record a copy of the process table on Mac or Linux the 'ps' command is used. On Windows, the Task Manager application includes a process tab which can be used to view running processes. However, the 'tasklist' command line utility is used to export a copy to a .csv file.

When using live acquisition tools it is a good idea to keep an eye on the process table entries. It's not beyond the realm of possibility that some smart malware, or a savvy suspect, has built detection routines to stop their activity if they detect certain security tools running. This includes commonly used live acquisition tools.

Kernel statistics

Operating systems divide physical memory into logical chunks called pages. Kernel statistics are used to keep track of the status of those pages and how they're being allocated. Tools that map physical memory and can tap into these statistics are used to collect them during a live acquisition. Examples of such tools include RAMMap, part of the Sysinternals suite for Windows, and memmap in the Linux world.

Memory

As already touched on a number of times, the contents of RAM have significant forensic value. So much so that we'll be covering this in detail in the entirety of the next chapter.

Temporary file systems

Some file systems are designed to be purged after a reboot, or in response to some other specific event. An example of this would be the '/tmp' folder on a Linux host. Temporary files can contain potential evidence generated by a running process that would otherwise be lost in the event of a reboot. Continuing with our '/tmp' example, this folder is usually writable by anyone, so an attacker, or malicious process, might use this location to store data knowing that it is both an accessible resource and one in which the contents will not persist.

The aforementioned page file (Windows) and swap files (Mac, Linux) are other examples of temporary files of interest.

Presented with a powered-on machine, an investigator should ensure that such temporary files and storage locations are included in the scope of a live acquisition.

Relevant remote logging and monitoring data

In Chapter 4 we noted the importance of remotely storing log data, the idea being that rapidly getting logs off a system which subsequently becomes compromised is incredibly important to ensure the integrity of those logs. This sentiment is further reinforced here, as such logs are closer to the least volatile end of the order of volatility.

Archival media

At the very end of the order of volatility we have removable media such as CDs, backup tapes and USB drives. Not surprising, really, as these are all common examples of non-volatile storage.

As a quick reminder, the forensic investigator or incident responder should always use their own trusted versions of any of the utilities we've listed above. These are known as static binaries.

NETWORK FORENSICS

The networks that connect our machines to others within our homes, offices, enterprises and across the globe via the internet have themselves become highly important sources of digital evidence. The internet is a tremendous equaliser. A teenager sitting in their bedroom can go toe-to-toe with a global enterprise and often win, at least temporarily. As a result, the forensic investigator needs to be equally familiar with ports, packets and protocols as they are with disks and slack space. Deep analysis of network traffic is not solely a post-incident activity, of course; many incidents are detected through proactive monitoring by the way of IDS/IPS systems and wire-data monitoring platforms. However, not everything network security related results in a nice alarm and notification. In fact, the most dangerous, damaging or illegal network activity can blend right in, a tiny signal buried deep within the noise of hundreds of thousands of other signals. With the right skill set it is possible for an incident responder or forensic investigator to isolate, capture and analyse those ever so important flows of data.

Finding evidence on the network

There are two primary sources of data that are significant from a network forensics perspective. The first is the network packets themselves. Machines connect to networks by way of a network interface, which is a piece of hardware or software that takes on the job of passing messages between the machine and other devices on the network. When it comes to hardware-based interfaces, the medium of connection can be either wired or wireless. In either case, monitoring and recording the activity that takes place at these interfaces is possible using various hardware and software tools. Typically, the process of using these tools to record network traffic is called performing a packet capture.

Packets

When data is sent between hosts it is split into chunks and placed into transmission units known as packets. The specific characteristics of a packet vary between the different protocols, but generally speaking they contain a header with routing information to ensure that the packet gets to the correct destination, various other header flags used to convey information about the state of the packet, the actual data being transmitted, information regarding data boundaries, and a means to detect transmission errors.

At this point in the book you might expect to find an overview of the OSI[56] model and pictures of the various packet headers, such as those found in Transmission Control Protocol (TCP) and Internet Protocol (IP) packets. You might even expect to find a list of common TCP port allocations. These are important foundational topics that will allow you to understand how networks function. However, these topics have been beaten to death in many other publications, and I want to dive right into the fun of actually understanding these packets in the real world, from a forensics perspective.

One of the most widely known packet capture tools is a piece of open-source software called Wireshark. Wireshark affords you the ability to capture and analyse the content of a packet in an extremely digestible format. For instance, say you capture an HTTP packet from a client to a server in Wireshark. Selecting that packet will allow you to see the following information:

- The content of the request, including the destination hostname, the HTTP content requested, the HTTP method and any cookies or headers sent along for the ride. This could, of course, include attack traffic if the client is attempting an SQL injection attack on a web server or is partaking in a DDoS attack.

- The TCP packet that encapsulates the HTTP request. This includes information such as source and destination ports, data length, flags and sequence numbers.

- The IP packet that encapsulates the TCP packet. This includes the forensically relevant source and destination IP addresses.

- The Ethernet packet that encapsulates the IP packet. This includes the source and destination hardware MAC addresses, which, as you'll remember from the ARP cache discussion earlier in the chapter, is of forensic relevance.

From one single packet it is easy to see just how much evidence could be present in these modular protocols. Wireshark is one very popular tool for capturing and visualising this data, but there are plenty more such tools, both hardware and software, that can be deployed across an enterprise to permit large-scale continuous packet capture. The expression, 'PCAP or it didn't happen' has long been used jovially between network engineers to suggest that without recorded evidence of a particular network event, it didn't occur. This, of course, is frequently used to deflect blame from the long-suffering network team. Joking aside, there's no reason to think that this same expression might not be used by a defence lawyer in the context of attempting to prove a suspect guilty of a crime.

---

[56] Microsoft Support (2017) *The OSI Model's Seven Layers Defined and Functions Explained*. Microsoft. Available from https://support.microsoft.com/en-us/help/103884/the-osi-model-s-seven-layers-defined-and-functions-explained [3 May 2018].

It is very easy to capture network traffic and create packet captures, but it may not be so easy to capture a specific protocol that you're interested in analysing. For instance, on your home network you're unlikely to find enterprise database protocols.

To overcome this problem the good folks at Wireshark have a wide selection of sample packet captures available for download on their website. These captures can be loaded into Wireshark and other tools that support the PCAP format. Each capture also includes a description of what is included in the file. See https://wiki.wireshark.org/SampleCaptures for the full list.

Additionally, the LMG Forensics Contest site offers a variety of network forensics challenges that make for great practice in the field of network forensics. You can find full details at http://forensicscontest.com/puzzles.

Encrypted traffic

Just as hard disk encryption can present us with a barrier to acquiring stored data, encryption in transit can hamper our ability to gain full visibility into network traffic. With an increasing amount of malware using encryption for its command and control traffic, and a number of incidents where data exfiltration has occurred over an encrypted connection, it is easy to see why this is a concern.

Let's consider a connection secured by Transport Layer Security (TLS), the protocol typically used to secure sensitive information as it is transmitted over the internet. It provides confidentiality by encrypting data using symmetric encryption with a unique key generated when the connection is initiated. It also provides data integrity, using a message authentication code to validate that the content of the transmitted data hasn't been altered in transit. Finally, the TLS protocol uses public-key cryptography to authenticate the identity of the server (or the client and the server) by the way of certificates.

The content of a TLS-encrypted connection can be viewed in the clear in the RAM of both the client and the server after decryption has occurred. This content might be of interest to us from an investigative perspective, so how do we access it? If we have access to the RAM of either the client or the server then a live acquisition of RAM will include that data, so that's one option. Another is to try and get in the middle of the traffic by way of a proxy device. A corporate web-filtering appliance, for example, can use an internal trusted certificate authority to essentially bypass the identity verification. The proxy device needs to do this to enable content inspection for the purposes of detecting malware and performing data loss prevention activities. If the client is configured to trust any certificate issued by that authority, we could use the packet capture and inspection features of a proxy to access decrypted content.

Secure Shell (SSH) is another example of a commonly used traffic encryption protocol. Such connections provide an encrypted tunnel designed to be used to transfer data across untrusted networks using public-key cryptography to authenticate remote computers. It can also use the same public-key cryptography to authenticate users, otherwise a password can be used. A popular feature of SSH is the ability to tunnel data via an encrypted connection. With no way of monitoring the content of the SSH tunnel this is a popular way to hide data exfiltration activities.

Wherever there is an encrypted connection but the investigator has access to neither client nor server, and therefore no access to the decrypted traffic, it can still be possible to make statements about what that connection might be being used for. Wire-data tools like ExtraHop or ntop (see Chapter 1) provide insight into the amount of data being transferred, and to where, even when that data is encrypted. For example, if I saw an SSH connection to a remote IP address on a web server not related to my business, with a few short bursts of data followed by a larger persistent transfer, I could surmise that I am looking at some commands being sent, followed by prolonged data exfiltration.

Wireless

The medium may have changed, but the principle is still the same. In wireless networks, packets are transmitted through the air using radio waves rather than being confined to a cable. When investigating wireless networks from a forensics perspective, using a wireless adapter in a special mode known as promiscuous mode allows a computer to see all the packets on the network, not just those addressed to it.

Logs

The second commonly sought-after source of network forensic data, network traffic logs, differ from the raw packets, but they can still offer valuable insight. The analogy I like to use is this: in a traditional crime, we might not be able to obtain a recording of the phone call but we might still be able to get phone records to show that a suspect called a victim. The recording would be a packet capture, whereas the phone records would be network traffic logs.

Logs can be obtained from a machine or from a piece of network hardware such as a switch, firewall or router. It is good practice to ensure that all logs from these sources are offloaded to remote locations, such as a syslog server, for the same reasons that we get operating system and application logs off computers as soon as possible. Log buffers on network hardware do not typically allow for expansive historical recording of network activity, and, as always, any self-reported data could be tampered with if left on a device that becomes compromised.

Critical network services such as the Domain Name System (DNS) or Dynamic Host Configuration Protocol (DHCP) can also record logs that are highly valuable in both forensics and incident response. There is nothing quite like catching remote access malware by detecting requests to its command and control domain at the DNS level.

Network log files can be parsed and compared to other evidence items to build an accurate picture of the communications a suspect machine was involved in for the purposes of your investigation.

SUMMARY

In this chapter we've studied the wide variety of factors that may force us to perform a live acquisition. This includes both technical and non-technical pressures such as full-disk encryption or a requirement from the business.

We also introduced the topic of network forensics, and the importance of being able to shift from the mindset of collecting evidence that is relatively static to working with highly important evidence contained in packets moving across the wire.

Volatile evidence is a topic that we'll continue to study in the next chapter, on memory forensics.

12 MEMORY FORENSICS

Virtualisation, smart malware, ephemeral containers, full-disk encryption – just some of the reasons that being able to navigate acquired memory images has become such an important skill for digital forensic investigators and incident responders alike. An incident can occur completely within the confines of volatile memory. Like the mythical bullet made of ice, the suspect intends volatile evidence to simply melt away without a trace once a victim has been claimed.

Unlike analysis of persistent file systems on hard disks and other archival media, the nature of volatile memory means that its contents are less structured. If looking for digital evidence on a hard disk is like looking for a needle in a haystack with the help of a map of the haystack, the same activity using volatile memory requires looking for that needle without any guidance. To add additional complexity to the mix, that haystack may as well be in the middle of a hurricane, since the contents of memory are constantly moving and changing with all the activity on the machine. The act of simply looking at the contents of memory alters the contents of the memory. The memory forensics discipline is young, evolving and increasing in importance. In this chapter we'll expand upon the live acquisition concepts introduced previously, exploring in detail the process of capturing and analysing the contents of volatile memory.

I want to point out that the topic of memory forensics alone is enough to fill many books. There are many subdisciplines involved that can be invoked when considering the topic. When I speak of the topic in this book, I'm mainly considering it from the perspective of a forensic investigator working to supplement an investigation with additional evidence seized from volatile memory.

UNDERSTANDING MEMORY DEVICES

Before we delve into how we capture and process memory, let's take a moment to understand exactly what we'll need to capture. Operating systems differ on how they represent memory objects, and therefore digital forensic investigators have to be aware of these differences before they tackle an acquisition. Just as with a forensically sound image of a persistent storage device, the objective is to obtain a bit-by-bit image file containing the contents of volatile memory.

A quick terminology note: images of memory are frequently referred to as 'memory dumps'.

Microsoft Windows

The Windows operating system presents physical memory as a device known as '\\.\ PhysicalMemory'; a second device, '\\.\DebugMemory', is also available. These devices can be acquired in order to create a raw image of the memory contents or an image formatted for use in a debugger, respectively. There's a sting in the tail, however: as of Windows Server 2003 Service Pack 1, user-space access to this device was curtailed; only kernel-space access is permitted. Therefore the live acquisition software tool must install a device driver to be able to access the memory entirely. This requires both full access to the machine and administrative privileges. That obviously makes a lot of sense from a security perspective. Limiting direct access to RAM from programs that are not part of the operating system can only serve to bolster defences against malicious applications. This is just another example of how security protections that we need and advocate as security professionals can require perseverance when the shoe is on the other foot.

Launching a tool from kernel space also allows for more complete results, as a number of applications use anti-debugging technologies to protect the content of their memory sets from being accessed by other user-space processes. Anyone who has ever used a 'game trainer' to cheat on a computer game has likely directly manipulated memory to give themselves extra credits or some other form of advantage. In the modern era of online games, where real money is often exchanged in return for content, and people play against each other in real time, it would figure that the developers of those games would want to protect them from the same type of manipulation. That's where memory protection mechanisms come in, providing another obstacle for us to navigate.

Linux

In the Linux world, just as disk drives are represented as a file, so too is memory. Two files are typically used to gain access to memory, namely '/dev/mem' and '/proc/kcore'. The first of these contains the raw physical contents of memory, while the second contains those same contents but in the core file format used by debugging tools.

Mac

Apple's design philosophy for their macOS operating system typically means that they like to 'hide' most of the behind-the-scenes functionality of the operating system from the end user. This philosophy is in full swing when it comes to accessing the raw contents of physical memory. There is no native way to do this, so third-party software must be introduced. Many Mac memory acquisition tools, including OSXPMem,[57] load a driver to virtually recreate the /dev/mem device found in other Unix-type hosts. This of course means that root permissions are needed, which can be problematic.

Beginning with Mac OS X (the predecessor to macOS) version 10.9, Apple implemented compression for physical memory. The aim of this was to reduce the amount of swap space used, improving performance and battery life for mobile devices. From the

---

[57] Stuettgen, J. (2018) *OSXPMem – Mac OS X Physical Memory Acquisition Tool*. GitHub. Available from https://github.com/ wrmsr/pmem/tree/master/OSXPMem [3 May 2018].

forensic investigator's perspective, this just means that physical memory becomes even more important since more potential evidence is crammed into physical RAM rather than being committed to disk by way of a swap file.

What can memory tell us?

Given all these constraints and challenges, one might be forgiven for questioning whether acquisition of physical memory is worth the effort. I can assure you that it most certainly is, and in some cases it's absolutely critical. Let's explore some of the useful artefacts that can be found in volatile memory.

Running process information

Not all processes will be revealed through inspection of the system utilities typically used to track them. In some cases, rogue processes such as rootkit-based malware will alter these utilities in an effort to hide its activity from prying eyes. Our best shot of detecting such malware is to carve through a raw dump of all physical memory looking for related artefacts.

Outside malware, process information can be relevant to a number of other types of case. It can be used to supplement the evidence found on a hard drive to give more context. For example, we might find evidence of peer-to-peer file-sharing software being installed on a machine. We can supplement our finding by confirming that a process associated with the software was running when the machine was imaged.

The names and types of files that are opened by a process can also be discovered, which again plays nicely into getting the full picture by allowing us not only to see that a file was accessed, but also to understand what was accessing it.

Passwords

Passwords that would otherwise be encrypted are often found in the clear in memory. This is especially true when it comes to full-disk encryption passphrases and keys. I don't really need to elaborate on why this is so very useful.

Contents of open windows

As I type these words into a document they're also being held in my computer's volatile memory. I'm a typical Mac user, so that means I also have around 5,000 application windows open at the same time. The contents of those windows will also be resident in memory – very useful if you consider that I have chat applications, terminal sessions and web pages open which, thanks to my full-disk encryption, will all be a lot harder to acquire the second I power down.

Network connection information

Before data transmitted across the network leaves via a network interface controller, it has to transit through memory. Therefore, the data itself and details about where it is going, such as IP addresses and ports, can all be found in a memory image. Very useful for determining if a process was transmitting data across a network.

In the midst of an incident response scenario or an investigation, a common investigative task is determining why exactly two hosts are communicating over a network. Of course, the majority of network traffic is perfectly legitimate, but there is nothing like an unexplained encrypted conversation occurring on a random high TCP port number to get the information security professional paranoia flowing. This feeling is amplified when you're looking at a machine you believe has been compromised.

Time may not allow a full memory capture and subsequent offline examination, so you'll need to be able to use a different live analysis technique to get to your answer.

- Unix-like

  - For Mac and Linux, a couple of commands can get you there. The first is 'lsof', which stands for 'list open files'. When used with the '-i' flag, the lsof command can be used to home in on a specific IP address or port of interest and will allow you to see the user and process IDs associated with a given connection. Running 'lsof -i :443' will show you all connections associated with port 443, commonly used for TLS communication.

  - Once you have a process ID, you can translate that into a friendlier process name using a second command, 'ps'. Say, for instance, we wanted to figure out which application is associated with process ID 1111 – we'd run the command 'ps -fp 1111'. In this example, if we saw the name of a web browser communicating over port 443 it would be much less suspect than an otherwise unknown application.

- Windows

  - The same results can be achieved in Microsoft Windows, again by way of a couple of command line commands. First of all, the netstat command. Executing 'netstat -a -n -o' will show a list of all active connections and the process ID associated with each.

  - To look up the process name associated with that process ID, the command 'tasklist' can be issued from the command prompt. This will return a table showing both process IDs and names.

Encrypted traffic, but in the clear

We're all familiar with the use of TLS to encrypt connections to web applications when exchanging sensitive data. To anyone outside the machine, and even if capturing from a network interface controller (NIC), those connections appear to contain nothing but incomprehensible data. The only place you'll be able to find a decrypted version is in the memory space used by the user's web browser.

Decrypted versions of files

If an encrypted file is open then a decrypted version of that file can be found in memory. This applies to both files encrypted at the file level, such as documents and spreadsheets, and those encrypted by way of full-disk encryption.

CAPTURING

The tools used to capture volatile memory exist in both hardware and software form. Hardware memory capture cards that connect directly to a machine's Peripheral Component Interconnect (PCI) Express bus can bypass the limitations of operating system lock screens and reduce the impact on running memory by connecting directly to the memory to be acquired. Direct memory access is a feature of the PCI Express standard. However, such hardware can come with a price tag that places it out of reach for some practitioners, and as a result software-based acquisition tools are more frequently used.

File formats

When you capture a memory image you have a choice as to which format you save it in. Typically, investigators stick to the standard EnCase evidence file (.e01) format, as they know that'll allow for maximum portability between forensic suites. However, other formats of an image might be useful so that they can be explored using standard, platform-specific debugging tools. We're going to cover memory analysis frameworks shortly, and one of the common themes with the majority of these is that they'll support a combination of raw, forensics-specific and debug dump file formats. The best advice is to always acquire a full raw copy of memory, since it is possible to convert these into debug formats later if required.

Generally speaking, a captured memory image will be offloaded to a removable storage device connected to the target machine. USB devices are frequently used for this purpose, which again require the investigator to make note of the impact of connecting the device to the target machine. Some acquisition tools also permit the memory image to be shipped to a remote host via a network connection.

Memory acquisition tools

Let's take a look at some commonly used software tools, both commercial and open source, that are capable of capturing the contents of volatile memory.

FTK Imager

FTK Imager by AccessData is capable of capturing memory on a Windows machine; however, at the time of writing it runs in user space and therefore cannot access protected memory. FTK Imager is free to download.

Belkasoft RAM Capturer

This tool is another free product capable of acquiring RAM from a Windows system. It uses a device driver to bypass user-space limitations; however, it has more impact on the operating system because of this.

OSXPMem

The OSXPMem utility allows for memory acquisition in macOS from both user and kernel space via a bundled driver. The tool is part of the open-source Rekall forensics framework, which is a widely used toolset for the acquisition and analysis of memory from a wide variety of operating systems.

dd

A renowned Linux command line utility, dd is a highly versatile tool and can be used to create bitstream copies of files, disks and physical memory. Using it against the physical memory device in Linux will produce a user-space-sourced copy of memory, so some protected memory regions will not be included in the image.

Fmem

A Linux kernel module, Fmem creates a new virtual device on a machine called '/dev/ fmem'. The investigator or first responder can then use dd against this virtual device without running into the same restrictions that would be present trying to directly obtain physical memory through '/dev/mem'.

Linux Memory Grabber

This tool is a script that attempts to automate a number of the steps that must be taken to acquire memory from a Linux system. The tool is designed to be run from a USB stick, and automates the installation of kernel modules and creates a profile for the open-source Volatility Framework, a memory forensics suite. Once the USB drive is mounted a single command can be issued to do all the work, making it suitable for folks who might not be as proficient in Linux. That said, a golden rule is to always understand the impact you're making on a system, so an investigator should still be aware of what they're doing whenever they run any tool.

VMware

In a VMware environment it is possible to snapshot memory directly using the built-in utilities in the VSphere client.

Crash dumps and hibernation files

A slightly different technique to obtaining a copy of memory involves working with dump files generated during a computer crash. We're all familiar with the so-called blue screen of death (BSOD) in Microsoft Windows. When this occurs, the default condition is for the operating system to dump some memory relevant for troubleshooting into a file on the hard drive for debugging purposes. This typically isn't a complete memory image, given sizing concerns; however, it is possible to have Windows capture the complete contents of memory as part of this dumping process. As a result, security researchers have demonstrated techniques that force a crash and subsequently produce a memory dump as a mechanism for collecting volatile data. Obviously, this has a considerable impact on the target system, but the tools used to cause the crash aren't trying to access memory directly and hence they're less likely to be detected by anti-forensic measures. This can include malicious processes, such as malware, that are actively looking for known forensics tools being loaded into memory, so that they can hide traces of nefarious activity. Some argue that this makes crash dumping a more reliable approach to memory forensics.

A similar, yet less dramatic, approach is to leverage the operating system hibernation features. Hibernation allows a computer to power down, yet be returned to the same condition the next time it is powered up, with the same programs open and processes running. Hibernation works by saving a copy of the memory contents to a hibernation file on a machine's hard drive. The contents can then be imaged along with the hard disk using standard acquisition tools. The downsides to this approach include potentially overwriting evidence in the slack space of a suspect hard drive and, in cases where disk encryption is used, not being able to access the file after the machine is powered off.

ANALYSIS

One we've captured an appropriate image from our target platform, it's time for the fun to begin. There is no single way to analyse a memory image. Indeed, it is a complex topic that can mean a variety of different things to different people, depending on their objectives. In some cases it can be as simple as searching for text strings in memory, or carving out files. In others it can involve a complex reconstruction of the state of the computer at a given time, perhaps for the purposes of reverse engineering a piece of malware.

There are a few things that anyone who is looking at a memory dump from a security perspective will have in common. For one, they'll understand the structures in physical memory, and the significance of several operating-system-specific memory locations. They'll also be aware of a couple of prominent memory analysis forensics frameworks and their capabilities.

In early 2017 security researchers at Kaspersky Lab uncovered a strain of fileless malware that was estimated to be affecting over 140 companies globally, mainly in the banking and telecommunications sectors. The malware was completely resident in memory and leveraged legitimate Windows utilities such as netsh to create a tunnel back to a command and control server operated by the unknown attackers.

The malware also took advantage of Meterpreter, a frequently seen in-memory payload that forms part of the Metasploit framework, and Windows PowerShell. An open-source memory string extraction tool called mimikatz was also bundled into the malware; this tool is used to extract passwords and Kerberos tickets from Windows memory.

Upon reboot of a compromised host all traces of the malware were removed from the machine. The only way that Kaspersky were able to analyse and reconstruct the malware was through analysis of memory images acquired from infected machines.

Exploring memory images

Before we open up a physical memory image we should first understand what we're about to see. The short answer to this is a collection of seemingly unstructured data, a cursory examination of which will reveal human-readable strings and other binary files. It is entirely possible to run file-carving tools over a memory image and extract photographs, for example. This can be useful, of course, but ultimately the real value of memory images will be if we can add some structure to that unstructured data. The ability to tell the difference between allocated memory in use by a running process versus unallocated memory that contains data from a terminated process can dramatically alter our understanding of the contents of an image. This is where having a memory analysis framework comes into play. Tools like Volatility and Rekall add structures based on an operating system profile. Each operating system will use physical memory in a different fashion, and those profiles bridge the gap between a raw image and something that can be parsed more effectively.

The key to understanding how an operating system allocates memory to a process relies on familiarity with the concept of virtual memory management. As one of its core functions a modern operating system provides a process with an abstracted view of memory resources. Processes do not access physical memory directly; instead, a virtual memory layer is presented, with its own addressing scheme. Each process uses its own isolated virtual memory, which makes for a more secure operating system. If all processes had access to all physical memory, things could get very messy very quickly. Pages in virtual memory, typically 4 kB in size, are allocated to a process as needed. The operating system then places those virtual pages into physical memory page frames. Crucially, the mappings between virtual and physical memory locations are stored in a table known as a page table. Generally speaking, there is a page table for each process. Sometimes, multiple page tables will point different virtual addresses to the same physical address in RAM, allowing processes to share the contents of memory. This is known as shared memory.

The page tables that manage the mappings are also present in RAM, and therefore will be included in any complete memory image that we acquire. Memory analysis frameworks can extract these tables and rebuild the virtual to physical mappings, which is how they allow us to better reconstruct the state of memory at the moment of acquisition.

Memory forensic analysis tools

The really neat thing about memory forensics is that it appeals to a wide variety of people, each with different objectives. There is a huge community of some of the smartest computer scientists you could ever wish to meet who're all super interested in malware analysis, for example. A positive outcome of this is that the majority of these folks make their tools available by way of open-source projects, or as plugins for other open-source projects. All of a sudden, the highly complex world of memory forensics is accessible to a much wider array of personnel thanks to these tools.

Two prime examples of this are the Volatility framework and the Rekall framework (which started off as a fork of Volatility, but has been mostly rewritten). The most-cited difference between the frameworks is that Rekall has a web GUI, whereas Volatility is solely a command line tool. These two frameworks use a community-driven array of operating system profiles and custom plugins for extracting the types of information discussed earlier. For instance, both frameworks have a plugin called 'pslist' that will display a list of all the running processes found in memory. It makes tremendous sense to practise with one or more of these frameworks before you use them in a real case. For this purpose there are plenty of memory images available for download and exploration online.

Commercial forensic software suites such as EnCase and FTK also support memory analysis via their respective GUIs, including the ability to pull out running process lists, data regarding active network connections and lists of open files, and bookmark them just as if they were any other sort of on-disk artefact.

Real-time memory analysis

A new generation of tools, aimed specifically at incident responders, which use an agent installed on a machine to track the contents of memory, are increasing in popularity. The idea is that these tools maintain an overview of running processes, open sockets and all the other good stuff that memory can offer. The agents report memory activity back to a central console, which uses a combination of signatures and threat intelligence data to alert on suspicious activity occurring in memory. In this vein, the creators of Rekall have recently released an agent designed to be pre-deployed to machines to acquire memory remotely.

We can expand the usage of such tools into the forensics realm, as many of them support the subsequent capture and remote storage of the contents of RAM. Examples of products with this ability include AccessData Enterprise[58] and EnCase Endpoint Investigator.[59]

SUMMARY

In this chapter we introduced the complex topic of memory forensics. Volatile memory is an area worthy of exploration and analysis as smarter malware and more advanced attackers use its rapidly changing contents as cover for their activities.

We talked about the tools that allow us to capture the contents of memory on various platforms, and how they overcome some of the limitations imposed by those platforms to access raw memory structures.

We'll move from one relatively modern forensics technique to another in the next chapter, as we explore the topic of performing forensics work in a cloud infrastructure.

---

[58] AccessData (2018) *AD Enterprise*. AccessData. Available from https://accessdata.com/products-services/ad-enterprise [3 May 2018].

[59] OpenText (2018) *EnCase Endpoint Investigator – Remote Forensic Security Solution*. OpenText Corporation. Available from https://www.guidancesoftware.com/encase-endpoint-investigator [3 May 2018].

13 CLOUD FORENSICS

There has been a significant increase in the number of organisations using cloud computing resources over the last decade, the result of a perfect storm of faster wide area network connectivity, the coming of age of virtualisation technologies and the need to architect systems in a way that will rapidly scale up to meet demand. A move to the cloud is often seen as a way to reduce the up-front costs associated with building out an IT infrastructure.

For a start-up, starting out in a cloud means that they can get by with the minimum amount of resources to develop their product, adding more compute nodes and storage as needed. For an established company, a common setup is that a cloud offering is used to supplement an existing 'traditional' data centre. Although a minefield of marketing terminology, clichés and a seemingly endless supply of proponents and opponents, the cloud is fundamentally built on the same underlying hardware and software that we're used to. The difference is the level of access we have to the equipment, which can vary based on the cloud model in use. As a digital forensic investigator or incident responder, this can have a fundamental impact on how we approach our work. In some cases the cloud makes the job harder, in others it makes it a lot easier. The good news is that no cloud model makes the job utterly impossible, as this chapter will discuss.

CLOUD COMPUTING TERMINOLOGY

Before we delve into how we adapt our forensic and incident response processes to handle cloud environments, we should take the time to understand the different types of cloud offering. The term 'cloud' can be used interchangeably to represent a number of different deployment models and service offerings. Therefore, the absolute first step when looking to conduct a digital forensics investigation that includes a cloud element is uncovering exactly what type of cloud you're working with.

Deployment models

The three most commonly used enterprise cloud deployment models are described below. Factors that determine which model is adopted by a particular organisation include security and compliance requirements, cost considerations and the type of workload being transferred to a cloud deployment.

Public cloud

The term 'public cloud' is used to describe cloud computing services that are offered to the general public over the internet. A service provider takes responsibility for operating the cloud infrastructure, including the networking, storage and computation, while the customer is responsible for the software and applications they run on that infrastructure. Amazon Web Services (AWS), Microsoft Azure and Google Cloud Platform are all examples of public cloud service providers.

Private cloud

A private cloud is a collection of computing resources that are used by a single tenant, typically an organisation. Private clouds can be hosted either internally or externally, and may be entirely operated by a third party. If you think this sounds like a traditional on-premises or co-located data centre, you're spot on. It is essentially just that, but in order to 'qualify' as a cloud it'll typically come bundled with a layer that provides orchestration of resources. For example, a private cloud could be used by a product development team to build, test and deploy their application without intervention by a dedicated hosting operations team.

Hybrid cloud

A hybrid cloud is simply a combination of public and private cloud resources being used together in some fashion. This situation is common in established companies, who may choose to use private resources for some functions and public resources for others.

Cloud computing services

The cloud can be used to deliver a single application, or can run almost every aspect of an organisation's information technology programme. It is this scalability and flexibility that makes it so popular. As an organisation's cloud footprint scales, changes to security policies and procedures must be made to reflect the organisation's situation. This is especially true when it comes to the incident response playbook. If you're in a public cloud, while the ultimate goals of an incident response playbook are the same, how you go about achieving them on a tactical level will be different. For instance, you might not be able to use a traditional hardware firewall to isolate a network segment in a public cloud infrastructure, but it's likely that you'll be able to do so using an API.

Infrastructure as a service

In this offering, frequently abbreviated as IaaS, service providers use virtualisation technologies to carve out networking, compute and storage resources from their vast pools of hardware. Customers then use APIs and remote management software to provision and operate their virtualised resources that sit atop the physical infrastructure.

Platform as a service

This offering, known as PaaS, is designed to take away some of the complexities involved with managing an application's underlying infrastructure. Rather than maintaining virtual machines and other infrastructure components, a customer of a PaaS will provide the application source code to be run on the platform and the service provider will take care of the rest.

Software as a service

In the world of SaaS, a service provider takes care of hosting an application for a customer to connect to remotely. SaaS applications are typically accessed via a web browser, and can include human resources information systems (HRIS), finance applications, office and productivity software, and customer relationship management applications.

In Figure 13.1 you'll see a visual representation of the three cloud computing offerings just discussed, and how responsibility is shared between the service provider and the customer.

Figure 13.1 The split in responsibility between cloud service provider and customer

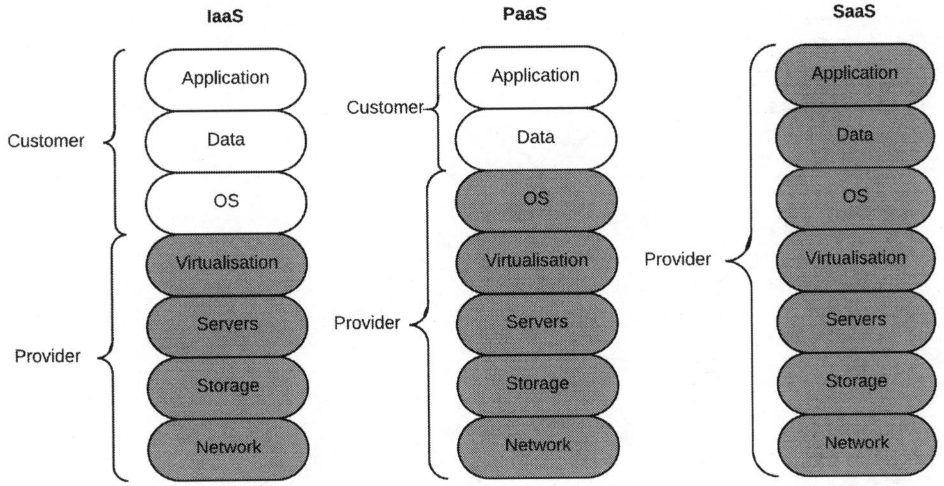

ACQUISITION IN THE CLOUD

Unless you're dealing with a private cloud fully owned and operated by the organisation affected by an incident, or requesting an investigation, physical access to resources is not going to be an option. This is the most obvious difference between digital forensics and incident response in the cloud versus traditional infrastructure. If you tried to walk into a data centre running any of the 'big three' public clouds to perform a hard disk acquisition there would be more than a few barriers in the way. Not only would you face significant resistance from the physical security measures in place at these facilities, it would be nearly impossible to find the disk containing the image of your acquisition target! Therefore, a new approach is needed.

Before an incident or investigation

Regardless of the deployment model or service offering used by an organisation, there is significant mileage to be had in performing detailed security-incident-related due diligence with a cloud provider before purchasing, moving to or building in their cloud offering. I'm not talking about the standard vendor security questionnaire, either – we should be asking direct questions about security incident response procedures, including determining who is responsible for what, and building relationships with cloud service provider security teams. These folks can be a tremendous ally in the event of an incident, and serve as a go-between to get you, as the first responder, access to information that might not be so accessible via traditional means. As an information security professional, the most important thing to remember when a cloud service is discussed is that you can always outsource the function, but you can never outsource the risk. A company running on-premises infrastructure can experience an incident that results in a data breach just as a company running a cloud infrastructure can experience an incident that results in a data breach. The end result is the same, and the lasting impacts on that company and its customers are just as damaging.

Amazon S3 (Simple Storage Service) is the primary data storage service offering from AWS. The S3 service is used to store many trillions of objects on behalf of AWS customers, and is used both to store data that is considered private, and subject to access controls, and data that is publicly accessible. A policy engine is used to set appropriate permissions on S3 buckets, a bucket being the highest-level organisational unit for a collection of folders and files in the service. S3 buckets are configured as private by default.

Throughout 2017, a number of organisations experienced incidents caused by inappropriately set S3 bucket permissions. Data that should have remained in the default private, access-controlled state had accidentally been configured with public permissions settings by the AWS customer organisation, meaning that anyone who found the URL unique to the bucket could access the files contained within it.

One company affected by such a mistake garnered particular attention because of the nature of the business they were in. Election Systems and Software, a voting machine supplier, confirmed that records pertaining to 1.8 million voters in the Chicago area were accidentally exposed via a misconfigured S3 bucket. Fortunately, the company was able to confirm that no ballot information was included in the data, but a great deal of other sensitive personal information was.

Given the increased scrutiny around voting system integrity and security following the 2016 US Presidential election, this was an embarrassing slip-up for a manufacturer of such systems.

IaaS forensics

It is crucial that an organisation choosing to use the cloud is deeply familiar with the logging options for the various service offerings that they are about to invest in. All major IaaS vendors allow for deep levels of monitoring and auditing, being acutely aware of the leap of faith some customers perceive they are taking and wanting to allay some fears. Just because those features are there doesn't mean that they'll automatically be enabled. As part of a cloud build-out an organisation should, of course, configure and, perhaps most importantly, budget for those features to be running constantly. You can log every single network flow that transits a virtual network, making network forensics a blast, but those logs still have to live somewhere. The pay-as-you-go model adopted by most IaaS providers means there might be a charge per log message, and then a further storage charge for the logs themselves. Those changes might be measured in fractions of a penny initially, but as more and more workloads make their way into the cloud they can build up significantly. That typically leads to the dreaded 'the cloud is getting too expensive; do we really need all this forensic data?' conversation.

Personally, I've seen both sides of the coin. I managed a security operations team responsible for incident response and investigations at a very large SaaS company for a number of years, and I've also spent time investigating incidents with origins or evidence in SaaS platforms. I can honestly say that the most important factor when working with a SaaS provider during an incident is the people you can get connected with. There is a mutual understanding between security teams that we'll help each other out when we can. The challenge is usually breaking through the layers of first-line support or account management to get in touch with that right person at the SaaS provider.

When I was working at a SaaS provider I adopted a mantra of 'the convenience of the cloud, but with on-premises level of detail'. I worked with customer security teams to get data out of our platform and into their SIEM solutions. This helped to keep them just as informed as if they were running an application in their data centre, and resulted in a great customer experience. It also improved security for all customers because it meant that, by way of the customer security team, we had more eyes on more events.

I'm not really much of a networker, but I will say that I can think of at least three occasions when a direct connection of mine, or a 'friend of a friend', helped to get me in touch with a security professional at a given company to get me better information for use in an investigation. If you ever find yourself thinking that a SaaS platform should automatically be removed from scope, or is too big to care about your investigation, don't give up. Talk to people at the company – you might be pleasantly surprised.

Cattle, not pets

As previously discussed, one of the most attractive features of hosting with an IaaS provider operating a public cloud is the ability to rapidly scale up available resources when demand warrants it. Businesses like this because it saves them money, but scaling up is not how you save money. You save money by scaling back those resources once the demand has passed. Suppose that an incident requiring forensic investigation occurs during peak hours but isn't discovered until a few hours later. The compute instance which processed the request that triggered the incident might not even exist any more. What does that mean for us from an evidence perspective?

Architecting for the cloud, and rapid scaling, requires a change in how we think about computing resources. A commonly used analogy to describe the difference in this approach versus traditional architectures was allegedly coined by former Microsoft engineer Bill Baker. Baker's analogy was that we should stop treating servers as pets, and start treating them as cattle. For instance, in many organisations if a server breaks down it is all hands on deck to make it feel loved, fix it and nurse it back to health. Conversely, if a cloud-based instance breaks it is unceremoniously taken out the back, shot and replaced by another 'cow' that looks exactly the same. Now, I know people who have pet cows, so I'm sure they wouldn't agree with this analogy completely, but hopefully you get the gist.

The compute functions of the cloud instance are built in such a way that they can be deployed, do their job when they are needed, and destroyed when they aren't, without data loss or adversely affecting the overall function they're involved in. Where persistent storage is needed, perhaps for a user-uploaded file or to maintain the state of a user's session, that information is stored away from the compute instance, perhaps in a data storage service or a hosted database platform. Going back to our evidence acquisition approach, this means that we have to get out of the mindset of a specific server being the sole source of all evidence, and understand the dependencies between the various services used in the IaaS platform. We might have network-layer logs, a file on a data storage platform and a database transaction log from a hosted database platform that provide just as much evidence as any file system when combined. All IaaS platforms will allow us to export and hash those files to prove forensic integrity if questioned.

Understanding each intricate detail of each cloud service is probably not a realistic goal for an investigator who works on multiple cases in a broad spectrum of environments; that said, cloud services are becoming as ubiquitous as SATA hard disks in some industries. Moving in step with technology trends is nothing new to digital forensics, and this is no exception. All of the major IaaS players offer something wonderful: a tier where registered users can play with their services for free if certain parameters are met. It could be that the number of CPUs in an instance are limited, or the amount of data processed by a service is kept under a certain level, but despite that it is still very possible to get a general idea of the offerings and how they can be configured. Before going into a real scenario that requires acquisition of data hosted in a public cloud, practise by playing in a free tier.

Forensics by default

The acquisition scenario described in the previous sections, roughly summarised as deconstructing a cloud deployment and picking up the various chunks of evidence from the various persistent services and logging tools, is likely to be the most commonly available approach to the first responder or forensic investigator. We're still in the relatively early stages of cloud adoption, and there is still much work to do for the majority of cloud customers in terms of fully embracing all of an IaaS provider's features. That said, there are an increasing number of cloud adopters who are in a more mature phase in their cloud deployment life cycle. The world's largest online video streaming company, Netflix, runs out of AWS, and is widely believed to be the largest AWS customer, storing petabytes of data and pushing out a tremendous amount of traffic at any given moment. Netflix have been in AWS to some extent for almost 10 years, and as a result have some pretty good experience with the platform. Not only did they migrate there, a lot of their products and operational tools have been built specifically for AWS over the years. Netflix's security team has even open-sourced some of their cloud-specific security tools. One such tool is known as Security Monkey, which hooks into both the AWS and Google Cloud Platform (used by Netflix as a backup) APIs to monitor for configuration changes that could introduce a security incident.

Security Monkey is a great example of a tool that can greatly assist a security team working in a cloud environment. Where things get especially powerful, however, is when those same APIs used to alert also take other smart actions designed specifically to benefit forensics investigation and incident response. Orchestration engines, such as AWS Lambda, can be used to create automated jobs that take input from one service and perform an action on another. It is entirely possible, for example, to react to a security incident indicator by isolating an instance, creating a snapshot image of both instance RAM and attached virtual disks, moving that snapshot into remote storage and notifying the first responder. The first responder will, of course, show up to an incident that is already contained, with forensics acquisition run by default. There are also third-party commercial products designed specifically to run these types of task in any cloud platform. It takes a while to get to this point, trust me, but it is possible. This forensics-by-default approach could be the future of cloud-based incident response, and it is what we've been pushing for all along!

People still have pets, though

While there are plenty of cattle, the cloud still has more than its fair share of pets: compute instances that run continually and are essentially just classic virtual machines running on someone else's hardware. In these cases, live acquisition techniques should be mirrored as closely as possible. An investigator probably won't be able to simulate the insertion of a live CD or USB in most cases, but there are ways to get tools into a virtual machine even in an IaaS public cloud. These typically involve using a shared network volume that stores the tools and static binaries. When working with clients who have a cloud presence I like to give them a standard machine image full of tools that would otherwise be on a live CD/USB, which I can have them run up alongside the target instance and connect to that resource from the target.

In addition to this approach, public cloud IaaS providers typically permit snapshotting, with or without rebooting. A 'without-reboot' snapshot is equivalent to a live acquisition, and a snapshot with a reboot is more like a traditional powered-off imaging process. The same decisions must be made when choosing which snapshot method to use: powered off is likely to pass the forensic integrity test if challenged, but powered on is likely to contain extra volatile evidence. Given that most instances running in the cloud are likely to be powered on by their very nature, it is likely that a without-reboot snapshot will be chosen most of the time. Forensics rules such as the ACPO guidelines translate well to the cloud in this scenario, and so the investigator is free to follow them.

PaaS forensics

When using a platform as a service an organisation has handed over control of more of the underlying operational infrastructure, such as servers, storage, networking and firewalls, to the service provider. A PaaS customer typically wants to be able to concentrate on building and deploying apps rather than running them and having to worry about issues such as operating system maintenance, load balancing or managing storage hardware. Therefore the risks to the PaaS customer are centred on their intellectual property (their code) and the data they're processing. For instance, it is more likely for a first responder at a PaaS customer to have to deal with a remote attack against their application than patching a critical operating system vulnerability – the security team at the PaaS provider should be taking care of the operating system patching responsibilities.

Our acquisition abilities will be limited to those resources to which we have direct access, so once again the best strategy is to build apps that are designed specifically for the platform they're running on. If logging that would typically be available at the network layer is not present in the platform then build it into the application and capture it during the normal course of operations. Forensic readiness takes on a whole new meaning in these types of service arrangements.

But what if we're arriving on the scene after an incident has occurred, the PaaS application wasn't built for forensic readiness, and the PaaS provider doesn't offer a great deal of monitoring data in their platform? Aside from grabbing any relevant files from the customer side of the equation, the next best strategy is to pick up the phone, call the provider and ask to get in touch with a representative of the security team. From there it can go one of two ways. More commonly than not, the PaaS provider, via their security team, will scramble to provide you with any data relevant to your incident, if they have it. It might also take a while for them to filter out data that pertains to other customers on the platform, to ensure that they are protected, so patience is required. It can also go the opposite way, and the PaaS provider might not be so forthcoming with information. There is usually a correlation between your annual spend with a provider and their willingness to help out in an incident.

This brings me on to the final option, the legal one – working with a lawyer to draw up a formal request for the PaaS provider to provide documents and data that could be relevant to the investigation. This can be costly, of course, especially if outside counsel is used. Such activity typically has to be approved by executive management at the affected organisation, so the investigator often has to make the case for doing so internally before the decision to engage legal professionals is made.

SaaS forensics

Acquisition of data from a SaaS platform affords an outside investigator the most limited options. There are no hard disks to image, no network traffic to capture and very limited authorisation to obtain artefacts from the application. Yet SaaS products can be used to affect financial transactions, and contain highly sensitive data, so are to be taken extremely seriously as a source of potential evidence. SaaS products typically feature audit logs that can be very useful when tracking user activity, but in most cases the deep details are hidden from the customer.

Working directly with SaaS platform security teams is an option. So too is the legal route. I can assure you that, having worked at a large SaaS provider, I got used to responding to a subpoena every couple of weeks, typically about when, and from which IP address, an account accessed the application. Most SaaS providers have built a process for responding to such requests, so it is not usually a big deal. It is also true that in multi-tenanted SaaS applications the provider will do everything they can to eliminate the risk of law enforcement showing up and asking to physically seize servers. Such an occurrence is built into many SaaS provider threat models.

CONTAINER FORENSICS

Many cloud-centric companies use an architecture model known as a micro-services architecture. The idea here is that instead of having one, bulky, monolithic application, a series of smaller application components and services work together to deliver the final product. This has advantages, as the individual components can be modified without having to rebuild the entire application and can be scaled out individually. Containers are an increasingly popular virtualisation technology used to facilitate the micro-services architecture in a number of instances. Rather than virtualising an entire machine, containers are an abstraction at the application layer that packages code and dependencies together. Multiple containers can run on the same machine, be it virtual or physical, and share the operating system kernel with other containers, each running as isolated processes in user space.

Capturing containers

Containers are designed to be ephemeral, and in fact multiple container security products play up this property as a security feature. If a container only runs for five minutes, even if an attacker compromises it they'll only have access for five minutes at a time. Personally, I support anything that makes the attacker's job harder, but I'd caution that relying solely on this feature of containers doesn't replace the need to fix the underlying problem that let them compromise the host in the first place. This property of containers runs contrary to the fundamental forensics need to preserve evidence. Container images that start and stop constantly represent not just moving targets, but targets that frequently cease to exist.

There is good news however: the majority of container platforms use a copy-on-write file system, which helps us tremendously when working with a running container. The underlying container image is stored in one location; this image contains the configuration data and applications that form the container image. Any changes made while the container is running will be written to a separate file and can actually be committed into a new image on the fly, without affecting the running container. If a container is believed to be compromised you can run that newly committed image to explore its contents. Note, however, that such an action results in the creation of a new container from the image, not the exact same copy of the container you committed from. This differs from a VM snapshotting approach, since running processes in the target container are not included in the image.

Escaping containers

There are several examples of vulnerabilities that would permit malware to escape a container image and access resources on the host machine. Security updates to container management platforms are frequent – as soon as each such bug is discovered it is patched. Therefore, if a container is believed to be affected by some sort of malware, or other malicious actor, an investigator may consider simply treating the container as 'just another compromised application' and image the entire host machine.

FORENSICS IN THE CLOUD?

All this cloud talk might have you thinking, 'could I use an IaaS provider to host my forensics processing tools?' The answer is yes, certainly, it makes some degree of sense. Big scalable compute instances for processing complex cases would certainly be cheaper than maintaining a server room full of bulky physical machines running constantly. I've even known people to use cloud-hosted graphics processing unit (GPU) deployments to crack passwords.

The challenges to doing so will likely come in the form of pushback from clients, or falling foul of some legal or regulatory requirement. For instance, if a customer doesn't use the cloud for their own contractual or regulatory reasons, they're likely not going to welcome a disk image from their environment making it into an IaaS platform during an investigation.

The key is to consider your client base and build measures that protect both the confidentiality (such as encryption) of your evidence and that all-important forensic integrity. Also, for forensics investigations that contain very large datasets and disk images, be extremely mindful of data transfer costs.

SUMMARY

In this chapter we reviewed the various cloud deployment models and service offerings, and how they can affect the way we choose to perform forensics investigations. With an increasing number of organisations moving to the cloud it is of paramount importance that we, as investigators, are prepared to embrace new ways of working to accommodate those organisations.

We also covered container forensics, an important and evolving topic to consider when working with an organisation that has adopted a micro-services architecture.

Along the same vein as cloud adoption, another relatively recent enterprise challenge is the widespread support of mobile devices, owned either personally or by the organisation. In the next chapter we'll explore how forensic investigators handle mobile devices that may fall into the scope of an investigation.

14 MOBILE DEVICE FORENSICS

If extraterrestrials arrived on planet Earth tomorrow morning to study humans, they could be forgiven for thinking that we somehow need our mobile phones for us to remain conscious. In the smartphone era it is rare to find a person without a device in hand, or at least very close by at all times. I'm guilty of using my phone constantly, and you could very well be too. The impact of this from a digital evidence perspective is that more important evidence is moving off our traditional devices, like laptop and desktop machines, and finding its way onto our mobile devices. Photographs, messages, emails, app data that covers every facet of our lives, and even location data that shows where we were physically at a given moment, can all be found on our mobile devices. Just as the sensitivity of the data on these devices has increased, so too has the quality of the measures employed to protect it. Full device encryption is standard on most devices, biometric authentication is well established, and the ability to remotely wipe data from a device from the other side of the world is an expected feature. This has resulted in a situation whereby investigators have to put on their creative hats once again.

The global smartphone market is dominated by two names: Apple's iPhone and closed-source iOS operating system, and Google's Android operating system, which is used by a variety of manufacturers, notably Samsung, Huawei and Google themselves. Smartphones are of particular interest to us, and are the focus of this chapter, since their functionality and performance is more likely to elevate them to the status of 'laptop replacement' devices, and thus they're more likely to contain that range of evidence discussed earlier. 'Traditional' mobile phones shouldn't be completely shunned, though. Cheap throwaway devices can be bought with cash, and provide a suspect with a degree of deniability when used in support of a crime. If any type of device provides an opportunity for people to store data on it, you can rest assured that people will store data on it, knowingly or not. The term 'mobile device' can be broadly applied to other equipment, including tablets, satellite navigation equipment and wearable computers like fitness trackers or smart watches. If it's any kind of computer that moves, and is relevant to the investigation, we should attempt to seize it.

MOBILE PHONE TERMINOLOGY

Usability is highly important in mobile devices, which is why, when compared to traditional laptop and desktop devices, they tend to require a lot less maintenance. You will typically get hardware and software that is designed together, and therefore the maintenance of such devices requires a lot less manual intervention. A side effect of this usability is that many people don't realise that the modern smartphone is a full-blown computer, just in a smaller form. As such, they don't realise that the threat surface of their mobile device is comprised of the same risks as traditional computers – mobile malware and client-side attacks specifically for mobile devices, to name but a couple of examples.

When a person buys a new mobile device, in a retail setting or online, the setup activity is minimal. Typically, a SIM card has to be installed, if it's not already pre-installed, and then the device must be activated, which can be done online without further human interaction. In the store an employee will usually do all this for you. Then you're free to go about your day with your new device. In the vast majority of cases, the next time you'll be back at the store will be when you become eligible for an upgrade and are ready for a new device, or if your phone suffers some unfortunate screen-shattering fate along the way. This whole experience means that even though we're using our phones more than ever, we're probably further abstracted from the underlying technologies than ever before. Given this, we should take a moment to recap some of the underlying technology concepts that keep us glued to our phones.

Cellular networks

Before we even get to mobile phone devices, we have to have a significant cellular communications infrastructure in place to make them useful. A telecommunications service provider is responsible for maintaining this infrastructure. Cellular radio towers are dotted across an area in a pattern that uses directional antennas to ensure maximum coverage. In a city a cell tower is typically able to provide up to half a mile of coverage, whereas in more rural areas, with fewer people and obstacles, a single tower can provide many miles of coverage.

The earliest cellular networks used analogue radio signals, which provided only voice support and offered nothing in the way of security. A simple radio scanner could be used to listen to calls. Nowadays those signals are digital, and have seen multiple enhancements in both performance and security over the years. The majority of cellular networks these days are built on third- or fourth-generation technologies. The Universal Mobile Telecommunications System (UMTS) is the third-generation (3G) technology, and supports voice, text and data at speeds of at least 144 kbps, with actual speeds typically being higher. Long-term Evolution (LTE) is the fourth-generation technology, which uses IP packets rather than the cellular-specific packet-switching network technologies seen in previous generations. With speeds of up 300 Mbps possible, some people are perfectly happy with a 4G LTE connection being their only source of personal internet connectivity.

From an investigative perspective, cellular networks can be extremely valuable sources of information. To support an investigation, telecommunications service providers can provide call detail records listing a subscriber's call activity during a given time period. Additionally, each time a phone registers with a given cell tower, either because it has been powered on or simply because it has moved around, the telecommunications service provider can use this information to provide a rough location for the device. Both of these use cases require that the appropriate legal authorisation has been obtained.

SIM cards

The Subscriber Identity Module (SIM) is a small removable chip that contains details pertaining to the identity of a phone. The SIM is used to store a number of important identification numbers and authentication codes.

IMSI

The International Mobile Subscriber Identity (IMSI) uniquely identifies a user of a cellular network. These numbers are a maximum of 15 digits in length and are made of codes that represent the home country and issuer of the device, along with a unique code to identify the subscriber's account. The IMSI is then used by the telecommunications service provider to route calls to the correct person. Given that the IMSI is a sensitive piece of information (it could be used to eavesdrop if compromised) it is sent only rarely. After an initial IMSI exchange, a temporary version called a TMSI (the T stands for temporary) is created and used in most exchanges.

Devices called IMSI catchers can be used to compromise transmissions between a mobile device and a cellular network, and work by performing a man-in-the-middle attack against the mobile device. Posing as the closest nearby cell tower, the IMSI catcher will trick the device into connecting to it. It then sends a special request asking for the IMSI to be sent from the device. The catcher can then act as a proxy between the device and the legitimate cellular network. Using encryption downgrade techniques the catcher can then eavesdrop on voice calls and intercept data. IMSI catchers are used by both law enforcement and intelligence agencies during their investigations.

PIN and PUK codes

SIM cards can store authentication codes that provide an additional layer of protection against SIM misuse. A SIM card with a PIN code set will require that same PIN to be entered to 'unlock' the card in order to make calls or send data over a cellular network. Given that the PIN is stored on the card, rather than in the device, that same PIN will need to be entered on any device in which the SIM card is used. A three-attempt lockout policy is in place for SIM PINs: if the wrong PIN code is entered three or more times in a row the card will remain locked; a second code is needed to unlock it from this point.

That second code is known as a personal unblocking key (PUK). These are obtained from the provider who sold the SIM card, typically through a web interface, and are the master key for the SIM card. If a PUK is entered 10 times or more incorrectly then it's game over for that SIM card. It will remain forever locked, and a replacement would need to be sought.

It is important to remember that a SIM PIN is different from a device PIN that can be set as part of a mobile operating system. Therefore, a device PIN may or may not have a lockout policy or, more worryingly from a preservation perspective, a device-wipe policy.

IMEI

The International Mobile Equipment Identity (IMEI) is a unique number given to a mobile device, as opposed to the subscriber (IMSI). The number is 15 or 16 digits in length and comprised of numerical sequences that can identify the manufacturer of the device, where the device was built, and of course the specific device itself.

In the UK and various other countries IMEI blacklisting is used to prevent devices that have been reported as stolen from connecting to cellular networks. In practice this means that a stolen device, even with a new SIM card, would be unable to make voice calls, decreasing its value. While the IMEI blocking technique undoubtedly helps, like every technical security control it is subject to constant attack. There are plenty of tools out there that allow an IMEI number to be changed, even though the act of doing so might be explicitly outlawed in some jurisdictions.

SEIZING MOBILE DEVICES

When an investigator makes a determination that a mobile device could contain evidence pertaining to an investigation, and has the legal authority to seize a device, the specific actions they take can vary depending on the state of the device at that particular moment.

Powered on and unlocked

By far the most ideal scenario, and therefore the least likely to materialise (this work makes you a little cynical, if I didn't already mention that), would be if a device is found at a crime scene, powered on and completely unlocked. In this case the investigator's aim would be to keep the device running as long as possible and prevent it from locking. A couple of useful but entirely non-specialised tools can help with this particular endeavour. If you've ever walked around any sort of information technology event where there is a vendor hall, such as a security conference, you can probably find both of these things available for free as promotional gifts handed out by the vendors. The first is a battery backup for a mobile device. These are typically small tube-like objects with a couple of USB ports on them, one for charging the battery and one for charging the device. The second is a device known colloquially as a 'USB condom'. These devices attach to a USB type A connector, often found on one end of a smartphone charging cable, and are actually little write blockers that allow USB power to flow through the cable but provide a physical barrier between the cable's data connectors. The idea is that you use them to protect your own devices from being accessed via the cable, when charging up at an airport for instance, but they work just as well in forensics settings.

Once the device is stabilised with power, all network connectivity should be removed. As the device is unlocked, this could theoretically be done by way of direct manipulation of the operating system settings – enabling aeroplane mode, for example. However, this isn't without risk. Making changes to the device settings, of course, directly affects the original evidence source, which is contrary to digital forensics principles. It also provides the phone with a chance to register a change that could indicate that it has fallen into someone else's hands – a software kill switch that knows to wipe the device if aeroplane mode is enabled, for instance. It's not likely in the majority of cases, but if a suspect were technically savvy enough, why not? For these reasons, a tried and tested method is to place the device in an RF-shielded bag that blocks the cellular and Wi-Fi signals from communicating with the device in a more natural 'out of range' manner. We do this, of course, to protect against remote manipulation, such as a suspect running a remote wipe on the device.

Finally, before we are ready to acquire the device we should prepare it for acquisition by enabling any USB debugging features, such as those found in the Android operating system. These features allow the device to communicate directly with a computer running the Android Software Development Kit, and as a result open up more options for Android acquisition tools. The investigator should also check whether or not a passcode is present on the device. If it is, and can be removed by the investigator, then it should be. As always, the investigator should detail the actions they take while removing the passcode. If a passcode cannot be removed then emphasis will shift to a manual examination.

Powered on and locked

This is the most likely condition for a mobile device at a crime scene and, in the case of a modern mobile device, one of the most challenging to deal with. Most modern devices require the phone to be unlocked by way of a passcode before attempting any sort of physical or logical acquisition. Without that code we essentially have a brick containing garbage data that will never be of any use to us. As with any rule there are exceptions, but those exceptions usually come at some significant cost – a commercialised zero-day vulnerability that can bypass the lock code of a smartphone could easily have a price tag in the millions of pounds.

So, do we just give up? No, of course not, that's not how we operate. Let's look at one potential way around this problem. Because our phones have become so important, we tend to back them up to another location, either to a cloud backup service or to another device. While a phone may be encrypted, there's no guarantee that the backup is. I've personally found entire backups of otherwise encrypted devices on seized laptops. Those backups contain pretty much all the same information as on the phone. They are taken at the logical level rather than being a physical image, so no slack space to carve, but given that we were faced with being locked out completely a few moments ago, we'll take it.

Thanks to cloud technologies our devices have been afforded more opportunity to present a unified front than ever before. Within the Apple ecosystem it is possible for all devices to run on their iCloud platform, meaning that a message sent to an iPhone can be viewed on a user's laptop, tablet and desktop machine all at the same time. Those messages may live in the cloud, but content is downloaded to the local machine for performance reasons. Therefore, we could very easily gain indirect access to content through this vector.

A powered-off device

Devices should initially be kept powered off if they are found in that condition prior to an attempt at physical acquisition. If physical acquisition is found to be a non-viable option then the device should be powered on, again in a network-isolated condition. The next steps will then be determined based on the lock status of the device.

Damaged

Everyone knows at least one friend who has a mobile phone with a perennially cracked screen. These things go everywhere and get dropped or otherwise mistreated at a consistent rate. Given this, what if a device cannot actually be powered up because it is so damaged? Techniques exist that may be the only option for forensic acquisition, and these are aimed at the chips and circuits within the device itself.

JTAG

An industry group known as the Joint Test Action Group (JTAG) was responsible for inventing a method for testing printed circuit boards in the 1980s that has forensics use cases to this day. A JTAG debug port may be included on a device's circuitry, and trained investigators can use this port, some solder and some specialised tools to instruct the phone's CPU to offload data found within its memory chips. Using this method it can be possible to obtain a full physical image of a mobile device, no passcode or working screen required.

This may sound remarkable, but don't forget that this isn't without its limitations. First, the device must have a JTAG port to start with. You can find these on Android phones, but you'll never find them on an iPhone. Secondly, it's extremely labour intensive. Also, if the device is encrypted then that physical image will also be encrypted, so you'd still need to know the passcode to get at the majority of the useful information.

Chip off

A chip-off method can also be used to recover data from mobile devices. This method requires removing a memory chip from the smartphone (i.e. taking the chip off) and placing it on a donor board, with the goal of using software on that board to access the data in the chip. The donor board is essentially an external reader that allows the investigator to read the contents of the memory chip directly. Again, it's a relatively painstaking process, requires specialised equipment and could be undone by device encryption. That said, it might be the only option available.

ACQUISITION TYPES AND TOOLS

A number of different mobile device acquisition techniques were alluded to in the previous section, namely manual, logical and physical. Let's take a look at each of these, and the tools that can be used to perform them.

Manual acquisition

An acquisition technique used by forensic investigators and concerned spouses alike, manual acquisition simply means scrolling through the contents of a phone and looking to see what you can see. Unlike the concerned spouse, a forensic investigator will typically film this entire process to create a record of the actions they took when acquiring the evidence. This approach has the advantage of requiring no special tools, simply using the operating system on the phone to access data as anyone would. The primary disadvantage is that the investigator is limited to accessing files and information that are visible to the operating system – no deleted files can be accessed, for example.

The Paraben PAP 8000 is a video camera designed specifically for forensics investigations. It allows the examiner to place the phone on an area that is exactly the correct distance from the camera.

Logical acquisition

This approach to acquisition results in a bit-by-bit copy of a device's file system, and thus contains only those files that are in allocated space. This, of course, is another way of saying that any deleted files in slack space will not be included in the image.

Logical images of phones can be acquired in a couple of different ways, using specialised and not-so-specialised tools. A device backup image, such as those created by iTunes in the case of the iPhone, would be considered a logically acquired image. Forensics suites such as Cellebrite's UFED[60] and Paraben's E3: DS[61] are designed to perform logical acquisitions by using the device manufacturer's APIs for exchanging data over a cable. The forensics software installed on the investigator's machine will communicate with the phone and build the image from the data that is returned.

Despite its limitations, a logical image will have an associated structure thanks to the file system, and therefore will be easier to examine when compared to working with a full physical image.

Physical acquisition

This is the mobile equivalent of taking a desktop hard drive and connecting to a write blocker for imaging. A full bit-by-bit image of a device, including slack space, is created during a physical acquisition. Unlike the desktop, however, there are no hard disks in a mobile phone that you can simply remove and attach to the write blocker. Instead, physical acquisitions are typically performed by using a custom boot loader developed specifically for forensics usage and bundled with a mobile forensics suite.

The commercial UFED suite of mobile device forensics tools developed by Cellebrite is a prime example of a tool that uses a custom boot loader. To perform a physical acquisition of an Android device the tool uses a cable connection to inject a custom boot loader. It then requires the examiner to install a blank SD card to which the contents of the phone will be imaged.

Removable media

Should a device feature removable media such as a Micro SD card for additional storage, it should be acquired using the best available method. That would typically be a full physical image; however, if the card is encrypted then a logical image from the operating system's mounted volume perspective would be likely to be a more fruitful approach.

---

[60] Cellebrite (2018) *UFED Ultimate / PA*. Cellebrite. Available from https://www.cellebrite.com/en/products/ufed-ultimate/ [5 May 2018].
[61] Paraben (2018) *E3: DS*. Paraben Corporation. Available from https://www.paraben.com/products/e3-ds [5 May 2018].

Acquisition of SIM data

Data can be acquired directly from a SIM card using a hardware SIM card reader and a software tool that understands the data structures on the SIM card. AccessData's Mobile Phone Examiner+ is one such software tool that can perform this function. The data found in SIM cards includes the IMSI and TMSI, as well as information regarding recent calls.

A few years back I worked on an incident that would be solved by evidence found on a mobile phone. A former employee of an organisation was suspected of using their historical access to manipulate data in a financial system. The former employee had not left the company on good terms, and it was suspected that they were messing with the data as an act of revenge.

Passwords had been changed, but still the employee had a way into the system. After some digging it was determined that an Oauth token had persisted on the employee's mobile device, meaning that access to the financial system had remained intact. The financial system used a globally unique identifier (GUID) for mobile devices that was stored both in log files in the application and on the device itself.

As the investigation closed in on the suspect, a warrant was issued to seize all computer equipment owned by them, including mobile devices. The mobile device was forensically acquired, and shortly afterwards, during analysis, that unique identifier was found in the app data, meaning the manipulation could be traced back to the device. Case closed!

SMARTPHONES

Given that the majority of devices we'll run into in the field these days are smartphones, we should be especially well versed in both Apple iOS and Android. I would be remiss if I didn't mention the fact that there are, of course, other smartphone operating systems out there, such as Windows Mobile and Blackberry OS, but only one of those is currently supported (Windows) and, unlike in the desktop space, the Windows Mobile market share is low. With this in mind, the balance of probabilities would suggest that you'll find an Apple or Android device at a scene where a smartphone is involved.

Android

In the world of smartphones the market share belongs to Android. Developed by Google based on the Linux kernel, the Android operating system is an open-source project used by many manufacturers. Those manufacturers will typically add proprietary code to the official Android distribution in order to add their own features to the devices they sell.

True open-source spins of Android that have been developed by the open-source community do exist, and are designed for users who wish to be free of any proprietary code.

Along these lines, a community has grown up who create software to 'root' Android phones. Rooting an Android phone involves using a custom boot loader to obtain root access to the device.

A boot loader is a program that loads a computer's operating system.

By using a custom boot loader it is possible to load the operating system with additional components and in a different configuration to allow different types of access to the device beyond those afforded by the standard boot loader shipped with a device. Since the operating system is Linux based, the root account has all the power that a root user on a server would have. Most Android devices allow for rooting because they don't ship with locked boot loaders. It is therefore something to be mindful of when working with an Android device. A rooted device would make it easier for that phone's owner to run anti-forensic tools.

Owing again to its Linux heritage, analysis of an Android device has a very similar feel to examining any other Linux machine. Elements of the Linux FHS can be seen when analysing a logical device image. Thanks to this standard the file system layout is roughly the same between devices, but there is always the possibility of slight variations.

- /data – contains user-generated data, including apps installed by a user. You'll also find key databases, in SQLite format, containing call logs and SMS messages. This is probably the most important location when it comes to forensic artefacts.
- /system – contains operating system device files.
- /sdcard –the mount point of the removable SD card.

Apple

Apple's iOS is the closed-source operating system for their iPhone and iPad devices. Like macOS, it is a Unix-like operating system derived from the open-source Darwin operating system. Apple maintains strict control over which apps can run on iOS through code signing and various other security features, which led to a movement in the early days of the operating system to create so-called jailbreaks. These use kernel patches to achieve root-level access to the devices to bypass Apple's security controls and install unsigned third-party software.

In the arms race between Apple and the jailbreaking community the tide seems to have swung in Apple's favour, with the most recent versions of iOS having escaped unbroken owing to improvements in security controls and a less active jailbreaking scene. What this means from our perspective is that iOS devices are extremely predictable. The iOS file system layout on one device will exactly match that on another. This predictability means that we can very easily visit common locations for forensic artefacts.

iOS stores the majority of useful forensic data in databases and .plist files (a property list, just like in macOS). Because iOS is Unix based it uses a Unix file structure and, as of 2017, the APFS file system. Some commonly reviewed locations in investigations include:

- /Library/CallHistory/call_history.db – contains call history records;
- /Library/SMS/sms.db – contains SMS messages;
- /Library/SMS/Attachments/ – contains attachment files;
- /Library/Safari/ – contains various Safari browser logs.

SUMMARY

In this chapter we introduced the topic of mobile forensics. We reviewed the underlying terminology and infrastructure that powers modern-day cellular networks, and how that infrastructure can play a role in our investigations.

We discussed how the state in which a mobile device is seized influences the acquisition options available, including some advanced acquisition techniques like JTAG and chip off. Finally, we reviewed some common storage locations on Android and Apple iOS devices that are of particular importance to an investigator because of the evidence they may contain.

While we've been focused primarily on technical topics to this point in our digital forensics journey, we're about to switch gears to another skill set that is just as important for any investigator: the art of reporting your findings in a clear and pragmatic way.

15 REPORTING AND PRESENTING YOUR FINDINGS

There is an art to taking deeply technical topics, such as those encountered during a digital forensics investigation, and crafting a document that can explain them to an audience that might not be so technically inclined. This is precisely what a digital forensic investigator must do as a final, yet critical, step in the investigative process. Although report production is typically reserved for once an investigation has reached its conclusion, the reporting process starts much earlier. Throughout an investigation the investigator should be making notes to track actions taken and findings alike. It is during the reporting phase that these notes will be at their most useful, as they help us to recall exactly what we did, when we did it and what we were thinking. Acquisition and investigation is exciting work, and the temptation can be to dive right in and look for evidence by any means possible, but a good investigator will always balance the desire to get results with the need for keeping an accurate record of how those results were obtained. We're taught from a young age to show our working when solving mathematical problems; this is no different.

Remember, a digital forensics investigation is a scientific process that must be repeatable. In order for that to ring true, a report with all the steps taken by the investigator must be readily available for any applicable third party that needs it to reproduce the findings. In this chapter report-writing techniques, layouts and content will be examined and the different types of audience for investigative reports will be discussed.

In talking about all the things a forensics report should be, it is worth reflecting on what it shouldn't be. Early on in my career I had a habit of, as one supervisor put it, 'writing reports as if they're Jane Austen novels'. It had been drilled into me that I had to be extremely detailed when reporting and, given that I was operating in my early twenties at peak eagerness and naivety, I had taken this a little to heart.

'As I arrived at my client's office building, my gaze was drawn to a Japanese maple that stood opposite me. The leaves had started to turn, and they precisely matched the shade of the hard-shell carry case used to transport my write-blocking equipment.' This is exaggerated, but you get the idea. Relevant details are good; superfluous information should be left out.

LAYOUT AND CONTENT

Let's start by examining how the report should be laid out and what should be in it. The exact layout can be influenced by various factors, including, but not limited to:

- The role of the investigator in the investigation. There will be a difference depending on whether or not the investigator is considered an expert witness (more on this shortly).
- A client's bespoke requirements. After all, they're the ones paying the bill.
- Any company standard reporting templates. This is especially important if working for a digital forensics service provider.
- The nature of the investigation.
- The number of people working on the investigation, and its complexity.
- The jurisdiction the investigation is occurring in.

Know your role

Depending on the nature of the investigation and the needs of the client, a forensic investigator could serve as either a technical or an expert witness. It is important to understand the nature of your involvement, as this will have a significant bearing on the content of the investigative report when it is delivered.

- A technical witness is able to give facts about what was discovered during the investigation.
- An expert witness is able to give opinions and conclusions.

Forensic investigators who work with law enforcement agencies typically act as technical witnesses. Their reports state facts about the evidence found and how it was acquired, but they do not draw any conclusions from their work. In such instances the aim of the report is to clearly articulate what was found in such a way that members of a jury can draw their own conclusions about the relevance of the evidence to a case. The completeness of the information is important in making sure that the report doesn't require an additional source to be used to correlate the stated facts.

In cases where an investigator is hired by an organisation to run an investigation the typical intent is to have them testify as an expert witness. It would make sense that the investigator is allowed to give an opinion based on what they discovered during an investigation. It is this expertise that the organisation is paying for, and is hoping will allow them to win whatever case they're trying to win. As such, the conclusions section of the report written by an expert witness is considered to be the most valuable section of the report. Digital forensics professionals can also be brought in specifically for trial, to review work conducted by technical witnesses and give an opinion.

In order to be able to testify as an expert witness the investigator's background will first be reviewed by the judge. Standards regarding the investigator's skills, experience, education and reputation must be met in order to fulfil the role. A common technique employed by a defence lawyer is to attempt to discredit a forensic investigator involved in an investigation so that their opinions or conclusions cannot be used in evidence.

Templates and timing

Where possible, an investigator should make use of a standard template for all the reports they produce. A template reduces the time spent on formatting a document, helps to build professional reputation and brand when used consistently (people start to recognise you and your work from the template) and makes it easier for the investigator to keep track of where in the report certain pieces of information can be found.

The earlier that report writing begins in the investigative process the better; some investigators even elect to write notes directly into a report template, which they later polish and format into the final product. Personally I prefer to keep a separate copy of my notes and transpose them into the report, so that nothing is lost during the formatting process. I also use handwritten notes the majority of the time, as it's quicker and easier to add diagrams and annotations inline. I will then scan them in and back them up at regular intervals. Everyone works in different ways, of course, so the key is to find an approach to note-taking that works for you.

Sections

The body of a forensic report should be broken into sections for easy digestion, and for the most part they should track the chronology of the investigation. The exception to that rule is the executive summary, which acts as a spoiler revealing the investigator's final determinations. This is for audience members who do not have a need to understand the detail but will be responsible for determining the direction to be taken following the investigation.

Introduction and overview

This first section of the report is used to set the scene. It'll explain how the investigation came into being and detail the role the investigator writing the report took in the process. For example, was the investigator involved from an early stage, and responsible for data collection, or did they provide analysis and consultation based on already acquired evidence?

> On Tuesday 17th October 2017, at 12pm local time, I attended the office of Example Company, located at 123 Fake Street in west London. I was called there to acquire digital evidence following an allegation of misconduct by an employee, Mr David Fakerson. Mr Fakerson was suspected of accessing pornographic materials on his work computer.

Executive summary of findings

As previously noted, the executive summary of findings is there to spoil the plot of the rest of the investigation, and is there for those who don't want to tune in to the whole report. The hard truth is that, as fascinating as the investigative process is to people like us, some folks don't have the time or the inclination to learn about it. They just want answers, and that is perfectly acceptable. If you're a CEO of a company that has been defrauded, for example, the last thing you're going to want is to be held in suspense while you try to decipher whether or not you have enough evidence to seek restitution.

The executive summary should be just that, a summary. If your summary is 20 pages long then it is not a summary. Try to keep the number of pages in the single digits. Bullet points are your friend; use them to lay out paragraphs of findings rather than wrapping the findings up with narrative. The use of technical terminology might not be entirely avoidable, but it should be limited during the executive summary.

- Several pornographic images were found on the computer used exclusively by Mr Fakerson, including some that had been deleted.
- Internet browsing history revealed that the user account assigned to Mr Fakerson was used to frequently access pornographic websites during business hours.

Acquisition and chain of custody

As we resume the chronology of the investigation, this section of the report is used to detail how evidence was acquired and details the chain of custody for each evidence item. The early investment we made in maintaining the chain of custody pays dividends here, as we lay out our records that can disprove any claims of evidence tampering. Remember, attacks on the chain of custody and associated records are a common technique to get digital evidence thrown out.

This section will also detail the steps taken by the investigator to reduce the risks of evidence spoliation. In the case of a live acquisition, for instance, this is where the detail regarding the technique used and the potential effects on the evidence would be reported. Photographs and sketches of the scene that were taken during the investigation would also be included here.

> Mr Fakerson's laptop was found to be in a powered-off state at his desk in Example Company's office. I took photographs of the laptop, and noted its model and serial numbers. I removed the 750 GB 2.5 inch Western Digital SATA hard disk from the laptop and recorded its serial number. I then used a Tableau T35u IDE/SATA forensic bridge that was in write-blocking mode to make a forensically sound image of the hard disk on my forensics laptop. I used Access Data FTK imager version 4.1.1 to facilitate the creation of the EnCase evidence file. I repeated this process twice, and both times validated that the SHA-256 hash produced from the data on the disk matched (50D858E0985ECC7F60418AAF0CC5AB587F42C2570A884095A9E8CCACD0F6545C).

> I then sealed the original hard disk in an evidence bag, completed the chain of custody documentation and transported the hard disk back to our facility, where it was placed in our secure evidence storage area. I went directly from Example Company to our facility without stopping; GPS tracking data for this trip is available.

> Prior to loading the disk image into our forensics analysis suite I confirmed that the integrity hash matched those that had been recorded at the time of acquisition.

Tools and techniques

This section of the report is important for establishing the scientific credibility of our work. The entire investigation should be repeatable, with the same conclusions reached, based solely on the information contained in the report. A huge part of that is detailing the various tools and techniques used along the way.

This can be as simple as describing which software tools were used, including version numbers, or it can be as complex as detailing a new technique that was devised specifically for the given investigation, and how that technique has been validated.

> The disk image acquired from the hard drive in Mr Farkerson's laptop was loaded for processing in AccessData Forensic Toolkit version 6.1. The data-carving processing option was enabled, specifically for JPEG files.

Findings and evidence

The meat of the report will contain examples of what was uncovered during the investigation to support our conclusions. Evidence can be considered either inculpatory or exculpatory. Inculpatory evidence implies that a defendant is guilty of a crime. For instance, if evidence found on a machine shows that a defendant paid in bitcoin for a DDoS-for-hire service then this would be inculpatory if they were being accused of orchestrating a DDoS attack. Exculpatory evidence is the opposite, and is used to exonerate a defendant. For instance, if evidence of malware was found on a suspect machine then this could be considered exculpatory, since the malware might have been responsible for whatever activity was sourced from that machine.

Exculpatory evidence holds a special status in most legal systems: should a prosecutor discover such evidence they have a legal obligation to provide it to the defence. For a forensics examiner, this same legal principle should be applied during an investigation. Remember, we always treat our work as if it'll have to be defended in court, and that includes adhering to professional and ethical standards from the very beginning. The rules on exculpatory evidence are a prime example of this. It would be unethical to withhold such information from a report, and that would ultimately transition into becoming illegal should the case end up in court.

Evidence artefacts are typically laid out in a numbered or lettered fashion so that they can be easily referenced later. Details pertaining to each artefact, including relevant metadata, are included inline, along with a sample of the artefact where applicable – for instance, a copy of the image when dealing with a photograph. The investigator will also give details as to where the artefact was located and, if giving a report as an expert witness, go into more details about why this is considered relevant to the case.

> Item A is a Mozilla Firefox history SQLite database found in allocated space; it contains a record of all the websites Mr Fakerson accessed over the 30-day period prior to the imaging of his laptop. The evidence shows that Mr Fakerson accessed a number of sites that are pornographic in nature during this period and, based on the timestamps (validated against the accurate system clock), these sites were accessed during business hours.

Conclusions and opinions formed

In this section we'll revisit the executive summary, and provide more technical details about each of our findings. Conclusions are typically listed in order of importance, with the most important finding at the top of the list. If serving as a technical witness, the report will not have a conclusions section as this will fall outside the investigator's scope.

The evidence discovered on Mr Fakerson's laptop overwhelmingly supports the claims that he accessed pornographic materials during business hours.

Appendices

Sometimes, in cases where there are many evidence items, including all of the data pertaining to them in the body of the report can result in many pages that are filled with binary or metadata. Having to flick through all these pages is inconvenient and can disrupt the flow of the report. Therefore, some investigators choose to add such information to one or more appendices. In such cases, those numbered or lettered evidence items can be cross-referenced.

It is also common to include the curriculum vitae of each investigator involved in the investigation in an appendix to the report. This is to assist in supporting the investigator's case for being recognised as an expert witness by the court.

AUDIENCE

The digital forensics report is a highly technical document that must be accessible to people of varying technical skill levels. This can run the gamut from a jury member who may never have received any formal computer training to a fellow investigator who has many years of experience. It is for this reason that your reporting style can be at least as important as your technical skill level. That might be a somewhat controversial statement, but think about it for a second. You can very easily extract digital evidence if you follow the processes in place and use a commercial forensics tool with the default settings. The case might feel like a slam dunk, only to see it fall down at the reporting stage.

The key is to think through everything you're writing and, each time you run into a technical concept or terminology, ask yourself if you believe someone with a standard level of technology knowledge would be able to digest what the report is saying without further research. Your mission should be to keep the person reviewing the report locked in, without them having to go elsewhere to search for the meaning of a word or an article on a particular process.

We often say that digital forensics is both an art and a science, and this is nowhere more apparent than when you sit down to write a report. A well-written report will afford you major professional respect, drive the right outcome for your client and possibly negate the need for you to take the stand in court to defend your work. Fewer things in this profession are more stressful than having to endure a cross-examination from a determined defence lawyer, who'll stop at nothing to discredit you and your professional abilities.

If you do find yourself in this situation, take a deep breath, think before you answer the question being asked of you, and believe in your work. Offer up the minimum information required to answer the question fairly and honestly. Do not become argumentative and, most importantly, don't take it personally. You just happen to be a person doing a job that you love, and so too is the person grilling you.

SUMMARY

In this chapter we introduced an often overlooked but highly important part of any forensics investigation: reporting. We covered examples of the content that should be included in any forensics report, and how those reports should be laid out.

We discussed the importance of knowing your role as a witness in a trial, and how that influences the content of any report or deposition that you can provide.

As we move to the final chapter in the book we tackle another non-technical topic, the impact of an investigation on the people involved.

16 THE HUMAN ELEMENTS OF AN INVESTIGATION

Throughout this book we've looked at deeply technical subject matter, but we've never lost sight of the fact that information security is undoubtedly a people business. People are, of course, the real victims in the event of a cybercrime. When we're dealing with data, in many cases each row of a database represents a human being and something about their life. When a security incident occurs, resulting in damage or disruption to that person's life, this becomes very apparent. Unfortunately, not everyone can appreciate this beforehand, which can also be a contributing factor to an incident. If you process sensitive information about a person, and you're not protecting data like someone's well-being depends on it, then you're doing it wrong. If not someone else's data, it'll be ours. The mantra 'treat data as you'd want your own data treated' sums up the best way to approach this particular topic.

Of course, people aren't just the victims, they're also the perpetrators of these crimes. The reasons that people commit cybercrimes are just as varied as the reasons that people engage in traditional physical crimes. Financial motivations are common. Revenge, bullying, stalking and abuse are four hideous categories of activity that can be performed, to devastating effect, with electronic help. Technology and the internet have undoubtedly brought us closer together and been a force multiplier for all that is good in society, but unfortunately the same is true for the worst in society.

Finally, the investigators of these crimes are people too. Just as police officers and other first responders are exposed to a variety of horrific scenes and situations as they go about their jobs, so too are those who work solely in the electronic realm. In some cases you could even argue that the impact is worse. The technician turned investigator might suddenly find themselves confronted by images of child abuse, something that is hard for anyone to prepare for, let alone a person who believed they were engaging in a purely technical career. In this chapter we're going to focus on victims, perpetrators and investigators, and some of the associated human factors that should be considered during an investigation.

VICTIMS

Our lives have never been more dependent on, and intertwined with, technology. The online presence of a single person spans multiple services and user accounts. Our finances, shopping, social lives, romantic lives, intangible assets, safety, security and identities are distributed across an array of servers and storage devices we'll never see. None of it is real, but all of it is real, and that becomes extremely clear the moment any one of these things is compromised. As a digital investigator you could find yourself working on an incident involving the loss of millions of records about people. Individuals seem so very far removed from the large SQL database dumps you're sifting through during evidence collection. You might start to tire, to wonder if you'll ever get to the bottom of the incident. Even if you don't, perhaps it doesn't matter. The incident has been contained, the company who brought you in is back to business as usual. If you ever start to develop these kinds of thoughts, pause for a second and think about who you're really working for. The victims. The real people, dealing with the anxieties, possible financial hardship and uncertainty brought about because of a security incident that wasn't their fault. If that doesn't motivate you, you could be in the wrong line of work.

Single-victim cases

Sometimes we're tasked with an investigation that involves a single victim. Perhaps someone got phished and is now at risk of identity theft. Perhaps ransomware landed on their computer, locking up gigabytes of family photos. It could be a young victim of cyberbullying, grooming or sextortion. In such cases our job as an investigator is to figure out if there is a way to undo the wrongs, find justice for our victims and restore their faith in technology and, depending on the circumstances, humanity. Victims are victims regardless of how they ended up with such a status, and that is always important to remember. Of course, some victims make it easier for themselves to end up in such a state. Password reuse across multiple websites, not using multifactor authentication and oversharing information on social media are but three examples of bad online habits that make a person a softer target. Sometimes, though, the victim's position is unavoidable. Perhaps an online service doesn't offer multifactor authentication, or enforce or support the use of strong passwords, or it suffers from some other information security failing.

Mat Honan is a journalist. In August 2012, while he was working for *Wired*, he was targeted by a couple of hackers who were interested in gaining access to his three-letter twitter account '@mat'. Mat wrote an article about his experience,[62] and in doing so shared how various security mistakes on his part, combined with some questionable security controls in services we use every day, led to his own personal data breach nightmare.

Mat noticed that his iPhone had unexpectedly shut down. He assumed the battery was flat and went to plug it in. When the phone booted up he was presented with the iOS setup screen. Frustrated, but not overly concerned, Mat entered his iCloud password to restore his phone from backup. The password was not accepted. Mat had a local backup available, so using that he was able to restore his phone. The first thing he noticed when he got back into his phone was a pop-up informing him that his Gmail password was incorrect. The phone then prompted him for a four-digit PIN, which he hadn't set. In Mat's own words, 'By now, I knew something was very, very wrong. For the first time, it occurred to me that I was being hacked.'

---

[62] Honan, M. (2012) *How Apple and Amazon Security Flaws Led to My Epic Hacking*. Wired. Available from https://www.wired.com/2012/08/apple-amazon-mat-honan-hacking/ [5 May 2018].

Mat made frantic calls to Apple support to try and rectify the situation. It was later determined that he wasn't the first person to have made a call to Apple regarding his account that day. Remember, the attacker had wanted access to Mat's Twitter account, so in order to get that he had to find out the email address used to log in to that account. Mat had a Gmail account that he used for this purpose, and this was easily discovered by the attacker on Mat's personal website.

The attacker then headed to Gmail and started to perform a password recovery on Mat's Gmail account. He didn't actually go through with the recovery, but was able to discover, via Gmail's on-screen prompts, that Mat had set up a 'me.com' account as a recovery email address; me.com was owned by Apple.

The attacker targeting Mat had also called Apple support on that fateful day and, while pretending to be him, had requested that Apple reset the password for his me.com email account. Mat discovered that Apple support had reset the password and given the attacker a temporary password in exchange for two pieces of information: the last four digits of his credit card and his home address. These are two extremely easy pieces of information to obtain. First of all, a home address is online in many places; in this case the attacker obtained it from the 'whois' record associated with Mat's personal web domain. The last four digits of his credit card were stolen from his Amazon account. The method used here was fairly ingenious, but frighteningly simple.

The attacker called Amazon and requested that a new credit card be added to Mat's Amazon account. All the attacker needed to provide to get them to do this was Mat's home address, email address and name. The attacker added a new, fake card to the account. Crucially, it was a card to which they knew the card number! The attacker then ended the call and called back, pretending to be Mat and telling Amazon that he'd lost access to his account.

In order to reset Mat's password Amazon wanted to know the home address, email address and last four digits of a card on the account. Of course, the attacker could simply provide the last four digits from the fake card they'd just added. They were then provided with access to Mat's account, and with that were able to discover the last four digits of Mat's real card, which were displayed in the clear on his account page. With Mat's home address and the last four digits of his credit card, the attacker was able to convince Apple support to reset his me.com password. With that, the attacker had completed the loop that allowed him to reset Mat's Gmail password, take over his Twitter account and remotely wipe his devices. Those devices included his only copies of photos of his one-year-old daughter. Incidentally, the devices were wiped for 'fun'.

Mat was able to establish communication with his attacker via Twitter, which is how he was able to learn about the methods used to attack him, and their motivations. A true example of how a person can be victimised, and how the lack of standards for digital identities can be exploited to maximum effect.

Youth, intimacy, trust and tech

It is often said that humans are the weakest link in the chain when it comes to digital security. We're often guilty of being too trusting of others, too quick to want to please and help, easy to alarm and prone to making poor decisions under pressure. All of these traits can play a significant role in allowing us to become victims. This is especially true in the case of youngsters. For the generation that has never known life without broadband internet it is seen as just another utility – a constant, like the water from a tap or the power to light a light bulb at the flick of a switch. The internet is so entrenched in daily life that using it is no longer seen as an 'event', as it once was. As a result, the boundaries between reality and virtual reality have eroded to the point of being non-existent in most cases. If you've never known life to be any different, this might catch you out. We've all experienced the pressures and stresses associated with puberty and the transition to engaging in sexual relationships, that's nothing new. However, the role of technology in this phase of life is relatively new and has been the source of more than its fair share of heartbreak, incident and investigation.

As incident responders and investigators it is not that unlikely that we'll be exposed to such activity. There are many examples of 'harmless teenage fun' exploding into significant, life-changing incidents for those involved. Examples of this include cyberbullying or sexting, where the exchange of explicit images, based on an often-misplaced trust or driven by peer pressure, becomes a significant problem when those images are shared with or accessed by someone other than the intended recipient. Teenage relationships are never the most stable; trust is established and eroded at a rapid pace. You always maintain full control over whom you choose to trust, at any age, but the second you press 'send' on an image you've forever lost control of it. In the case of a sexually explicit picture of an underage person, the ultimate destination of such an image can have a significant bearing on the lives and livelihoods of both sender and recipient. As investigators in a digital forensics investigation we're given unfettered access into the life of a person through their computers and data. That could be a victim or otherwise, but in all cases it is a privileged position, and a position that affords us the opportunity to make a very real difference to the victim. The best way to do this, if we find ourselves coming into contact with such material either directly or consequentially as part of an incident, is to ensure that law enforcement becomes involved quickly, for the protection of all parties.

Prevention is, of course, the best cure, and we can also leverage our unique position to educate youth about the risks associated with risky online behaviour. Using first-hand experience of investigations and their effects on victims is a great way to educate and enthuse about online safety. We can do this through educational institutions, in our communities and through family connections. I can assure you, it's time well spent.

In August 2014 Apple's iCloud storage platform found itself in the crosshairs of suspicion as 500 private, and mostly intimate, photographs of young female celebrities were leaked to the internet. These images were soon identified as having been stored on iCloud, which led many to question whether a flaw in the service had allowed it to become compromised.

Apple promptly investigated, and determined that there was no flaw in the service. Instead, a targeted attack on the victims, most likely a phishing or brute force attack, had been the root cause. In a statement a couple of days after the incident was revealed, Apple shed some light on their investigative process:

After more than 40 hours of investigation, we have discovered that certain celebrity accounts were compromised by a very targeted attack on user names, passwords and security questions, a practice that has become all too common on the Internet. None of the cases we have investigated has resulted from any breach in any of Apple's systems including iCloud® or Find my iPhone. We are continuing to work with law enforcement to help identify the criminals involved.[63]

The actress Jennifer Lawrence, one of the victims of the incident, said during an interview shortly afterward, 'Anybody who looked at those pictures, you're perpetuating a sexual offence. You should cower with shame.'

Some of the victims were also underage.

The incident served as a reminder of the value of multifactor authentication, and to always be aware of where your data is being stored. Cloud backups can be so tightly integrated with a device that some users may not be aware they are enabled.

Medical data and identity safety

In recent years, thanks to a number of serious incidents mainly with US-based medical insurers, there has been a renewed focus on the safety and security of medical data. The theft of medical data has the potential for more significant and longer-term problems for victims. The reason is that a medical record frequently contains all the information someone would need to be able to steal the identity of the person who is the subject of the record. Identity theft is a serious crime, allowing criminals the ability to obtain cash and other goods by opening lines of credit using the stolen identity, which the victim must then fight to prove they didn't request.

Because of the rate and speed at which stolen or compromised credit cards can be blocked, identities are increasing in popularity as the prime target for a determined attacker. A quick perusal of the dark web will yield numerous identity records being traded; records typically include names, addresses and national identification numbers.

Medical records may also contain deeply sensitive personal information such as a given person's HIV status or history of drug abuse. Given this, there is always a risk that such information could be used to blackmail or otherwise compromise an individual. Imagine if someone who worked in intelligence was forced to reveal classified information in exchange for a deeply embarrassing medical issue being kept quiet. Stolen medical data could very well become weaponised in this way in the coming years.

---

[63] Apple (2014) *Apple Media Advisory: Update to Celebrity Photo Investigation*. Apple. Available from https://www.apple.com/newsroom/2014/09/02Apple-Media-Advisory/ [5 May 2018].

PERPETRATORS

It is easy to forget that digital crimes are, of course, ultimately committed by humans. The machines didn't rise up one day and decide to start scanning a web application for vulnerabilities, at least they haven't yet, anyway. Any illusions that we may have about this are shattered the moment we come into direct contact with suspects or perpetrators. It's not a pleasant situation for anyone to find themselves in, but often we have little choice. The suspect could be someone who up until a few hours ago was a trusted colleague. You might be faced with presenting evidence in front of a person on trial. You might need the cooperation of a suspect or their family in your investigation. The best advice I can give in all these cases is to be polite and conduct yourself professionally. Be impartial, and never make assumptions. Sometimes otherwise good people can make bad choices. The apparent anonymity afforded by technology can often lure people into doing things that they wouldn't ordinarily have done. Just look at any comments section on the internet if you need any proof of this – some people make a habit of posting sexist, racist and downright disgusting commentary from behind the safety of a keyboard. They say things they wouldn't dream of saying in public. This hobby is known as trolling, and the people who engage in it thrive on the reactions they get from disgusted people.

Personal safety

The most important consideration when coming into contact with a suspect or perpetrator is your own personal safety. It is easy to understand why someone you're in the process of investigating might be hostile towards you. Personal safety is your number one priority at all times. If at any point you feel like it is in jeopardy, just leave. You should never find yourself in a situation where you're alone with a suspect, and if you do, again, just leave. It's not worth the risk of either physical harm or any other type of conflict.

The suspect's family

Perpetrators and suspects have families, and it's important to remember that they themselves aren't suspects. In fact, they're frequently victims too. They might be dragged into a suspect's activities, or try to blindly defend the suspect out of sheer love. It is well documented, both on paper and in Hollywood, that love makes normally level-headed people act erratically. This, of course, puts you at the same level of risk as if you were alone with a suspect. It has never happened to me, thankfully, but I've known of instances of fellow investigators being harassed by family members after giving expert testimony against a suspect. In a situation where a suspect family is likely to be nearby, keep your head out of your phone and maintain situational awareness.

In one investigation I was imaging a laptop belonging to a woman suspected of stealing confidential information after she'd been made redundant. The laptop was personally owned, and as a condition of the payment of her redundancy she had agreed to the forensic examination of the device to confirm that there were no traces of the confidential information, and no evidence that the information had been moved off the device onto a USB drive or otherwise.

The imaging venue was set. It was to be performed at her solicitor's office. I arrived, along with my client's staff and legal representation. She was present, with her solicitor and, to my surprise, her teenage son. In front of all these people I removed the underside of the laptop and unscrewed the hard drive. I felt as if a million eyes were upon me, judging what I was doing. Of course, in this particular laptop the drive was connected by a fiddly, non-standard adapter. After doing battle with that thing for about five minutes I was thrilled to see that it was a 750 GB hard drive. It took almost three hours to image using my mobile imaging equipment. Throughout those hours the teenage boy just stared at me. He never looked away. He didn't play with a phone, just maintained a strange fixation on me. In my head, with nothing else to concentrate on, I began to question if he was attempting some mind control trick. It was incredibly disturbing. The progress bar on my imaging software took forever to move a couple of millimetres. I think it may even have jumped backwards a few times.

To break the silence I occasionally offered a thrilling update on the progress, giving the percentage complete and time remaining. I prayed hard that the imaging process wouldn't fail.

It didn't, and after what seemed like a year and a half I was out of there. Not before making sure the computer was able to boot back up after I reinstalled the hard drive. It was absolute agony for someone who doesn't enjoy conflict or awkwardness. I couldn't even run into the nearest pub afterwards because I had to get the seized materials back to the lab so as not to break the chain of custody!

Everyone makes mistakes

No matter who we are, many of us have done things that we later regret doing. Obviously, for most people that doesn't involve committing a crime, but I've always found it necessary to bear this truth in mind when working through an investigation. As an example as to why, consider the following: under pressure, an organisation might attempt to coerce an investigator into giving an opinion that a suspect conducted an activity deliberately. The cure, as always, is to stick to the facts, never make assumptions and maintain your impartiality. Never say something that cannot be backed up with hard data. To reference a quote often attributed to American engineer and author William Edwards Deming, 'without data, you're just another person with an opinion'.

In probably the most emotional and gut-wrenching experience of my own career to this point, I once dealt with a perpetrator whom I firmly believe was a good person who had made a mistake. A big mistake for sure, but one that could ultimately have been rectified.

I was working on a suspected financial incident. A young operations engineer was the sole person responsible for ensuring that a financial process completed successfully. Only one customer used this particular process and they were to be migrated from it within a few months, so it hadn't been considered prudent to train others on it. The engineer was responsible for uploading a file containing banking information to a payment processing service. The file essentially contained account numbers and cash amounts to be paid into those accounts.

At some point, the engineer had realised that they could manipulate the file to transfer funds into their own bank account. After that, each time the process needed to be run they'd modify the file and siphon some cash. Eventually the scheme came to light through monitoring and a brief investigation. It was a pretty cut and dried affair. The evidence collected was handed over to law enforcement and within a few hours the person involved had admitted their actions. A trial date was set, and the evidence was collated into witness statement format.

One evening, a few weeks after the incident, I received a call that even as I recall it now, several years later, gives me that sick-to-my-stomach feeling. On the end of the line was another person involved in the investigation. They informed me that the suspect had taken their own life. Rather than pleading at trial and facing justice, they'd elected a different, and very final, route. Later, I came to discover that the money had been stolen to help the family after the primary breadwinner had passed away. Obviously this doesn't excuse the actions at all, but I think it gives some insight into what was going on in the suspect's mind at the time.

Although I never knew this person personally, I bear this story in mind when working with both victims and suspects. Digital crimes happen in the digital realm, but this is the clearest example that I have about the real-world impact they have. I don't need another one.

INVESTIGATORS

To conclude, let's take some time for ourselves. We've called out the stresses and strains of this work throughout this book. There may be late nights, there may be inconvenient travel, and there may be time spent away from home locked in a Faraday cage so you can't even check the football score. So, why do it? Well, hopefully that question has been answered over the course of the last 16 chapters. This is hugely rewarding work, with real purpose and outcomes that many who work in IT, and even other areas of information security, can only dream of. We operate at the bleeding edge. We have to be network engineers, database administrators, lawyers, developers, desktop support technicians, cloud architects, virtualisation engineers, mobile device experts and politicians, and sometimes all in one day. Incident response and digital forensics are never boring.

Mental health breaks

As much as you may love it, it is incredibly important to take time away from the job when you can. Sometimes you'll just lie in bed at night unable to sleep because you're thinking of an investigation. Did I do everything properly? Have I looked everywhere? Did I use the correct technique? What time zone should the system clock be in? The questions are endless, and they'll keep coming up as long as you let them. It is incredibly hard to do, people in this field are incredibly passionate, but you have to always remember that this is just a job and that your health and the health of your family must come first.

I've found that a great way to achieve this is to allow your family into your work – just a little, don't go sharing anything overly horrific! Give them a sneak peek of what you're working on every once in a while. This probably isn't something any other textbook will teach, and strictly speaking it's against the rules and may violate confidentiality agreements, but let's just move past that for a second. You can still respect a client's privacy while explaining the gist of what you're working on. For example, you don't need to name names and you don't need to give industries, but you can still give enough detail to convey accurately the pressures you're facing. It is important to have someone you trust to offload on. A significant other will, of course, be concerned when you're stressed or upset about something you're working on. To say 'I can't talk about it' isn't always healthy. Personally, I've found that sharing little pieces of information about what I've been working on with my wife is a great way for her to develop an understanding of why, when the phone goes off midway through dinner, I might have to up and leave to deal with an incident. Through my descriptions of work she has learned that speed is important, and she's learned to trust me when I make a call about dealing with something then and there as opposed to waiting until the morning.

If you really don't want to bring a family member into your world of work, talk to your employer about them offering you access to counselling or other wellness services. Many incident response and forensics companies do this, and all government departments and police forces (in the UK at least) do too. There are plenty of documented cases of post-traumatic stress disorder (PTSD) affecting digital forensic investigators.

Whatever you do, just remember to look after yourself. I promise you'll be a better, more effective, investigator for it.

It's a people business, after all.

SUMMARY

In this chapter we concluded the book by tackling an issue that has just now started to register as an issue for forensic investigators: the impact on the humans that are part of an investigation, including suspects, victims and investigators.

We have seen, particularly in the case studies, that while investigations occur in the digital realm, they have repercussions on real people's daily lives.

INDEX